the kitchn

COOKBOOK

the kitchn

COOKBOOK

RECIPES, KITCHENS & TIPS
TO INSPIRE YOUR COOKING

**SARA KATE GILLINGHAM
& FAITH DURAND**

Photographs by Leela Cyd

CLARKSON POTTER/PUBLISHERS

NEW YORK

We dedicate this book to our readers

Copyright © 2014 by Apartment Therapy LLC
All rights reserved.

Published in the United States by Clarkson Potter/Publishers, an
imprint of the Crown Publishing Group, a division of Random
House LLC, a Penguin Random House Company, New York.
www.crownpublishing.com
www.clarksonpotter.com

CLARKSON POTTER is a trademark and POTTER with
colophon is a registered trademark of Random House LLC.

Library of Congress Cataloging-in-Publication
Data is available upon request.

ISBN 978-0-7704-3443-4
eBook ISBN 978-0-7704-3444-1

Printed in China
Book and cover design by Danielle Deschenes
Interior and cover photography by Leela Cyd

10 9 8 7 6 5 4 3 2

First Edition

CONTENTS

INTRODUCTION

The kitchen is the most important room of the home. It's the space where we nourish ourselves and we feed the people we love. It's where families tell each other about their day while the pot of pasta boils or where friends gather before the meal is even served. But a lack of basic cooking skills is a real obstacle to enjoying these moments of togetherness, not to mention eating wholesome, healthy meals, and without a properly set-up kitchen space, cooking those meals on weeknights after a long workday will never compete with the temptation of the takeout menu.

The Kitchn began in 2005 as a sister site to Apartment Therapy, a website intended to help people live better in their homes, and to help them create healthy, beautiful, and organized spaces. And what is more important to a healthy home than the kitchen?

Throughout the early days of Apartment Therapy, Sara Kate sat down to write weekly stories about how life takes shape in the kitchen, but she had no idea what would follow. As a food writer, she thought she was just adding more context to a website about home design, honoring the place of the kitchen in the home and helping people cook more. But it quickly became clear that life in the kitchen deserved its own conversation—and website. We took a leap, and created The Kitchn.

In the early days Sara Kate wrote the site alone, either from her famously tiny apartment or in Apartment Therapy's funky shared office space in Tribeca. She posted recipes, tidbits of culinary news, musings on the whys and whats and hows of home cooking, answers to readers' questions, cookbook reviews, and tours of people's kitchens. When her daughter was born in 2006, the team grew as well, to include Chris Phillips, who now runs sales and marketing for Apartment Therapy, and Faith Durand, the executive editor of The Kitchn, and cowriter on this book.

Faith came to Apartment Therapy and The Kitchn first as a reader, as she fell in love with the warm, practical advice and community crystallizing around these young websites. She joined in the conversation as a reader, then a commenter, then a writer, and now an editor who understands firsthand that The Kitchn is created by our readers as much as our writers.

The Kitchn was meant to be a destination on the web for people like us—home cooks who like to get their hands dirty while they cook and who desire a communal table online to ask questions and share their experiences. We longed for a virtual place to gather with others who care about the quality of their food, and how it affects their health and the health of the planet, while keeping in mind the realities of home cooking across America. As Apartment Therapy's sister site, we were also naturally interested in design, so The Kitchn quickly became a clubhouse for cooks who care about making their kitchen not only useful, but also beautiful. It was, and still is, a place to dive in deep and embrace the joy of one of our basic needs: food, the kind cooked at home, and the kind served with spirit.

Miraculously, our readership has grown from our mothers, our best friends, and Sara Kate's high school English teacher to people all over the world; today The Kitchn is read by millions of cooks. They are beginning cooks and experienced cooks. They are cooking in their dorm rooms; they are single guys learning to make chicken for the first time. They are large families hosting potlucks and Thanksgiving; they are new families, busier than they could have ever imagined, but committed to the nourishment of homemade food.

We publish posts daily that inform and inspire every aspect of home cooking, from recipes and cooking lessons to product reviews, kitchen design, and renovation advice. The website comes together each day thanks to a vibrant, diverse team of writers, recipe developers, and photographers from across the country. Many of them contributed to this book.

After almost eight years and over thirty-five thousand posts, Faith, our recipe editor

Emma Christensen, and Sara Kate wanted to boil down some of our greatest recipe hits and the most essential information into a book you can use when you unplug. Although we publish a website, we believe in cookbooks. With so much information behind a glass screen, this book of curated content feels even more necessary. We wanted you to have something to hold and keep by your side as you cook, when you're curled up in front of a fire, dreaming of asparagus season.

This book is also meant to be a go-to resource for someone who wants to understand how to work the keys to their kitchen—the first-time apartment renter, or the new parents, or the empty nester. It's a book to splatter with grease, to stain with the bottom of your teacup. It'll help you organize and personalize your kitchen so that you can quickly get in and out and have more time at the table to enjoy the good food you've made, or so that you'll want to spend even more time in there mastering new techniques and cooking side by side with friends. Once you experience the magic of a truly efficient kitchen, it's our hope that you'll cook in more often.

The book begins with a meaty section about setting up and caring for your kitchen. Here you'll find hints, tips, and lists of tools that will make your cooking life breezier, such as how to make your own natural cleaning solutions, how to recognize a smart kitchen layout, and how to keep your kitchen in usable and inspiring shape every single day.

Once you feel at home in your kitchen, our attention turns to the practical skills of everyday cooking. The second section of the book is your launchpad for cooking safely and more efficiently, your personal trainer with a bonus guide to your new exercise routine. We talk you through stocking your pantry and refrigerator, with tips for planning meals

around what you have, and then our Cooking School shares what we feel are fifty of the most essential techniques for cooking.

The cookbook comes next. One hundred and fifty recipes, including some favorites from the site, but many updated (we give many new variations for our one-ingredient ice cream!) plus dozens of new recipes developed with you in mind: a curious home cook who cares about food and is working to fit home cooking into a busy schedule and competing demands on your time.

Finally, we talk about Gatherings, the term we use loosely to refer to any kind of entertaining: quiet meals, dinner parties, picnics, and all-out shebangs. Here's where we talk about the importance of candles, cloth napkins, and a good playlist, and we hope you leave the chapter feeling free and ready to get your kitchen floor dirty.

Sprinkled throughout you will find five gorgeous Kitchen Meditations by Dana Velden, our resident priestess of all things moving and heartwarming about the kitchen. We also bring you a voyeuristic peek into ten kitchens across the country where you'll see real people in their real kitchens; imperfect and beautiful.

At the end of the day, cooking is about putting something in our bellies in order to survive. How lucky are we that such a simple, basic act inspires so much attention, so much design, so many parties, such color, and such joy? Know that each time you cook for someone—whether for yourself or for your whole neighborhood—you are making a profound offering. You are sustaining life, and, one hopes, providing joy to everyone at the table.

We are honored that you come to us when you decide to spread that spirit.

The Kitchen

SETTING UP *the* KITCHEN

The kitchen feeds our most basic needs, and it is often the magnetic center where family and guests drift, drawn irresistibly from the larger gathering spaces of living room and dining room. Most of us spend hours in our kitchens, standing at the sink or at the stove, chopping, stewing, and washing up.

So let's take a moment to stand back and survey this most essential space. Perhaps you're setting up a kitchen for the first time and are scratching your head over how to do it well. Maybe you have lived in your kitchen comfortably for a long time but would like to freshen it with a new battery of equipment or storage so organized it makes you feel delighted to open your pantry.

We're going to tackle the essentials for setting up a great kitchen space—wherever you live. A little creativity and ingenuity can help give any kitchen a soul and make it truly feel like home.

First, let's be clear: You will never be done setting up and caring for your kitchen. This is good news, because the unavoidable nature of kitchens is that they cannot stay pristine and perfect, and there will always be an endless need to add to and edit their contents. The other good news is that there is great joy in creating a kitchen over time, adjusting and revising it to the inevitable changes your life will bring. A kitchen truly is the heart and hearth of your home in ways that comfort and reassure.

So the best kitchens aren't the ones that are fresh off the assembly line or just on the other side of a remodel. The best kitchens have had a chance to age and take on the character of the people who live, cook, argue, love, laugh, cry, and throw parties in them. Like the Velveteen Rabbit, kitchens and the tools they hold will show some wear and tear because they are well used, and needed, and loved.

Some of us will have sleek and spare kitchens, and some will fill our shelves and cupboards with a hodgepodge of collections and memories. Our kitchens might look like laboratories, or they might be unplugged and rustic, or wild and cluttered and always full of people. Or they can be a quiet corner in a small apartment. But no matter how your kitchen looks and feels, no matter how big or small, I hope you will remember to always have something beautiful in your kitchen, something that will remind you to stop for a moment in order to fully appreciate how lit up and wondrous it all is.

As with most of the great things in life, your kitchen will grow, change, shrink, expand, and become more refined and expressive over time. You will break things that you love and cannot replace, and you will hold on to things for years out of sentimentality or laziness, or the conviction that one day you will really, really need them. We hope your kitchen will contain a few pieces given to you from a favorite grandmother or an old friend. We hope that much of what you consider useful will also be beautiful. We hope you will learn that the best pot is not the most expensive pot or the latest model, but the one that makes you feel good every time you reach for it.

Kitchen (and people) maintenance is not very complicated. It boils down to two basic precepts: Handle fragile things with care, and clean up your messes as soon as possible. Anything else is extra.

WHAT MAKES A PERFECT KITCHEN?

Put aside images of gleaming kitchens from magazine spreads with their lavish expanses of marble and stainless steel. Size and opulence do not necessarily characterize a well-planned kitchen. The best kitchen for you is a place that makes you want to cook, and it is one reasonably equipped so that you can prepare foods with ease and joy.

Everyone has his or her own idea of what a perfect kitchen should look like and how it should function. If you're lucky enough to build your own dream kitchen (or if you already have!), it will be much different from someone else's customized kitchen. And right now, the kitchen you already have—rented or owned, whatever its weaknesses or flaws—might have the potential to become the best kitchen for you.

Ask yourself: How do I use my kitchen? This is the first step to find or create a better kitchen. Do you like to cook with friends? If so, then a small galley kitchen, closed off from the dining room, is not ideal. Do you like to grill? A kitchen with easy access to the outdoors should be a priority. Do you have kids? You may want a space open to the living or family room, so you can keep an eye on young ones while cooking (or better yet, include them!). Do you love cocktails and mixology? Space for a bar (and a good icemaker) is a priority. Is it just you cooking and cleaning up? Or do you need space to cook while someone else is washing the dishes? Do you like to shop every day? Or do you stock up on food by shopping once a month?

These are just a few examples of the routines that determine your own perfect kitchen. A small, humble kitchen that is well suited to your habits is a better pick than a fancy space that is not built right for you. If your priorities don't align well with your current space, ask yourself why, and whether you can make a change to better accommodate your daily life.

THE KITCHEN WORK TRIANGLE

The kitchen work triangle is the space created by three points: the stove, the sink, and the refrigerator.

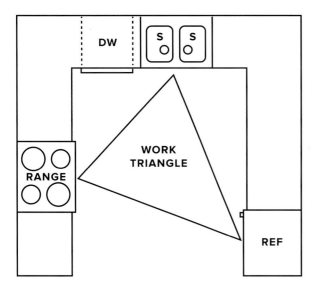

These are the three places in the kitchen that cooks use most frequently, and cooks wear virtual paths in the floor moving between each point. These points also correspond with basic categories of kitchen work: preparing ingredients, cooking, cleanup, and food storage.

Look at your kitchen and mark each point in this triangle. Where are they in relation to each other? How far apart are they? In a classic galley kitchen, you may have the refrigerator and sink on one wall, and the stove facing them. In a larger kitchen, perhaps each point of the triangle is on a different wall.

Kitchen design experts recommend that there be at least four feet of space between each point of your work triangle (e.g., between your refrigerator and sink) but no more than nine feet across the furthest points (think about how inconvenient a ten-foot walk between your sink and stove would be!).

So what's the point of this exercise? The kitchen triangle can help you when you are searching for a new kitchen: Does the proposed triangle work for you and the way you cook?

But if you already have a kitchen, you probably don't have much control over your work triangle. If your refrigerator is actually located in the dining room, or your sink is crammed up next to your stove, what can you really do without major renovations?

First, remember that the concept of the kitchen triangle isn't a hard-and-fast set of rules; it is more of a diagnostic tool to help identify potential problems and solutions. I had friends who needed to go through two exterior doors to get to their refrigerator, for instance. To ease their workflow, they stored commonly used vegetables like onions and garlic near the workspace and stove, instead of in the fridge or pantry. Other kitchens have a refrigerator with a door that opens in the wrong direction. In these cases, it's possible to reverse the hinges on most refrigerators, making the door open from the left instead of the right or vice versa.

"I think the most important thing is having adequate counter space close to the stove. You shouldn't take more than a step or two to put your prepped items in a pan or into the oven. And the same goes for plating the finished food when it's done. Having my sink opposite the stove helps, too. Super handy for draining pasta. I just turn around and dump it out." —tmunar

On the other hand, don't be bound to the idea of the triangle if it doesn't work with your cooking style. Some people prefer to have each major kitchen point in a straight line. Others give counter space priority above all else. Perhaps you bake far more than you use the stovetop. Or you want the fridge well out of the cooking area so your kids can help themselves to snacks without getting in your way.

It helps to occasionally stand back and scrutinize your kitchen, identifying what gets in your way.

7 QUESTIONS TO ASK
WHEN YOU'RE IN THE MARKET FOR A KITCHEN

If you are house-hunting or apartment-hunting, take along this list. These are also helpful diagnostic questions to ask yourself when thinking about improving an existing space.

— 1 —

How does the kitchen relate to the rest of the home? Do you want a kitchen that can be closed off when the dishes are dirty? Or do you want your kitchen as open as possible?

— 2 —

Do all the appliances work? Don't forget to inspect the appliances when checking out a new place. Do all the gas burners light quickly and fully? Does the oven open and shut easily?

— 3 —

How much counter space is there? Countertop workspace is perhaps the biggest factor that sets a difficult kitchen apart from an easy one. Look for a kitchen with at least twelve inches of counterspace on at least one side of the stovetop, and the same amount near the refrigerator. In an ideal world, all kitchens would have at least one four-foot stretch of uninterrupted countertop, separate from the dishwashing area.

— 4 —

Is there natural light? When possible, spring for a kitchen with sunlight. A window in the kitchen instantly makes it feel more inviting.

— 5 —

Is there an eat-in space? Consider sacrificing a bit of storage space for a small eating area in the kitchen; what you lose in storage you gain in coziness and a little more time enjoying the kitchen.

— 6 —

Is there adequate storage—in the kitchen or elsewhere? Dismayed by storage options in the kitchen itself? This is actually only a small problem if there is storage elsewhere in the home. The secret to kitchen storage is that very few things actually need to be within arm's reach at all times. Think of converting an underused coat closet into a pantry or putting shelving in the dining room. You may actually find that you have plenty of storage, even if the kitchen itself is small.

— 7 —

How close is the nearest grocery store? Living an inconvenient distance from the grocery store can hamper even the greatest kitchen in the world. If this is your situation, then create space in the kitchen or pantry so that you can stock up more extensively on daily staples, if possible.

SETTING UP YOUR KITCHEN
for the Way You Really Cook

Now that you have a kitchen, what's the best way to get it set up and ready for cooking? We'll talk much more about specific tools you need (and don't need) in a later chapter, but for now you should consider your major cooking zones. These relate to the idea of the kitchen triangle, but they also depend on how you cook.

Sit down with a pad of paper and a pencil, and walk through the last few meals you ate at home.

What are your daily routines? Do you make oatmeal every morning? Do you prep a salad to take to work with you? What kind of dinners do you make? Do you like to sauté? Bake? Stir-fry? And what about more complex cooking—how do you start, progress, and finish? What kind of specialty cooking is in your repertoire? Do you bake bread every week? Do you decorate cakes? Do you cook ahead for a whole month at a time? Each of the major ways you cook deserves a cooking zone.

As a quick exercise, identify your primary cooking habits and activities, and write them down, ordering them by importance and frequency. (For instance: stir-frying, soup making, bread baking, and then canning.) Think through the ingredients and tools you use for each of these activities and whether you can group them. Which are most important? Now you know your cooking zones.

Here are some examples of cooking zones and the space they need:

> **Fruit and vegetable preparation:** If you eat a lot of fresh fruits and vegetables, then it's important to have some counter space near the sink and the trash can (or compost bucket). Knives, cutting boards, and storage containers for cut-up produce should be nearby.

> **Salad making:** If you eat salads regularly, a salad zone would include oils and vinegars, salt and pepper, and big bowls for making and tossing your salads.

> **Baking:** If baking is a key activity in your kitchen, it helps to have a drawer or cupboard with all your baking staples (flour, sugar, and spices) near your baking equipment, such as a stand mixer and bowls.

In a truly small kitchen, the idea of cooking zones can sound a little absurd, since you may be able to touch all four walls of your kitchen without moving! But the principles of organization still apply. Think through your daily, weekly, and monthly cooking habits, and try to store items you use regularly together. Reduce your steps while cooking daily meals by recognizing what you use most frequently, and placing those things at the center of your workspace.

FAITH:
My Cooking Zones

▼

I do a lot of quick cooking on the stovetop. I often stir-fry vegetables or cook sausage to toss with pasta, so I keep the basics for these kinds of meals on the countertop, including salt, pepper, olive oil, and a bowl of garlic cloves. In the drawers below I store my favorite knives, a Microplane (for lemon zest and Parmesan cheese, which I use constantly), and mixing bowls. To the right of these basics, at arm's reach, is the stove itself. Below the stove I store my pots and pans, as well as my spatulas and wooden spoons.

Without moving more than a step, I can chop garlic and sauté it with olive oil, cook my dinner, and season it with salt and pepper. This cooking zone is set up for how I cook on a daily basis.

Less frequently used bakeware, such as cake pans, and appliances, such as my food processor, as well as baking ingredients are stored progressively farther away from the center of my daily cooking activity.

10 SMART STORAGE SOLUTIONS *for Any Kitchen*

Once you've identified your cooking zones, the next step in creating a great kitchen is finding the right place for all your gear. We've cooked in tiny kitchens and in large ones, and we've found that no matter the size, the avid cook often wishes for more space for her treasures and has a need to organize her space intelligently. Here are ten ways to create space for everything, no matter the size of your kitchen.

1. **Wall shelves.** Your walls are the first place to look for storage. Store books and dishware up above.

2. **Island or cart.** One of the best ways to improve nearly any kitchen is to add a small, movable, butcher block island, which gives you extra storage and counter space and can be pushed against the wall when not in use.

3. **Pot racks and Peg-Boards.** Hang a pot rack from the ceiling or, if you're short, the wall. The great Julia Child had a Peg-Board with a place for every tool, pan, and utensil. A painted Peg-Board is also an opportunity to bring a big splash of color into the kitchen!

4. **IKEA pullout pantry.** IKEA's AKURUM cabinets include an inexpensive tall cupboard that is very narrow (fifteen inches). Nearly any kitchen has fifteen inches to spare somewhere!

5. **Steel wire shelving.** Big box home improvement stores like Home Depot sell sturdy, freestanding chrome wire shelving that can be set up anywhere and used to hold baking dishes, small appliances, and linens.

6. **Armoire or hutch.** Storage can be beautiful, too. A family heirloom hutch or old-fashioned Hoosier cabinet looks handsome in the dining room and holds a multitude of cooking essentials.

7. **Big baskets.** Farmhouse chic baskets hold cutting boards, trays, baking sheets, or kitchen linens.

8. **Hooks and towel bars.** On the smaller side, don't forget about hooks and towel bars for kitchen towels and potholders.

9. **Backsplash organization.** There are many solutions for storage on the backsplash, such as IKEA's affordable GRUNDTAL system, and moving up to Rösle's handsome (and pricier) system. These usually consist of rails mounted on the wall, with S-hooks for hanging containers and cooking utensils.

10. **Cabinet tops.** Look up! There is often room between the tops of the cabinets and the ceiling—prime space for storing cookbooks, cake plates, and other less frequently used items.

"Best thing I ever did for my small kitchen was get a wooden kitchen cart. It's from IKEA, a hundred bucks and SO worth every penny. I can store pots under it and have a huge cutting surface, plus it's not too big to put in a corner or in the middle of my tiny kitchen as an island." —*jmh26*

MORE WAYS TO IMPROVE CHALLENGING KITCHENS

The storage solutions we've outlined above are good ideas for nearly any kitchen, but what about problem kitchens? Here are some particularly challenging kitchens and more specific solutions.

THE EXTRA-SMALL KITCHEN

If your kitchen is less than fifty square feet, you may be desperate for more workspace or storage. Here are some ways to get it:

> **Buy a cutting board and colander that fit over the sink.** Use the sink as workspace.

> **Cover the stove.** Get a large butcher block or nonslip cover so you can prep on the stovetop when it's not in use.

> **Install an island or petite rolling butcher block.** If there is enough floor space in the center of the kitchen, bring in a small island.

> **Install fold-down tables.** Create an eating nook by installing a fold-down table.

> **Open up space between the studs.** If you own your home and are handy with drywall, knock out some drywall between the studs on an inner wall, install shallow shelves, and use this nook for storing spices or canned goods.

> **Install a hanging pot rack over an island, butcher block, or sink.**

THE RENTAL KITCHEN

Renters have it the hardest, especially in the area of aesthetics. Stuck with a boring, bland, or dark kitchen? A kitchen outfitted with the lowest builder grade of fixtures? Here are some ideas for making the place your own:

> **Replace the faucet.** It is actually a simple one-hour project to swap out a faucet for a better one. (And to swap it back out when you move.)

> **Add a tall cabinet.** See the storage suggestions on page 20. A tall IKEA cabinet can squeeze into a tiny corner and triple your storage space.

> **Paint.** If you have an amenable landlord, nothing cleans up a kitchen faster than a fresh coat of paint.

> **Paint cabinets.** Many landlords are happy to have their tenants freshen up the kitchen cabinets with paint. If you get permission, be aware that painting cabinets is a bigger job, and it takes time and space to do it right. But the result of high-quality cabinet painting will transform your space.

> **Put down floating flooring, such as parquet or sticky tiles.** Bad kitchen flooring can be covered up by inexpensive rugs, parquet, or click-in-place tiles, and they are all removable later.

> **Replace light fixtures or light covers.** If you want to invest a little more, replace the light fixtures or cover ugly bulbs with new glass covers.

"To me, a modern kitchen is 100 percent functional and well designed (easy to work in, easy to clean up) and GETS USED! If it doesn't get cooked in, it's not a kitchen—just another room decorated with very expensive stuff." —*splatgirl*

THE ONE-DRAWER KITCHEN

Many small kitchens, especially in the city, have a dearth of drawers. Sara Kate has just such a kitchen, and here are a few of the ways she's found to store her kitchen gear:

> **Jars for cooking utensils and cutlery.** Use big jars or crocks to hold silverware and cooking utensils.

> **Baskets for small dishes, linens, and napkins.** Baskets can slide under benches and dining room seating, and hold glasses and linens.

> **Hang a knife strip or block.** Use wall space and a magnetic strip to hold knives. Alternately, look for knife blocks that can be mounted below an upper kitchen cabinet. Some swing up and hide away completely when not in use.

> **IKEA GRUNDTAL hanging system.** In the one-drawer kitchen these backsplash hanging systems really come in handy. Go beyond the backsplash and use these hanging containers for all those little gadgets like the can opener, citrus reamer, and Microplanes.

THE TOO-LARGE KITCHEN

How can a kitchen be too large? We can hear cooks in tiny urban kitchens snickering now. But in suburban homes this is actually a real problem: Many large kitchens are designed poorly, with the fridge ten steps from the sink, and the stove located awkwardly on the third wall. Following are some tips for a too-large kitchen:

> **Move the fridge.** This is an easy fix for some awkward kitchens. Changing the location of the refrigerator to a more convenient corner can vastly improve your kitchen space.

> **Move the stove.** This is actually a reasonable option, if your stove is electric. Moving the stove so it is closer to the sink or to your longest stretch of countertop can revolutionize your work triangle.

> **Add a movable island.** As in small kitchens, an island workspace is helpful here, creating workspace just steps away from the stove or sink.

THE BUDGET KITCHEN RENOVATION

If the home you own came with a difficult kitchen but you don't have the budget for a full renovation, these projects can make a huge difference while renovating on a dime.

> **Is your kitchen closed off?** Do you want a more open space? When appropriate, open up space between your living space and the kitchen. This sounds like a huge project, but if the blocking wall is non-load-bearing (check your house plans or consult an engineer), you can knock it down yourself. It will take a weekend day, a couple friends, and some crowbars. Prepare for massive dust and use drop cloths to protect any adjacent rooms. Be sure you know ahead of time how you will dispose of the construction debris, too. It's a fairly simple project, and any drywall repair to the ceiling should be inexpensive.

> **Paint or reface cabinets.** Instead of replacing cabinets, which can cost thousands of dollars, look into having your existing cabinets professionally painted or refaced. A good cabinet refinisher can replace drawer slides and touch up nicked wood and make your kitchen look amazingly new—for a fraction of the cost of replacing cabinets.

> **Seek out IKEA kitchen systems.** If you do replace the cabinets, IKEA's kitchen cabinet system can't be beat for value. We've installed IKEA cabinets and love their high-quality hardware and smart assembly. It takes time and energy, but an IKEA kitchen can save you tens of thousands of dollars. To get a custom look for a budget price, buy the IKEA boxes but use custom drawer and cabinet fronts from a company like Semihandmade or Scherr's Cabinet and Doors.

> **Don't move appliances.** Moving gas, electric, and water service can significantly add to the cost of a kitchen renovation. Leave appliances where they are, if possible, and improve the aesthetics of the surrounding walls, cabinets, and floors.

> **Put in windows.** If you're going to the trouble of a kitchen renovation, don't ignore windows. Spend a little to bring in some sunlight. Does your sink face an outside wall? Put in a window—it will vastly improve the kitchen.

> **Resist the impulse to upgrade everything at once.** If your budget is limited, upgrade appliances and fixtures one by one instead of buying lower-quality options. Start from the ground up (don't skimp on the flooring!) and focus on materials like the cabinets, countertop, and the layout of the space. Ovens, stovetops, dishwashers, and lighting fixtures can easily be replaced later.

> **Add a pantry without adding walls.** Instead of enlarging the kitchen, look for space that you can designate as a pantry. A small kitchen with everything at arm's length is actually quite convenient and easy to cook in. But if storage is a problem, try creating a pantry from a closet or part of the entryway. Move your stuff, not the kitchen walls.

Don't be afraid to have beautiful things in the kitchen. Everything wears out eventually, so enjoy pretty objects even in this functional room.

WHY (AND HOW)
a Beautiful Kitchen Means Better Food

A kitchen's first task is functional: it is a place to produce good food with cleanliness and efficiency. But functionality and beauty go hand in hand. We've met people who seem afraid to have beautiful things in their cooking space—they react in shock and dismay when they see paintings or rugs in a busy kitchen. "What if it gets ruined? That's so nonfunctional!" We couldn't disagree more. Everything in life decays and wears out eventually. Having something you consider beautiful in the kitchen is a nudge toward enjoying the act of cooking, a reminder that food is more than fuel.

A beautiful kitchen also helps us remember to clean regularly. When you enjoy your space, even in some small way, it's so much more pleasurable to keep it clean.

Once you've worked on your cooking zones and storage capacity, find creative ways to make beauty and functionality go hand in hand. A kitchen you enjoy is one that will motivate you to nourish your household. Here are a few ways to bring a bit of beauty into even the dingiest of kitchens:

> **Enjoy the beauty of food itself.** Heap oranges or persimmons in a dish on the countertop (this also will remind you to eat them promptly!). Tomatoes, onions, even sweet potatoes have an earthy beauty that grounds a kitchen. Store herbs with their cut ends in a shallow glass of water, which will keep them fresh and handy for snipping, as well as add a splash of green to your workspace.

> **Cover ugly countertops with a huge butcher block.** If you have a tiny and hideous laminate countertop, cover it up with a hefty cutting board, which is more beautiful and also of course very functional.

> **Hang a vibrant work of art.** No backsplash? Frame an inexpensive print and hang it behind the stove. Yes, the glass will get greasy eventually, but it's easier to clean glass than a painted wall.

> **Line drawers and cabinets with colorful fabric or paper.** Apply fabric wallpaper to the backs of your cabinets using fabric starch; the cloth wallpaper is both washable and removable (see more detailed instructions at Apartment Therapy). Line drawers with pretty paper from an art supply store.

> **Enhance the sense of space with a mirror.** A big mirror hung on one wall or over the kitchen table reflects light, helps make up for the lack of a window, and increases the feeling of spaciousness.

> **Lay down a rug.** You may think it will get irredeemably dirty, but a patterned rug will hide stains and is easy to vacuum. With a nonslip rug pad beneath, it's also nicer to stand on than hard, cold tile.

> **Adorn the table or windowsill with living plants or fresh flowers.** Fresh flowers are a simple grace note for any kitchen. Splurge on them to make your space feel more special, or snip evergreen twigs or even flowering weeds from your backyard or on your walk home. Anything alive makes the kitchen feel more welcoming.

"My roommate, who does not cook at all, often leaves me a few surprise flowers in a small jam jar on the windowsill in our kitchen. Makes me smile EVERY time."
—*nyalli718*

> **Paint!** Paint is a major tool for the cook with an ugly, dark kitchen. Don't forget the ceiling, where color can instantly make the room more cheerful (think sky blue, lemon yellow, pale washes of bright colors). Painting the entire room can seem daunting, but with careful cleaning, taping, and priming, you can do an expert job by yourself.

> **Supply music or a radio.** The companionship of radio is something we appreciate in our kitchens. Faith keeps a Tivoli radio on her windowsill and listens to NPR and podcasts while she cooks; she plugs in an iPod for dinner parties.

THE FLOURISHING KITCHEN:
5 Ways to Grow Food in Any Space

The last element of a great kitchen is something living. Not everyone can have (or wants!) a garden, and gardening indoors is not as practical and easy as some would have you think. It's actually rather difficult to grow tomatoes on a patio and not terribly cost-effective, either. But here are a few growing projects that truly make sense indoors:

> **Sprouts.** Growing sprouts like alfalfa takes just a few days and requires only a jar, some cheesecloth, and the seeds. It's the indoor gardening project literally anyone can do.

> **Microgreens and salad lettuce.** Microgreens can be easily grown at home in empty yogurt containers or tea tins for far less than it costs to buy them at the store, and because they are harvested long before they are full-grown, they don't need much room. Lettuce is similar: plant a variety of lettuce seeds in a window box and you'll have a salad mix variety that can be cut and used as the lettuces grow.

> **Mushroom kits.** Mushroom kits are a simple and low maintenance way to bring some life into the kitchen; companies like Mushroom Adventures, Fungi Perfecti, and Back to the Roots sell kits that require only sunlight and a daily misting of water.

> **Select herbs.** Chives, thyme, and oregano are hardy enough to be grown indoors. Avoid basil and rosemary unless you have quite a lot of sunlight.

> **Edible flowers.** Nasturtiums are edible and delicious in salads and a beautiful topper for cakes. Grow them indoors if you have plenty of sunlight and room for their trailing blossoms to cascade.

Kristen Ossmann and Jackie Werner

Kristen Ossmann, a florist and artist, lives with her partner in a small walk-up rental apartment off a busy street in Brooklyn. Within its walls is a menagerie of her own artwork, antique mirrors, and other bits and bobs she finds around the city, sometimes on the street, and of course a plethora of plants. Everything here is petite, including the occupant and the antique kitchen table and chairs she lugged up her steps by herself from the sidewalk. But somehow the apartment feels spacious and full of sweet-smelling air.

On weekends the apartment fills with friends and neighbors for her famous brunches; Kristen is known for making perfect Spanish tortillas and vibrant salads and for serving tumblers of champagne. Behind her cabinet doors are heaps of herbs and tinctures; she is truly a nature artist, consuming them for flavor, for health, and even for a bit of whimsy. "Fenugreek will make you smell like maple syrup," she tells me.

With light, open shelving and unique flea-market finds, Kristen creates a strong sense of home in her rental kitchen.

The kitchen table is the center of the home.

There is magic everywhere. Tucked into unexpected corners and shelves are cuttings, branches, and bouquets that bring the outdoors in no matter the season. "I have always had a strong affinity for light and airy spaces," she says. "It is important to me to have a relaxed feel to my space while still keeping it somewhat elegant."

The kitchen is the hub of the home, with its roughly assembled collection of appliances (such is life in a rental), bumpy plank wood floors, painted-over tin ceiling, and hanging plants. The backsplash, in funky subway tile with green trim and a built-in porcelain soap holder reminiscent of those found in a shower, was covered in paint when she moved in. A lucky ding to the wall revealed the secret behind the paint and she spent a weekend chipping it away.

Her cooking style is influenced by her love of herbs and healing foods and also of the natural colors and flavors that arrive with each season. During the winter when her flower business is at rest, she brings color and fragrance into the kitchen with lots of citrus dishes and highly flavorful cured foods from her chef friends. But what drives her most to cook is to gather people around. "Nothing too fussy," she says. "I love making salads and soups and having lots of different dishes that complement each other and fill up the table in a beautiful way."

While her favorite things about her kitchen are the light, funky wood floors and the tin ceilings, her least favorite aspect is the lack of counter space. To compensate, she uses creative ways to expand the surface area of the kitchen and says her best tip for creating a warm, inviting kitchen on a budget is to put up shelves. She tells me, "Kitchen items are really beautiful and look so nice displayed, such as stacked white ceramics and little French glasses."

Finally, it goes without saying that plants are a very affordable way to bring life into a kitchen, and Kristen certainly makes up for what she may lack in space or matching appliances with a strong sense of vitality and nature.

Kristen packs a lot into a tiny space: a pantry full of grains, herbs, and homemade remedies lines one wall, and next to the stove a cutting surface doubles as storage.

Kim's sleek white kitchen is surprisingly durable, cranking out three meals every day for her husband and three small children.

Kim Kushner

Kim Kushner is a trained chef, culinary instructor, and practiced home cook. Her cooking style is what she calls a "study in modern Orthodoxy," as she maintains a kosher kitchen in line with her upbringing and heritage. She brings a fresh perspective to kosher cooking, with a focus on fresh produce, eye-catching colors, and bright flavors. These are not the first thoughts that come to mind, she admits, when thinking of a kosher diet. Her cookbook, *The Modern Menu*, pays homage to the bold seasonal flavors that can come from a kosher kitchen.

Kim lives with her husband and three small children in what is, by Manhattan standards, a very large apartment. When they moved there in 2007, it was a brand-new development and had a glimmering marble and dark wood kitchen. After two years she decided the layout wasn't right for her. In four weeks they completely gutted the kitchen and remodeled it, keeping the original appliances but adding a second dishwasher and sink to help make the kitchen kosher.

Though the room has beautiful finishes and high-end appliances, Kim feels strongly that what defines her as a cook is what comes out of the kitchen, not what the kitchen looks like or what brand her knives are. Her favorite cookware is a mishmash of pieces passed down to her from her mother, mostly from flea markets in Israel.

Aside from the separate sinks and dishwashers, she keeps the kitchen kosher by labeling some of her pans and utensils "meat" and "dairy" in order to keep the two separate. At first glance you might think this is a typical upscale kitchen that doesn't get a lot of use—white lacquer cabinets, shiny stainless appliances—but open the pristine drawers and cabinets and you'll find endless well-loved cooking utensils and dinged up pots and pans. Kim admits that the kitchen definitely has signs of use and wear: "There are dings and scratches everywhere." While the kitchen feels luxurious, it's not precious; look closely and you'll see a stash of Nescafé instant coffee jars she keeps for shaking up vinaigrettes, and a refrigerator covered in family photos and drawings.

At one end of the long Caesarstone quartz counter is a lower seating area with benches that slide out; this is where her children do their homework and students of her culinary courses sit as she demonstrates at the stove. At the other end is a tower of baked goods in a tiered glass stand, including her renowned and ever-present Crunchy Biscotti with Chocolate, Pecans, and Coconut, a recipe she perfected over the years with a secret ingredient.

Kim's kitchen is one of only a handful we have seen that is ready for the pages of a design magazine yet gets used every single day to cook homemade food from scratch. Asked what she would do in her next kitchen, she answered, "I hope to be here for life."

Kim's kosher kitchen has two sinks and two sponges, tons of tools, and always a few treats on the counter.

Nancy Neil and Ethan Brostedt

Nancy Neil and Ethan Brostedt live with their two small children in a valley close to the ocean, on an 88-acre orchard in a cabin built in 1903. Nancy's cooking makes use of the lavish produce of the orchard: cherimoyas, avocados, passion fruit, sapotes, guavas, plums, apricots, persimmons, and oranges. "At any time of year there's something," says Nancy. Nancy also grows many of their own herbs and vegetables and keeps chickens; they shop at the farmer's market for meat, fish, and other supplies.

With this wealth of fresh food so close at hand, the kitchen is the heart of the home. "After we had kids, it became even more of the center," says Nancy, who made her own baby food and spends a great deal of time in this room. As a photographer she works several days a week in Los Angeles, and she has created a home she is eager to come home to from the city. "Some people need to do yoga when they get home from work at night," Nancy says. "I just need to be in my kitchen."

Nancy and Ethan's home is a modernized and expanded
cabin nestled in a canyon near Santa Barbara, with a
subtropical microclimate that nurtures citrus and other fruit.
Nancy grew up juicing oranges every day with her mom,
and she has carried on this tradition with her own kids.

Living on a farm has helped her create small rituals with her children. They check on the chickens and look at the trees, talking about the cycle of growth. They bring fruit back to the kitchen to juice with Nancy's heavy-duty juicer, a Mother's Day gift from her husband. "My mom and I also had this daily ritual," Nancy explains. "We had an orange tree and we made my juice together every day."

Nancy does most of the cooking, and her style is simple and nourishing. "I don't use a lot of ingredients. I like to cook low and slow. My favorite pan is our Dutch oven. I just toss in vegetables, olive oil, and herbs de Provence and roast them or make a stew."

The kitchen looks out on a huge wraparound covered porch. "We spend seventy percent of our time on the porch, and we eat outside a lot," Nancy says. "We sit down and have dinner as a family every night. Even if we have to go back and work later, this time is always together."

Above and left: The home was originally built in 1903 with old railroad ties.

Opposite: The dining table lives in a huge wraparound porch just outside the kitchen, where Nancy's family spends most of their mealtimes.

TOOLS

You can learn a lot about a cook by looking at his or her cooking equipment. Maybe there is a wok in a place of honor, a granite molcajete, a grandmother's silver spoons, or cast-iron skillets seasoned by fifty years of cornbread and bacon. Our collections of cooking equipment form a quiet autobiography of our lives as cooks, and each piece tells a story of daily life in the kitchen.

What do your tools say about you? Do you have everything you could ever want in the kitchen, or are you just starting out, looking for the best tools to help you cook well?

In 2009, a twenty-something reader named Mandy who was moving out on her own wrote to us with this question: "While I have a lot of hand-me-downs coming my way, one thing I have to buy myself is a set of cookware—pots, pans, skillets, baking sheets. What do you recommend for affordable (but quality) cookware?" We've seen some form of this question many times, and we love the excuse to get down to business and talk kitchen gear. In this chapter we're going to go beyond the lists of pots and pans that often get stuck in the fronts of cookbooks, and talk more nitty-gritty details of which equipment we prefer and why. And we'll share some of our own personal favorite tools, so you can see how much one well-equipped kitchen (and cook!) can differ from another.

OUR KITCHEN PHILOSOPHY

You don't need a lot of kitchen equipment to cook well. In fact, having too many gadgets and gizmos in your cupboards can actually slow you down, burdening you with a shifting pile of unused distractions.

But a good tool or appliance, if you use it regularly and take good care of it, is invaluable. We've seen cooks sniff at other cooks who use an expensive blender, or a garlic press, or a stand mixer. "I've cooked for years without one!" But what works for you and for others may be different. Sara Kate relies on her Vitamix blender daily for her morning smoothie, while Faith scarcely touches her hand-me-down blender. Faith, on the other hand, uses her food processor every other day, while Sara Kate rarely pulls hers out of the cupboard.

The best tools and appliances are the ones that help you cook the food you want to eat. Don't let anyone tell you that you should or shouldn't have a tool. Only you can be the judge of that.

But if your kitchen arsenal needs some reinforcement, where do you start? Here are some thoughts on the kitchen equipment we find most useful day to day. Although these tools and pans work well for us, you will create your own style of cooking and your own kitchen autobiography, written in tools.

OUR ESSENTIAL KITCHEN TOOLS

If we had to start from scratch—that is, if we were shipped off to a desert island with only one box of kitchen tools to keep us company—here's what would be on the list. Again, while these are the things we rely on day to day, there may be other tools that are indispensable to you.

> **Knives.** A chef's knife and a paring knife are like extensions of a cook's hands. You don't need a lot of knives, or even expensive ones, to cook well. In fact, we think it's a mistake to buy a whole set of knives at once. You will probably end up spending less money if you build your knife collection gradually, adding new knives as needed. To start, you need only one really comfortable chef's knife and a sharp, substantial paring knife to do 99 percent of your cutting and chopping in the kitchen.

> **Knives are very personal, and, again, only you can judge what works best for you.** There are three important questions to ask when looking for both a chef's knife and a paring knife: How does the knife feel in your hand? Can you control it easily? And can it be sharpened well? (For more on choosing a knife and learning to use it well, see that section of our Cooking School, page 109.)

> **Cutting boards.** Cutting boards play many roles in the kitchen. Not only are they surfaces to chop on, but they can also be casual serving boards for cheese, roasted meat, or dessert. For this reason, we prefer wooden boards over plastic. Stay clear of glass cutting boards; they are bad for your knives! Bamboo is easy to care for and has antibacterial properties; this is a good material to start with. We like having at least one really large board so that we can spread out. But make sure, when buying a large board, to check whether it will fit in your sink for cleaning!

"A giant cutting board is a must in a small kitchen with a double sink. Mine is big enough to almost double my available prep space. I keep it propped behind the sink because putting it away would be pointless."

—*matchbookhymnal*

> **Sheet pans.** The most frequently used pan in Faith's kitchen is the sheet pan, which is good for everything from baking cookies to roasting pork chops. The best sheet pans are the commercial pans found at restaurant supply stores. These pans are made of heavy-gauge aluminum, with a sturdy lip on the sides. They won't warp in the oven, and they are usually sold for $5 to $10. They aren't nonstick, however; we suggest skipping the nonstick finish and using parchment or a Silpat

SARA KATE uses an 8-inch Felix Solingen knife that was her mother's. It has a red handle and used to be sharpened by her grandfather every time he came over. She likes to give little chopping jobs to her young daughter, who uses a New West KnifeWorks Mini Chopper Chef Knife. This knife is short like a paring knife, but a little wider, so she can control its movement.

EMMA fell in love with a 7-inch Wüsthof Santoku knife the first time she used it; it felt right in her hand, comfortable and balanced.

FAITH has used the Victorinox 8-inch Swiss Army Chef's Knife for years. It retails for about $25, is comfortable to grip, and sharpens well.

DANA found a hand-me-down carbon steel knife that she has adopted as her favorite. Carbon steel needs a little extra care to keep it from rusting, but it can be honed to a sharper edge than stainless steel and holds that edge longer.

ELIZABETH PASSARELLA, one of our longtime writers, says her favorite knife is her Wüsthof paring knife, especially for cutting grapes and cheese for her toddler. "These are all things a lesser knife could handle, but the task is so much faster with a good, sharp paring knife. It's quick and super precise."

when baking delicate things. When purchasing sheet pans, pay attention to size. Full sheet pans are too big to fit into a home oven. Half size, at 18 × 13 inches, is just right for most home ovens, although Sara Kate has only quarter sheet pans, since that is the size that fits her 20-inch oven. When we specify a baking sheet in a recipe, we assume you're using something about 18 inches long, or a little smaller if your oven is smaller, like Sara Kate's.

> 9 × 13-inch baking dish. Many recipes, from casseroles to cakes, call for a 9 x 13-inch pan (the standard volume for this pan is three quarts). A pretty ceramic or enameled pan can double as a serving dish.

> Sauté pan or skillet. If we had to choose just one pan, it would be the 10-inch sauté pan. A sauté pan is a skillet with high sides, deep enough to simmer a batch

of tomato sauce or chicken stew. If we were allowed two pans, however, we'd supplement the sauté pan with a cast-iron skillet, or an extra-wide 12-inch skillet, which gives you plenty of room for browning meat. When looking for a sauté pan or skillet, the no-set rule applies here as well. We never buy pans in sets; it's better to build your collection as needed so you don't pay for pans you never use.

> "Definitely cannot live without my Lodge cast-iron skillet and 6-quart enamel-coated Dutch oven (red, of course)." —pventura

> **Saucepan.** We have saucepans in several sizes and find the most essential is the 2- or 3-quart saucepan, which are both large enough to heat soup or milk, but not too large for making a small quantity of sauce. Again, avoid nonstick, and look for a heavy, solid pan with a matching lid (see our thoughts on the importance of weight in pans on page 46).

> **Stockpot or large Dutch oven.** Everyone needs one big pot! A 4- to 6-quart pot is essential for soups, stews, braises, and pots of pasta. A big, heavy Dutch oven—which is usually constructed of smooth enamel over cast iron—conducts heat exceptionally well and also looks beautiful when brought to the table. Dutch ovens can be pricey, but they will last a lifetime, so they are worth the money.

> **Measuring cups and spoons.** We like sets of solid metal measuring cups and spoons, especially the steel measuring cups from Lee Valley, which have the measurements imprinted in the metal, so they won't rub away in the dishwasher. Look for narrow measuring spoons that will fit into spice jars. A 2-cup glass pitcher for measuring liquids is also essential.

> **Big bowls.** Big mixing bowls, 6 to 8 quarts in size, are constantly in use in our kitchens for mixing up salads, dough, and more. Faith buys her utilitarian metal bowls from a restaurant supply store. But if you can have only one, then look for a pretty ceramic bowl, since it can double as a serving bowl.

> **Utensils.** To round out our basics, we need cooking utensils! What's absolutely necessary? A long wooden spoon (or two) for stirring. A medium wire whisk for making dressings and sauces. Metal tongs for handling food on the stovetop, and a whippy metal spatula for flipping pancakes and removing cookies from their baking sheet. Last but not least, a silicone or rubber spatula for scraping down bowls (we love the GIR—Get It Right—spatula; it is all one piece, with no seam between the handle and the head to get gunky).

OUR MOST-LOVED KITCHEN TOOLS

While we offer you a basic list of the most essential tools, we also wanted to share our own personal favorites. They also illustrate the different ways we cook.

SARA KATE

Wood spatula. Also called a "turner," I use this more often than my wooden spoons because its flat edge makes scraping a sauce or moving quickly cooking garlic across the pan so much faster. It'll even flip an egg and is kind to my nonstick surfaces.

Thick end-grain chopping block. It's not a tool, but it's absolutely essential to the way I cook. It's my blank canvas, and it comes alive with every meal I make. Having a permanent (it's so big and heavy that I never put it away) space where I can spread out and cook gives me freedom. It has also been the surface for many years' worth of recipe photographs on The Kitchn. Look for something at least an inch thick and apply mineral oil often.

Ramekins. I have a large assortment of ramekins that I use as prep bowls while I'm cooking. I also use them as serving pieces for little first-course soups, dipping sauces, and individual baked desserts or small portions of ice cream.

FAITH

Mesh strainer. Multiuse and lightweight, this is my go-to tool for draining pasta, washing fruit and greens, and straining tea and soups.

3-quart pots. For nightly cooking, I reach for my 3-quart pots. The sauté pan is just right for frittatas and cooking meat and is big enough for small batches of pasta and soups. When you're cooking for just two or three, this is a handy size to have around. (Mine are from Sur La Table's now-discontinued Lagostina line.)

EMMA

Side-wing corkscrew. I'm of the opinion that a splash of wine or beer in your food and another glass for dinner is essential for a good meal. I like the simplicity and functionality of a simple side-wing corkscrew.

Reusable parchment paper. My mom gave me a packet of reusable parchment as a graduation present and I've used it ever since. The sheets of parchment are nonstick, reusable, and easy to roll up for storage. Almost everything that goes into my oven gets baked on one of these.

6.5-quart Dutch oven. Like my chef's knife, this pot almost never gets put away. If it's not in the drying rack, it's on my stove with something cooking inside! I use it for everything from sautéing a few vegetables to making a big batch of soup.

Baking stone. My baking stone lives in my oven. I like the even heat it puts out, and I cook everything on top of it. It's stained from years of sliding pizzas and loaves of bread on and off it.

HOW TO CHOOSE GOOD COOKWARE

Here are a few things we look for when investing in new cookware.

> **Weight.** The most important quality of a good pan, whether it's a stockpot or a frying pan, is weight. Look for heavy pans with thick cladding on the bottom. For the most part, heavy cookware will conduct heat better and more evenly. We prefer stainless steel or multi-ply, which combines a copper or aluminum core with a stainless-steel exterior and interior for extra strength and even heat conduction.

> **Nonstick versus cast iron and stainless steel.** Nonstick is a controversial thing in the kitchen, as many cooks remain dubious about the purported health risks of nonstick coatings. We certainly don't use nonstick for everyday cooking; cast-iron and stainless-steel pans brown food far better. But a nonstick finish is helpful in a few types of pans used for specialized purposes: muf-

fins, eggs, and crepes, for instance. These pans require extra care, as they need to be washed gently, and you should use only wood or silicone cooking tools—not metal—with these pans, or you will mar the finish.

> **Lid.** We try never to buy a pan without a lid, especially a really basic, everyday piece like a 10-inch sauté pan. We lean toward metal lids, as opposed to glass, since we are more comfortable putting metal lids in the oven.

> **Oven-safe cookware.** We prefer all our cookware to be oven-safe. Cookware is more versatile when you can use it to sear food on the stove, then slide the pan into the oven.

> **Price.** Quality cookware is justifiably expensive. But we look for a good match between the price and piece. We feel that $50 to $100 is just about right for a really good skillet we'll use every day. Two hundred dollars is a lot of money, but it's not too much for a Dutch oven we will use all the time. Of course, if we can find it half off at a discount store or online that's great, too.

THE BEST SOURCES FOR KITCHEN SUPPLIES

If you're equipping your kitchen for the first time, consider shopping at a restaurant supply store. Nearly every big town has some sort of restaurant supply outlet. If not, you can also buy items online (see Resources, page 286). These stores are great places to pick up inexpensive essentials such as metal tongs, metal mixing bowls, baking pans, and industrial-quality knives.

We also like shopping on Amazon.com; we find that Amazon often has the best prices on small electronics and gadgets. Other online resources include Overstock.com and Wayfair.com, especially for kitchen fittings such as faucets and sinks; and design emporiums such as Fab.com for tableware and accessories. Etsy.com's craft marketplace is a wonderful resource for handmade tools such as wooden spoons and salt cellars, and also for table textiles.

For good-quality pans and Dutch ovens, browse discount stores such as T.J. Maxx and Marshall's. They often have name-brand cookware at half off or more. Faith is gradually building up a collection of All-Clad cookware, bought at deep discount at T.J. Maxx.

"These are my five favorite tools in my Mexican kitchen: I use my espresso maker every morning as my law student beau needs his café. I'll also heat up some tortillas on my comal for his breakfast burrito. My cast-iron pans will be heirloom kitchenware for my children and their children if I continue to care for them properly. I prefer my molcajete to a food processor when making mole. A citrus reamer has made many a margarita and sangria." —*gabrielaskitchen*

"My Vitamix blender is the workhorse of my kitchen. I hardly eat cooked food anymore."
—*SydneyBristow*

We highly recommend scavenging yard sales as well as eBay and Etsy's vintage marketplace for treasures like old Le Creuset Dutch ovens. When shopping online, always double-check the dimensions and look carefully through photos for signs of worn enamel, rust, or discoloration.

We don't mention local kitchen specialty shops here, since you would know your local shopping scene better than we do. Shop your local store first if you have a good one nearby. Such shops can be invaluable resources, and it's a good thing to support the little guy!

5 RESTAURANT TOOLS WORTH HAVING AT HOME

There are several tools that are commonly found in professional kitchens that will help you cook better, with more speed and control.

1. **Scale.** Hard-core bakers love their scales, but a scale is good for more than just weighing flour and sugar. A scale is a precise way to weigh ingredients, instead of measuring by volume; it can actually be much faster and simpler.

2. **Bench scraper.** The bench scraper is a wide, flat piece of metal with a handle that pro cooks use to scrape their countertop clean, and to divide dough into equal pieces. We use ours to transfer chopped vegetables from board to pot, and to scrape up dough.

3. **Little bowls.** We keep a stack of small ramekins on hand to portion out chopped herbs or spices when setting up a recipe. Setting everything out ahead of time (a practice called mise en place) pays off.

4. **Instant read thermometer.** A good thermometer gives you control and peace of mind. We really love our Thermapen, a very fast, very accurate thermometer with an extra-thin probe. It's expensive at about $90, but we've come to rely on it. It's not just for meat, either; we use it to check the temperature of breads as well.

5. **Masking tape.** What's in the freezer, and when did I put it there? Avoid these questions by labeling bags and bowls with a quick scrap of masking tape and a marker.

BEYOND THE ESSENTIALS

You don't need a lot of equipment to cook well. We've enjoyed delicious meals whipped up in teeny vacation rentals with not much more than a dull knife and makeshift measuring cups made from yogurt pots. And yet the right tool can significantly contribute to your enjoyment of cooking. Beyond the essential knives and sauté pans, here are a few more tools that we think you might find a place for in your kitchen.

THE JOY OF GADGETS

Single use uni-taskers like the waffle maker are often scorned as frivolous space wasters. And it's true that having too many gadgets in your drawers can hold you back—if you don't use them. But let us pause for a moment to give some praise to gadgets, the tools we like despite ourselves; those that remind us that cooking should be fun as well as serious work.

"I use my old OXO cheese plane multiple times a day. It rarely sees the inside of the drawer because I seem to always be reaching for it. I love the easy way it cuts pieces of cheese that aren't too thick. Just right for crackers or melting on tortillas for my kids." —aprilf001

Sara Kate, for instance, is an unabashed fan of her garlic press, which doubled as a terrific toy for her toddler daughter. Faith loves her French nutmeg grater, which has just one purpose: to grind nutmeg, and it does so very well. She also adores her Chef'n Veggichop Hand Powered Food Chopper, which is a manual chopper, powered by a pull string in the lid. It's actually not really a uni-tasker at all; it's easy to pull out, use, and wash, so it's almost constantly in service for chopping nuts and making salsa. But it really can't be beat for sheer gadgety fun.

We come around to the same refrain again: If you love it, and if you use it, even the most goofy of kitchen gadgets can be a valuable tool.

CARING FOR YOUR KITCHEN EQUIPMENT

Now that you've invested in your kitchen collection, make sure to keep it in good shape. Here are a few notes on caring for your most important tools and equipment.

> **Hone and sharpen knives.** A good knife is a sharp knife. Keep your knives wicked sharp by honing them before every use. Honing doesn't actually sharpen the knife; it just realigns the microscopic edge into a straight line. To do this, run your knife down a honing steel (buy one at a good knife shop and have the salesperson show you how to use it). Get your knives professionally sharpened at least once or twice a year. You can learn to do it yourself, or you can drop them off and support a trained professional. And a tip: Don't forget your kitchen shears and slicers, like the blades in your food processor. You should be able to have any blade in your kitchen sharpened by a pro.

> **Oil cutting boards.** Wood cutting boards get dried out by repeated washing and drying, and if you want them to last a long time without cracking, it's best to oil them regularly. Every few weeks, rub in a small amount of mineral oil with a clean rag. Let the oil sit for a few minutes, then wipe off any excess.

> **Scour stainless-steel pans.** A good wash is enough to clean a pan, but simply washing a pan may not get all the burnt-on spatters off. From time to time we give our stainless-steel pans a little extra care by scouring them with Bon Ami, a gentle yet thorough cleaning powder that will buff the burnt-on stains away.

WHEN TO GET RID OF TOOLS AND COOKWARE

Sometimes, though, there's no way to bring a worn tool back to life. How do you know when it's time to get rid of a pan or utensil? When do you acknowledge that no, you're really never going to use that countertop griddle? Here are a few questions to ask yourself when you're lightening your kitchen of unused gear.

> **How recently have I used it?** With the exception of seasonal items like Christmas cookie cutters, if you haven't used a kitchen tool in six months or a year, then it is probably a good time to donate it to a better home.

> **Is it flaking, cracking, or peeling?** In the case of nonstick cookware, any flaking or peeling of the nonstick surface means you should throw it out. Don't donate it; it's not safe to cook in.

> **Does it still do its job?** Old countertop appliances like mixers and food processors with broken blades or frayed cords can often be repaired, but don't hang on to smaller tools once they wear out or stop doing their job well. When the markings on measuring cups and spoons are rubbed off (is that ¾ cup or ⅔?) it's time to let them go.

OUR ESSENTIAL SERVING-WARE AND TABLEWARE

The tools help you cook dinner, but servingware helps you put it on the table. So far we've noted many of the instances in which a piece can be used both for cooking and for serving. A pretty gratin dish can come to the table straight from the oven and look beautiful. But we also have a cupboard stocked with serving dishes. Here are our essentials.

> **Platters.** Nearly any dish looks gracious when spread out on a generous, beautiful platter. We look for oval and rectangular platters that are big enough to hold a roast chicken or a round cake. Crate & Barrel and CB2 are excellent sources of simple, inexpensive white platters.

> **Bowls.** We find it helpful to have at least a few 2-quart bowls in white china or stoneware for serving side dishes. When not doing duty as a serving bowl, one bowl might sit on the countertop to store fruit or onions.

> **Glass pitcher or swing-top bottles.** One of our rules for dinner parties is to always have water on the table. We use swingtop bottles (like IKEA's inexpensive Korken bottles) to hold water and iced tea.

> **Serving utensils.** A couple serving spoons, slotted spoons, and forks are helpful for serving at the table. We like to scavenge eBay and Etsy for vintage silver serving utensils at inexpensive prices.

> **Linens.** There's no substitute for cloth napkins. They look and feel so much better than paper napkins, and they are, of course, reusable. We gravitate toward linen napkins, like the handmade sets widely found on Etsy. They are a little more expensive than cotton, but they last longer and wash better.

We talk much more about our thoughts on setting the table in a gracious yet casual manner in the Gathering chapter (page 271).

A well-equipped kitchen is one that helps you cook with joy and ease, whether you have room for one pot or ten; and as our personal lists of favorite tools illustrate, each of us has a different style of cooking, with kitchen gear we love more than others. So build your kitchen as you see fit, and as need arises.

There are times in life, however, when you have to start from scratch. Cross-country moves, a first home, a divorce—major life changes can necessitate setting up a whole new kitchen. If you'd like a complete list to help equip a kitchen from scratch, see our handy checklist in the Resources chapter (page 286).

Vicki Simon and Tim Cohrs

Vicki Simon and her husband, Tim, spent over ten months renovating their dream home in Portland, where Vicki works as an interior designer. They gutted the back of their small cottage and combined the old space with a former porch to create a larger kitchen with a sense of the past, but updated for a modern cook.

Vicki has a passion for unique, vintage fittings, and she had a vivid sense of how this kitchen should look and feel. "My inspiration was the butler's kitchen I saw in a Rhode Island mansion," she says. "It was a furniture kitchen with a big table in the middle and pots and pans hanging from the ceiling." Vicki deplores built-in kitchen cabinets; she wanted every piece in this space to feel like a stand-alone piece of furniture. "I don't like the transition between horizontal and vertical that happens at the intersection of countertop and wall because this is a place that collects dirt."

Over a period of ten months, Vicki and Tim renovated their Portland kitchen completely, opening it up into a cozy, family-friendly space.

For her kitchen, Vicki placed a Craigslist ad asking for "old-school master craftsman" carpenters. She worked with a pair of carpenters who helped her restore, refinish, and build nearly every piece for the kitchen. They carefully tore up layers of linoleum and repaired some of the wood floor planks, and added additional salvaged wood that now show their age with a gentle patina of dents and scars. She worked with them to design and build expansive shelving. She found antique storage cabinets and painted them in her palette of soft creams and grays. "Everything had to be tall," she says. "I wanted to accentuate the height of the room."

The heart of her kitchen is the butcher-block island, which she and Tim have carried from home to home. "I don't want to bring out a cutting board; I want to cut right on the surface," says Vicki. "I'm a fast, practical cook—I want to have things ready to go." Tim keeps the island looking good; he cleans it with soap and water and a few times a year he oils it with mineral oil.

Vicki has a story for every piece in the kitchen, a mix of salvaged and new finds. You'll find art on the walls, much of it from Creative Growth Art Center, a nonprofit that serves adult artists with disabilities. Yet Vicki is always practical; everything beautiful also serves a purpose. She uses her family silver every day, leaving it out on the island within arm's reach. "I want everyone to use their silver!" Vicki exclaims.

The kitchen is full of small, thoughtful touches, such as handsome hooks next to the stove for towels and oven mitts, a custom set of dividers for baking pans and platters, and a reproduction sink.

Vicki prepares Thai steak salad, one of her family's favorite recipes.

Lauren owns a modest bungalow home in a suburb of Portland. Her kitchen has the advantage of a dining nook with a view of her garden.

Lauren Chandler

Lauren Chandler has two loves in life: cooking and climbing. She is a full-time cooking coach at Whole Foods Market in Portland, Oregon, explaining new foods, teaching classes, and offering resources to shoppers. In her time off, she is a rock climber looking for new challenges in the outdoors.

At home, Lauren's love of sunshine and earthy, simple foods is on display, as well as her laid-back approach. "I have an improvisational, 'throw things together' cooking style," she says and laughs, as she walks us out to the garden behind her small bungalow. She picks broad leaves of spring sorrel, new chard, and baby kale for a salad, pointing out how the kale is sprouting up naturally from last year's crop. "I love volunteers!"

Back in her kitchen, it's crowded and warm. Lauren lives with two roommates, Eric and Kara. Her roommates love the food Lauren cooks, but Eric has many food allergies, including one to gluten, which forces Lauren to be creative and resourceful in the meals she makes to share. "Eric pushes me as a cook—it's good for me."

Lauren's kitchen is small—a galley pass-through to the cheery, sunny dining room, which is ringed with shelves of cookbooks and kitchen supplies. The kitchen itself has a few touches to make it feel more homey and personal. Lauren took the doors off the cabinets so her collection of beautiful stoneware plates and vintage glassware can be seen, and she painted the ceiling a warm terra-cotta color that casts a glow over the space. Art hangs on the walls—much of it made by friends.

Lauren slices up bright watermelon radishes and tosses them with good olive oil and the greens from the garden. "My friends call me the salad whisperer," she laughs. The salad, slices of mango, and a plate of salmon that a friend brought her are brought to the table, and she and her roommates gather in the sun to eat.

Lauren removed the doors from her kitchen cupboards to make the kitchen more open, and to display her collection of handmade and vintage ceramic dishware, plus her jarred grains and spices.

A dining table and porcelain teapot collection (above) sit where a wall used to be.

Bridget Potter

Bridget Potter has lived in the same apartment across the street from New York City's Museum of Natural History since she and her now ex-husband bought the place in 1976. Bridget recounts, "The city was about to go into bankruptcy—everyone thought we were crazy to buy a place in the city."

She raised her family here and built an illustrious career in show business as a producer for HBO, NBC, ABC, and Warner Brothers, but when her second daughter left home thirteen years ago, she found herself alone in a big apartment with a strong desire to shake things up. Born in England, Bridget has no other family in the States. Once she got into the swing of life as an empty nester (while earning her bachelor's and master's degrees from nearby Columbia University), she decided that she had a great excuse for creating a new kind of family, one of friends and community, and that kind of family needed a new hangout.

She briefly considered moving to a new apartment, but couldn't find anything that felt like home. Around the same time her mother passed away and left her some money and antiques. She decided to renovate, starting with the kitchen, where she would incorporate some of the pieces inherited from an era when "no one bought anything; everything was handed down."

She knocked down the walls that separated the smaller original galley kitchen from a maid's room and a tiny bathroom and made one large, open kitchen. Getting rid of a bathroom and an extra bedroom in a New York City apartment is risky, she says, but all it had ever been was a teenage clubhouse. "The kids would play video games in there, piled on top of one another. Too many smelly hormones!" For her new life in the kitchen she wanted something glamorous, so she added chandeliers. But she also wanted whimsy and a certain casualness: "I don't need formality around food," she said; "it should be communal."

Though the kitchen was created in the spirit of big family gatherings, Bridget has become somewhat of an expert at cooking for herself. She doesn't skimp, either. Her favorite meals are turkey burgers she makes in bulk and freezes, stir-fries, and piles of sautéed broccoli rabe. In the winter she uses her crockpot often, cooking large batches of food and freezing it in individual portions.

Evidence of her British heritage is apparent throughout the kitchen—from her mother's teapot collection and nineteenth-century cabinet to the jars of Marmite and Lyles Golden Syrup she dips into every day. The recipes that were handed down have mostly gone by the wayside. She says she learned some things from her mother, mostly English dishes that she no longer makes, such as steak and kidney pie. When it comes to Great Britain, she is more attached to the antiques than the culinary style.

Bridget had a pantry custom-built by a local carpenter. Smart cabinetry design uses up every possible square inch: above, a skinny drawer for little things.

The mix of surfaces—wood, glass,
stone, stainless steel—makes Bridget's
kitchen warm and inviting.

Chris and Gretchen's kitchen is a sleek yet playful demonstration of their love for good design, art, and the outdoors.

Gretchen and Chris Hotz

When Chris and Gretchen Hotz open the door of their house in a quiet suburb of Portland, Oregon, the first thing a visitor sees is the kitchen. A sitting lounge flows directly into a long, open kitchen, with glass windows at the end and skylights overhead. The spotless kitchen and a view of their lush Portland garden form the backdrop for this friendly couple's exuberant art collection and lively family. Their son, Arrow, and dog, Ohio, love to run in and out and around the long, bright island, which is the centerpiece of their sleek and minimalist kitchen.

Chris, who owns a graphic design firm, explains that the kitchen fittings were custom-made by a woodworker friend, who built the cabinets to lie flush with the walls, with no handles visible. "We like that clean look," says Chris. When the couple renovated the kitchen, they also opted for a mirror-smooth Corian countertop, and an electric stovetop that nearly blends into the surface.

The whole family loves to cook together. Gretchen prefers to bake, especially comfort food such as chicken potpies. Arrow favors no-bake cookies like chocolate haystacks, and Chris likes to create fresh, colorful dishes, like a stacked crab salad that he and Arrow assembled together for us. Chris chopped red pepper, onion, and lettuce, and helped Arrow layer the vegetables with fresh avocado and crab.

Behind the sleek cupboard fronts there is strict order as well. "I minimized the stuff in our cupboards," said Gretchen. "It feels a lot more sane to just have a few things in their place." Gretchen opened the most organized Tupperware drawer we have ever seen. "I realized you have to keep yourself organized in the Tupperware drawer," she said, "or you can't find the lids! I threw away a bunch of mismatched pieces. All the lids fit the sizes now."

This streamlined kitchen is still playful, with Cole & Son's birch tree wallpaper and a huge bulletin board covered with art from Arrow and others. The most delightful pop of color is the faucet, which is neon yellow, a DIY project that Chris is proud of. "I bought a Hansgrohe faucet, took it apart, and had the metal components powder-coated for thirty bucks," he told us.

And in case it wasn't clear that this is a kitchen for good times with family and friends, you have only to look at their speaker system. "There's always music in this kitchen!" said Gretchen.

A GE Profile electric cooktop is nearly flush with the Corian countertop and a custom built-in pantry makes use of a tiny sliver of space.

CARING *for your* KITCHEN

From the very beginning of The Kitchn we have been cheerleaders for the importance of keeping the kitchen clean and organized, not just for hygienic reasons, but also because this is the room that nourishes you and provides vitality.

The kitchen is a temple of sorts, a sanctuary for your health and happiness. By keeping it clean and organized, you are apt to spend a lot more time there, which translates into fewer meals eaten out and ordered in, and more home-cooked meals. When your kitchen is well-stocked, your knives are sharp, and your oven is clean, you set yourself up to be a better cook. You are not just caring for your kitchen; you are caring for yourself and your family.

Before you restock your cleaning supplies and make resolutions about new habits, let's talk about why it's important to keep a clean kitchen and what "clean" really means for this room.

CLEANING PRODUCTS

We often seek out natural cleaners because as cooks we don't want to introduce chemicals into our food by using toxic cleaning products. Many store-bought natural products and DIY solutions are proven to work as well as, if not better than, their commercial and chemical counterparts, so why not use the more earth-friendly ones?

BUYING CLEANING PRODUCTS

If you're buying any cleaning products at all, the only products you need to clean the kitchen are an all-purpose cleaner (for everything but glass and mirrors), dishwashing liquid, and dishwasher detergent (if you have a dishwasher). If you have windows or other glass surfaces in your kitchen, add glass cleaner to the list.

Seek out these natural cleaners, which are our go-to products for keeping the kitchen clean and for protecting our health and the environment.

All-Purpose Cleaners

> **Method All-Purpose Natural Surface Cleaner.** Works on everything but glass.

> **Bon Ami Powder Cleanser.** For all surfaces (except wood) including countertops, tile (including floors), sinks, and appliances. It is not abrasive but still works pretty well for caked-on stains.

Dishwashing Liquid

> **Seventh Generation Free & Clear Natural Dish Liquid.** One of the most basic, unscented soaps you can find. It also comes in some pleasant scents like lavender and citrus.

> **Earth Friendly Products DuoDish, Lavender.** Another good option, though not as widely available as Seventh Generation.

Dishwasher Detergent

> **Seventh Generation Automatic Dishwasher Powder.** This is a commonly stocked brand that works well and has few harmful chemicals.

> **Nice! Dishwasher Packs Single Dose Detergent.** if you prefer the pod form of dishwasher detergent, this brand gets high ratings for effectiveness and low toxicity.

Glass Cleaner

> **Whole Foods Market glass cleaner, unscented.** The generic Whole Foods brand does the job well.

> **Simple Green Naturals Glass & Surface Care, Rosemary Mint.** A brand often carried at hardware stores.

Keep an eye on the Environmental Working Group's ratings on household cleaners for updates on the latest and greatest eco-friendly products. http://www.ewg.org/guides/cleaners.

MAKING YOUR OWN CLEANING PRODUCTS

It's easy—and cheap—to make cleaning solutions that can tackle just about any task in the kitchen, and since The Kitchn always has an eye toward the environment, we often post recipes and write about how to make these products at home.

Homemade cleaning solutions made with lemon should be stored in the refrigerator and will last up to two days. Vinegar, baking soda, and salt all last indefinitely, but when combined into a solution the mixture may degrade over time, so make small batches that you will use within a month or two and shake the contents before using. Any recipe containing both vinegar and baking soda should be used right away since combining the two ingredients creates a reaction that eventually fizzles out. Keep your homemade products in labeled sprayer bottles and jars.

Homemade Oven Cleaner

MAKES ENOUGH TO LIGHTLY CLEAN ONE STANDARD 30-INCH OVEN

2 cups baking soda
1 teaspoon natural liquid dishwashing liquid
¼ cup or more water

In a medium bowl, combine the baking soda, dish soap, and enough water to form a thick paste, like shampoo. It should be heavy, but not dry.

Start with a cool oven. If you have a gas oven, turn off the pilot light. Remove any dried debris with a hand broom or vacuum. Using a clean paintbrush or the back of a sturdy spoon, apply the paste to the inside of the oven. Let the mixture sit on the stains for a few minutes. For tough baked-on stains, let the mixture sit overnight. Scrub the inside of the oven, using a toothbrush to break up tough stains, then wipe the oven clean with a damp cloth, rinsing and wringing it out several times along the way.

Homemade Glass Cleaner

MAKES ONE BOTTLE

White vinegar
Warm water

Mix equal amounts of white vinegar and water in a clean, dry spray bottle.

Spray the vinegar solution on the window and wipe it with a clean lint-free cloth or a piece of crumpled newspaper.

Homemade Pot Scrubbing Solution

MAKES ENOUGH TO CLEAN ONE POT

½ cup to 3 cups water, enough to fill the pan halfway up to the highest stain (or ¼ inch deep if stains are only on the bottom)
½ cup to 3 cups white vinegar (use the same amount of vinegar as water)
1 to 3 tablespoons baking soda, enough to sprinkle a thick layer across all the stains

Place the water and vinegar in the pan and bring to a boil. Remove the pan from the heat and dump all but a few tablespoons of the solution into the sink. Add the baking soda. Scour the pan with an abrasive sponge. For stubborn stains, make a thick paste with baking soda and water, apply to the stain, wait a few minutes, and then scrub.

"I use white vinegar to clean countertops, wash the walls, get lime scale out of the coffeepot and teakettles, wash the vinyl siding outside, and for a homemade car wash. What else can you use to pickle vegetables AND wash your car? I always keep a couple gallons on hand." —Schwed

Here are a few things you might already keep in the kitchen that double as excellent cleaning solutions.

> **Boiling water.** Don't overlook the pure magic of boiling water. Pour a little over a greasy stovetop, let it cool, then wipe away the grime.

> **White vinegar.** Vinegar is an acidic cleaner that works for everything from walls to sinks.

> **Lemons.** A lemon rind ground in the sink disposal will freshen it, and lemon juice mixed with salt rubs away grease and stains on pots and countertops.

> **Baking soda.** Baking soda makes a good poultice for getting stains out of the countertop (scrubbed with a warm, damp scouring pad) and burned-on food off the oven or stovetop (see page 71 for full instructions).

> **Salt.** Combined with an acid, like vinegar, salt scours away stains and grease.

MORE IDEAS FOR EASY HOMEMADE CLEANING

By now you can tell that between warm water, lemon, vinegar, baking soda, and salt, you can pretty much clean anything. Some kitchen surfaces call for a specific approach, and we can thank generations of kitchen alchemists for helping us perfect the right formula for metal, wood, tile, and other surfaces.

> **Stainless-steel appliances.** Vinegar is the magic ticket for shiny stainless steel. Dilute the vinegar with water and store the mixture in a spray bottle. Use a microfiber or other low-/no-lint cloth to clean and to dry. This vinegar solution will remove smudges and fingerprints.

> **Granite and marble countertops.** Clean both granite and marble with a simple wipe of a nubby cloth or, for big spills and debris, use a sponge soaked in soapy hot water. You can also spritz granite with vinegar and wipe the surface dry with an old T-shirt or microfiber cloth. NOTE: Avoid acidic cleaners on marble. Hot soapy water works best.

> **Laminate countertops.** Clean textured laminate countertops with a brush and perhaps a mild soap. Stains can be lifted with a 3:1 mixture of baking soda and water. Be sure to dry the countertop after washing it to avoid water damage at the seams.

> **Wood cabinets.** Clean wood cabinets with a soft cloth soaked in warm water and a mild dishwashing liquid or all-purpose cleaner. Wipe dry with a soft dry cloth in the direction of the grain.

> **Tile floors.** Sweep regularly and use a damp mop soaked in a gallon of hot water mixed with a few spoonfuls of a mild all-purpose cleaner or floor soap. Rinse with warm water. To make it shine, wipe it dry with a soft cloth.

"I used the Bon Ami powder on my old stove all the time. My roommates would always leave gunk everywhere: caked-on oil, burnt-on grime, food and grease. With ten minutes, Bon Ami powder, and a sponge, I could get the stove even more clean than it was when I moved in."

—*chelseaellen*

HOW TO CLEAN THE KITCHEN

We approach cleaning our kitchens in two ways: we either go on a daylong cleaning spree, or we tackle one easy task in the kitchen every day. With a Daily Cleaning Plan you can keep your kitchen clean if you dedicate yourself to very light cleaning tasks every day. You can also combine tasks and consolidate a bunch of tasks into a weekend afternoon.

DAILY CLEANING PLAN FOR A CONSTANTLY CLEAN KITCHEN

☐ DAY 1	☐ DAY 2	☐ DAY 3	☐ DAY 4	☐ DAY 5	☐ DAY 6
Wipe down the outside of large appliances (refrigerator, oven, dishwasher) and small appliances (toaster, stand mixer, blender, food processor, and rice cookers).	Clean the inside and outside of the trash can.	Tidy the cookbooks, aprons, and towel and linen drawers.	Wipe down the baking containers (flour, sugar, cornstarch).	Clean out the refrigerator. Wipe down shelves and tidy the freezer.	Dust and polish the cabinet fronts and wipe down the range hood.

☐ DAY 7	☐ DAY 8	☐ DAY 9	☐ DAY 10	☐ DAY 11	☐ DAY 12
Mop the floor.	Scrub out the sink and wipe down the faucet.	Clean the inside of utensil holders and the top of the refrigerator.	Clean under the refrigerator and stove as well as possible. Some appliances can slide out, but be sure this is safe before proceeding.	Clean the seals on your dishwasher, refrigerator, and garbage disposal with a toothbrush.	Clean the windows and wipe down the sills.

☐ DAY 13	☐ DAY 14	☐ DAY 15	☐ DAY 16	☐ DAY 17	☐ DAY 18
Wipe down decorative accessories and pictures.	Mop the floor.	Wipe down the fronts of large and small appliances.	Tidy the pantry, canned goods, boxes, and bags.	Clean or wash cleaning tools (the sponge, towels, etc.).	Wipe down the interior cabinet shelves.

☐ DAY 19	☐ DAY 20	☐ DAY 21	☐ DAY 22	☐ DAY 23	☐ DAY 24
Wipe down the walls.	Dust and polish the cabinets and wipe down the range hood.	Mop the floor.	Wipe down the fronts of large and small appliances.	Organize the pots, pans, or other frequently used items in cabinets.	Scrub out the sink and wipe down the faucet.

☐ DAY 25	☐ DAY 26	☐ DAY 15	☐ DAY 28	☐ DAY 29	☐ DAY 30
Clean out the refrigerator, wipe down the shelves, and tidy the freezer.	Clean the inside of the microwave and clean the oven or set it to clean.	Wipe down the baseboards.	Mop the floor.	Wipe down the fronts of large and small appliances.	Dust the light fixtures and vent covers; clean the switch plates, removing with a screwdriver if possible.

ORGANIZING THE KITCHEN

Now that your kitchen is clean, it's time to organize it. Do you know where everything is, and can you reach the things that you use frequently? When you open a drawer is it cluttered with seasonal items like corncob holders and snowflake coasters? People are often stumped by how to organize their kitchen, and we always tell them the first step is to clean it out. (See our earlier chapters Tools [page 41] and Setting Up the Kitchen [page 13] to determine what you really need to have in your kitchen.)

The best time to organize your kitchen is when you do a deep cleaning. Put on some music, roll up your sleeves, and pull everything out of the cabinets and drawers. Tackle ingredients and tools separately. In both cases, decide what to keep and what to give away or toss. Then if, say, you're organizing tools and equipment, make piles on your dining table, floor, or even your bed (if that's the only place to spread things out) of baking tools, utensils, mixing bowls, and any other category that your stuff fits into. Wipe down the surfaces where they used to be stored, then put everything back in a way that makes sense. It might be exactly the same or it might be radically different. Now do the same for your ingredients, both in the cabinets and in the refrigerator and freezer.

BOOSTER SHOTS

Booster shots are manageable projects that upgrade your kitchen and help you maintain its health, appearance, and functionality. You can make a real difference with a small project, whether you have a few minutes, an evening, or an entire weekend to devote to your kitchen.

If all you have is a few minutes, choose one or two projects from the Daily Cleaning Plan on page 73 and make that combined task your booster shot. Even if you have only half an hour, you can still clean your entire refrigerator!

30-MINUTE REFRIGERATOR CLEANING

1. **Unplug the unit and vacuum behind it.** If your vacuum has a slim crevice tool, use it to vacuum under the front of the unit. Take a damp rag soaked in a capful of multipurpose cleaner and wipe down the sides and top. For brushed stainless steel, use a rag soaked with distilled white vinegar. Rinse the rag, wring it out, pour another capful of multipurpose cleaner on it, and slide it along the floor under the front of the unit, mopping away any remaining food particles and dust.

2. **Take everything out of the refrigerator.** Throw away or compost anything that is expired, moldy, or smells off. (Our conservative rule of thumb for composting is what comes out of the earth goes back in: raw fruit and vegetable scraps, natural papers, etc. More experienced composters process cooked foods and other items through their systems.) Clean out and recycle recyclable containers.

3. **Slide out the drawers and shelves and put them in the sink (if they fit) or the bathtub.** Soak them in warm, soapy water.

4. **Spray the inside of the refrigerator with multipurpose cleanser.** Don't forget the butter compartment. Wipe down each and every surface. Use a retired toothbrush to scrub the corners of the inside of the unit and the folds of the rubber door seal.

5. **Scrub the drawers and shelves.** Set them upside down on rags to dry.

6. **Soak a clean rag in a mixture of warm water and a capful of multipurpose cleaner and wring it out.** Wipe down all the jars and bottles that were in the refrigerator.

7. **Plug in the unit.** Replace the drawers and shelves. Return all saved items to the shelves and drawers.

ONE-EVENING PROJECTS

> Clean or replace hardware, such as drawer and cabinet pulls.

> Replace the kitchen faucet.

> Oil the cutting boards and butcher block with food-grade mineral oil.

> Sharpen your knives and scissors. You can do it at home on a sharpening stone (most knives like a seventeen-degree angle) by sliding the blade carefully back and forth, maintaining the angle. Or take your blades to a professional sharpener.

ONE-WEEKEND PROJECTS

> Paint the walls.

> Do a deep clean. Tackle all the steps of the Daily Cleaning Plan on page 73 in one weekend.

> Go through the kitchen and remove unneeded items. Review Chapter 2 and take stock of what tools you really need in your kitchen, then have a yard sale.

> Build/create a pantry from a closet.

"I have one chore per card, customized to my house. Every day I do one chore. On weekends or if I'm at home, I do three. It works pretty well to maintain order if not super cleanliness. —*Charlotte*

TRASH AND RECYCLING

Whether you like your trash and recycling in decorative cans (did you know you can spend $200 on a trash can?) or tucked away neatly under a cabinet, big kitchens have plenty of space for holding the trash and recycling; many kitchens even have a built-in arrangement. There are challenges inherent in having more than ample space for trash and recycling: The temptation to go large can actually present its own set of problems, primarily that with larger bins, odors build up.

However, if there is minimal space, fitting a trash and recycling center into a small kitchen can be a big challenge. If you have an under-sink cabinet, try putting in two office-sized cans (usually 12- to 14-quart size). Or, if you only have the cabinet door free, use a mountable frame that is designed to hold plastic grocery store–sized bags. This arrangement takes up minimal space and requires very little cleaning. For regular bins, we recommend frequent wipe-downs with a vinegar and water solution.

"I live alone in a tiny apartment, so my space is limited, but then so are the number of items I recycle. I try to reduce and reuse as much as I can. Plastic, glass, and metal all end up in the same bin, so I toss them all in a cloth tote bag that hangs inside the door to the cabinet under my kitchen sink. Once every few weeks I wash that bag out."

—*The Green Cat*

BASIC KITCHEN SANITATION

The big sanitizing question most cooks have is how to handle meat. How many recipes do you see that instruct "rinse and pat dry"? Many. A very famous chef at Sara Kate's culinary school once threw a whole chicken into the oven and, when asked why he didn't first wash the bird, said: "If a 400-degree oven doesn't take care of any bacteria, I don't see how tap water and a paper towel will." She hasn't washed a chicken since.

What about cleaning up the counters after handling meat? At that same culinary school, she was also taught to wipe down all counters and tools with a bleach and water solution after preparing meat, but since you don't have to worry about a food inspector in your own home, scalding hot water with an occasional spritz of white vinegar and then 3% hydrogen peroxide works best. These two fluids are effective at disinfecting countertops, but they will work only when used one after the next. *Science-News* magazine notes that you should never mix the two into a solution because you will create a toxic chemical called peracetic acid.

Those who are on an allergy-related diet have more strict kitchen sanitation requirements. This does not mean dousing it with chlorine bleach. Shauna Ahern, founder of the wildly adored website Gluten-Free Girl and a longtime friend of The Kitchn, says prepping a kitchen for gluten-free cooking isn't that hard. The only thing you have to do is give the kitchen a good scrub and avoid using any wood in food preparation: wooden cutting boards, spoons, and rolling pins trap gluten.

No matter how tidy we are, sometimes pest invasions are unavoidable. It happens to all of us. But take care of the problem promptly; lingering pests will only discourage you from using your kitchen. Fruit flies and pantry moths are the two most commonly reported pest problems we see in kitchens. Here are some natural solutions for mitigating an invasion.

EVICTING PESTS: FRUIT FLIES, PANTRY MOTHS, AND ANTS

You're making a beautiful meal and you find a pantry moth in your flour or ants along your counter. Not appetizing! Here are a few tips on banishing bugs.

> **Fruit Flies:** Remove the offending pieces of fruit. If the fruit is simply overripe, make a cobbler or a smoothie. Overripe bananas are perfect for Banana Bread (page 147). Now make a trap by filling a glass with apple cider vinegar and adding a few drops of dishwashing liquid. Place the cup near the flies.

> **Pantry Moths:** These moths infest flours and grains but can also turn up in other dry goods such as dried fruit and pet food. Adult moths are grayish-brown and smaller than a pinky nail. The larvae and eggs look like webbing. Discard anything that's infested. Remove everything else from the cabinet or shelf where you found moths and clean every nook, cranny, and corner with a vacuum and then with warm soapy water. Dry the area thoroughly before replacing the containers. Discard the trash and vacuum bags outside the home. To prevent further infestation, rub a few drops of peppermint, citronella, eucalyptus, or tea tree essential oil around the corners of the pantry areas. Store foods in airtight glass, metal, or plastic containers. Slip a few bay leaves inside food canisters and tape them inside your cabinets. Consider storing dry foods such as flour and cornmeal in the freezer. Some say this method only places the moths and larvae in a dormant state, and once brought to room temperature they are, in a sense, reborn. But at the very least they will be isolated from other ingredients.

> **Ants:** Make sure your kitchen is clean, but know that even the most clean kitchen can have ants. Scrub their scent trails with white vinegar. Follow their trails back to their point of entry, then use clear caulking (found at most hardware stores) to plug up the holes. Some people swear by using Borax in the holes before caulking. If you live in a house and can locate the trails outdoors, make a solution of sugar and honey (¼ cup each) and dissolve on the stovetop or in the microwave, and then stir in ¼ cup Borax and place the cup near the lines of ants outside. Keep this away from pets.

Rozanne Gold

Rozanne Gold began her cooking career in her early twenties as chef to then–New York mayor Ed Koch. She cooked for presidents, prime ministers, and world dignitaries. She put in years at the former Rainbow Room atop Rockefeller Center and the former Windows on the World in the north tower of the World Trade Center.

When not cooking in these legendary kitchens, she is in her home kitchen, a modest space in a 125-year-old Brooklyn brownstone where she has pumped out twelve cookbooks over the years. Most recently she and her teenage daughter Shayna hunkered down in the kitchen and wrote a cookbook called *Eat Fresh Food: Awesome Recipes for Teen Chefs*.

The kitchen is quirky: it still has its original parquet floors, along with solid oak doors and wainscoting, and stained glass above the expansive windows. The ceilings are thirteen feet high. Two walls are lined with antique porcelain serving platters, mostly English or early American, which she and her husband, restaurateur Michael Whiteman, have collected over the years.

With open shelving everything is on view, which is incentive to keep things neat and clean.

When Gold and Whiteman renovated their brownstone in 1971, Rozanne's friend James Beard looked at the 14 × 19-foot kitchen and said, "It's too large unless you have roller skates." Move the working area into half the space, he advised, with a large counter so at least two people can work around it without getting their arms tangled, and keep the sink close to the fridge. So that's the way she proceeded, using the other half of the kitchen to create a casual eating space.

Off the kitchen is a very narrow bathroom, only about thirty inches wide. "Beard was a mountainous individual," says Rozanne. "If he had ever tried to use it, he would have become permanently wedged in." In his honor, Rozanne and Michael named it the James instead of the john.

Like James Beard and Julia Child, Gold and Whiteman hang their pots on Peg-Boards for easy access. Whatever doesn't fit on the Peg-Boards is stored on open shelves to minimize playing hide-and-seek with their pots.

The kitchen is completely low-tech. Rozanne chose to install two five-burner ranges since she cooks at such volume, but other than that you'll only find a food processor, a stand mixer, a blender, and a coffeepot. There is no microwave or dishwasher. There are also no drawers. Everything in this kitchen is on display.

The family often has a dozen people to dinner, "which can generate a fearsome number of dishes." She feels that waiting for load after load to finish in a dishwasher would take more time than doing them by hand, and she notes that she keeps fancy hand cream near the sink to ward off chapped skin.

"We enjoy doing things by hand because it reminds us psychologically and physically of what it takes for the universe to create our dinner." In a world where modern innovations and automated tools are a valued part of kitchen design, Rozanne's way of doing things is a welcome exception.

Left: *Instead of an expensive double-wide range; Rozanne simply installed two regular ranges side by side.*

Above: *All of Rozanne's published cookbooks.*

Mother and daughter share tea and Rozanne's famous wine cake after school beneath their collection of platters.

Beatrice and Ramsey live in a Los Angeles cottage that also happens to be their dream home. "This house makes me feel like I'm on vacation," says Beatrice, who wanted the space to feel like an old country kitchen in Mexico.

Beatrice Valenzuela and Ramsey Conder

Beatrice Valenzuela's dream house is a cottage in the Echo Park neighborhood of Los Angeles. "I always wanted to live in a tree house when I was a kid," she said, "and this home feels like one." On an upper floor, with windows looking out onto the rolling hills of Los Angeles, her kitchen is the magical center of her small treetop abode, with Moroccan-tiled countertops, turquoise walls, and jars in artful rows.

Beatrice, who was born in Mexico, explained her inspiration for this kitchen, which she and her husband designed together: "I wanted an old Mexico kitchen, or one from Spain or Portugal—what a country kitchen used to look like. This house makes me feel like I'm on vacation. You would think that you were somewhere else, in another country."

Beatrice's collection of clay mugs comes from Puebla, Mexico, where they are handmade by women artisans. The tile in the kitchen is from a local Los Angeles shop that sells small lots of tile and other decorative items from Morocco.

Beatrice found a deep sink and added brass fixtures: "The brass faucet is like a little piece of jewelry." She traded in the kitchen's old stove for an antique yet classic stove they found in Burbank, and her husband built all the shelves. There are no cabinets in the kitchen—just open shelving, and a small pantry for the things that can't be kept in jars. She explained: "When I have cabinets I never use things—they're hidden. Mason jars make it really easy to know what I have, what I need to get, and what's been there for too long."

Beatrice loves to cook and entertain, and she has a small daughter, who loves to be in the kitchen with her. They keep chickens and quail, so Beatrice is a crack chef when it comes to eggs. When we met she was making bird in a nest (egg fried in toast) for her daughter. "I make everything with eggs you can think of," she laughed.

Her everyday cooking is influenced by her Mexican childhood, but also by the time she spent in France. "There's a bit of overlap. Instead of lettuce or cabbage I'll put arugula on something."

She often serves masala chai she buys from a friend; she brews it with a drizzle of rosewater. Rosewater went into the orange and grapefruit margaritas she served us, too, with a dried chili pepper on the side. "My favorite ingredients are orange blossom water and rosewater. I love using them in Jamaica tea; it's such a nice thing to treat people to iced tea and it makes people feel really sexy. I could be drinking flowers!"

What's the best part about cooking in her kitchen? She can lean out her Dutch door and gather herbs from the pots on her expansive deck, or step outside and pluck figs from the tree below.

"When I have cabinets I never use things—
they're hidden." says Beatrice, who designed
her kitchen to be full of open shelves.

John Kelly and Marianne Lannen

John Kelly and Marianne Lannen are photographers in Los Angeles who live in a coveted Spanish-style house. They follow a vegan diet and have created a kitchen to fit their specific cooking needs.

They say their cooking style is a combination of being inspired and being informed, which means they seek out mainstream recipes and simply alter what works for their vegan lifestyle. An iPad features prominently above a prep counter, but its contents are not limited to vegan recipe sites, and their refrigerator isn't dominated by vegan replacement foods such as seitan and tempeh. They just make most meals from scratch—salad dressings, soups, pesto, and their classic marinara sauce—all vegan, of course.

The renovation of John and Marianne's kitchen brought cleaner lines, more counter space, and a more classic design.

John and Marianne's kitchen is a cooking haven. It started out beautiful and functional (they raised two daughters here) but recently went through an extensive renovation to increase space, light, and functionality.

Before the remodel, their "pantry" was a few shelves in a closet opposite the washer and dryer, so it was very hard to reach and not very functional. By relocating the laundry upstairs and removing the powder room that was in the same space, they increased the kitchen size by almost half. That gave them plenty of room for a proper pantry with sliding shelves, making everything easily accessible without taking up a lot of floor space.

Their favorite thing about the new kitchen is how it is both well organized and aesthetically pleasing. Because of the custom knife and spice drawers, they never have to go searching. The added square footage and the extra light are especially nice. "Once the attached laundry and powder room were gone, the amount of natural light must have doubled,"

Marianne says. In addition to the increased sunshine, nighttime cooking is more comfortable with recessed and under-cabinet lighting. Replacing the old counter tiles with a distressed granite slab is a striking idea, and it's much easier to clean.

There really aren't any defined roles between this husband-and-wife team. Usually one of them will be the inspired chef, and the other lends a hand as sous-chef and wine pourer. Their vegetable-heavy dishes require lots of prep, so expanded counter space and self-closing doors and drawers keep the traffic flow uninterrupted so they can work together without being in each other's way. Thirty years of marriage later, they're bumping into each other just enough.

A tower of colorful plates complements their Mediterranean-style house. A simple still life becomes art.

YOU'VE FINALLY ARRIVED:
your kitchen is clean, organized, and beautiful. Now what?

You made a huge effort to get your kitchen in shape for cooking, so now we need to talk about the food itself. Sure, you can call it "cooking" when you toss a package of ramen noodles into the microwave, but is that cooking well? Our goal is to get you to a point where you can really cook in a healthy and inspired way without breaking your back or the bank.

How to
Cook Well

STOCKING *the* PANTRY
& PLANNING MEALS

How does one cook well? What a huge question, and one that is essentially the reason The Kitchn exists. We ask ourselves that question almost every day, and we are constantly working to be more nimble and creative in the kitchen, more apt to cook than to order takeout.

This chapter will offer some advice for getting your pantry in shipshape, and then we'll talk meal planning. We bring you real-life tips from our writers and our readers, people who are engaged, as you are, in the challenge of cooking daily. These are the ingredients, the processes, the skills you need to cook well, with or without recipes.

The best way to be a good cook is not to worry about being a perfect cook. In order to cook well, give up on perfection, or at least any ideas you may have that perfection is a fixed thing against which you must measure everything you do. Nothing we cook will look exactly the same as a picture in a magazine or taste the way our friend's dish did. Even a familiar recipe will not offer the same result from one day to the next time we make it.

Each day is brand-new, so is each potato or cup of flour or whole chicken. They are not the same potato or cup of flour or whole chicken we worked with last week. Ingredients will vary in quality and freshness; they will be drier or moister, or larger or smaller. Certain items will go in and out of season, or vary according to manufacturer. Good cooks and happy cooks take pleasure in responding to these changes and variations.

Further, your kitchen might be cooler or hotter than before, or you might have a new oven or a different knife in your hand. And, just as important, you are not the same person day to day, or at least you are not dealing with the same set of moods, energies, and priorities. The nature of the world is that everything is in motion; everything is in flux. Perfection, by extension, is a moving target as well. This is both the beauty and the challenge of cooking.

So cooking well, and indeed living well, involves responding with grace and agility to whatever circumstances present themselves. Which means we have to have a certain amount of openness and trust, and a willingness to be attentive and curious. It means we have to look more closely, be more aware and alert, and more forgiving. With our eyes open, we can then discover how each moment, each circumstance, has its own perfection: this particular lemon, this pot, this rainy/sunny/snowy day; this body today, this mind, this simple, extraordinary human life.

While there is no one right way to cook well, cooking always encompasses a vast set of skills. It involves shopping for groceries and stocking the pantry, storing and preparing ingredients, mixing and whipping, heating and searing, seasoning and drizzling, studying the nuances of texture and flavor, salt and acid, science and creativity. Cooking well means taking some risks and accepting your own compromises on evenings when you need a little help. And you can't learn it all in one go; it's a slow, daily accumulation of discoveries and learning with a simple goal: to feed you and yours with whole-some, homemade food—however you choose to define that.

But despite enticing fantasies of warmth and togetherness in a showroom kitchen, cooking is not always a romantic jaunt through a culinary won-derland. Home cooking today occupies a fraught landscape of America's "obesity epidemic," egged on by wacky television chef-entertainers and besieged by product marketing that tells us that cooking from scratch is really, really hard and we need a package to do it for us. The competing pressures are fierce: time, budget, skill, our culture's conflicted rela-tionship with both gourmet food and convenience products, and the strident, often conflicting, com-mands from health experts.

In the midst of that are the daily pressures of feed-ing yourself and perhaps a family, too. Eating never stops; the need for food arises at least three times a day, and the home kitchen is the place where that nourishment is best found. So how do you come home from work, open up the refrigerator, and just cook?

The daily grind of cooking will always have its nitty-gritty challenges and small defeats—the sod-den muffins, the eggplant slowly turning to mush in the back of the fridge, the carefully prepared dinner that your child sighs over and pushes away, all those funny moments where you throw up your hands and order pizza. And yet—the bone-deep satisfac-tion of home cooking is one of the most rewarding endeavors we know. We get so jazzed when we figure out a way to use up the ends of three ingredients at once, or take home-cooked leftovers for lunch. It's a pleasure to turn out delicious meals that you linger over with a friend or partner, scraping your plate and pouring one last glass of wine, feeling in that moment that the dinner table is the center of the home, and of your world.

Cooking well leads you to that moment, whatever you're eating. You've cooked. Let's make it happen more often. Here's where we begin. You need a pan-try and a plan.

HOW TO STOCK A PANTRY

A meal begins with your ingredients. What's in your pantry right now? Canned beans? Spices? A jar of tomato sauce? Congratulations—you have everything you need to make dinner right now (we're thinking a saucy stew of chickpeas and tomato over pasta or sautéed kale). A helpful pantry is one that helps you cook on the spur of the moment, even without a lot of fresh food in the house.

> **Chicken and vegetable broth.** While we love home-made stock, we also depend on a good-quality store-bought broth. We look for low-sodium broths and use them in quick soups and sauces and as the base of stews.

> **Canned legumes.** Beans are hearty, satisfying, and inexpensive protein. Toss a can of chickpeas with a little olive oil, lemon juice, and a cup of chopped vegetables and you have a quick and tasty lunch.

> **Canned tomatoes and tomato paste.** We make quick tomato sauce out of canned tomatoes, onion, and garlic, and add tomato paste to stews and sauces for greater depth of flavor.

> **Canned tuna, salmon, or other fish.** Canned fish is a delicious way to dress up a pasta dish and make it more substantial, or to make a quick sandwich.

> **Pasta and noodles.** What's a pantry without noodles? They're a nearly instant dinner, whether it's fettuccine with fresh vegetables, or Asian rice noodles with peanut sauce.

> **Rice, brown rice, and quick-cooking grains such as quinoa.** We like to make a big pot of brown rice on Sunday and then use it throughout the week in our meals.

ESSENTIAL COUNTERTOP STAPLES

Not exactly pantry staples, but always (always) on hand, these staples often sit on the countertop where we can grab them quickly.

> **Onions and shallots.** Onions form the base of so many savory dishes. We also like to caramelize a lot of onions at once and freeze them for later use in salads, pizzas, and sandwiches. Shallots are milder and sweeter than regular onions; we eat them raw in salads.

> **Garlic.** This goes in everything but cookies.

> **Salt and pepper.** We like to have at least three salts around: fine salt for baking and cooking; kosher salt for sprinkling on roasted vegetables and meat; and flaked, delicate sea salt, such as Maldon, for garnishing finished dishes. Invest in a nice peppercorn mill (avoid plastic single use mills): Faith keeps a Peugeot on the counter-top and Sara Kate prefers a Perfex filled with whole black peppercorns.

> **Olive oil.** Extra-virgin olive oil is delicious, but regular olive oil is fine for cooking. We buy economical olive oil in big tins to use for cooking, and finer extra-virgin oil for drizzling and finishing dishes. (Some favorite finishing oils include Laudemio and A l'Olivier).

> **Potatoes and sweet potatoes.** You'll often find potatoes and sweet potatoes in a basket in a dim spot in our kitch-ens (low light and good air circulation help keep pota-toes fresh). Roast a sweet potato and top with greens for a super-healthy dinner, or make an impromptu gratin by baking white potatoes, skins on and sliced, drizzled with a little milk, olive oil, fresh herbs, and salt.

ESSENTIAL BAKING STAPLES

> **All-purpose flour.** Most of the time, all-purpose white flour (we prefer unbleached) will be adequate for anything you're baking, be it cakes, cookies, muffins, or brownies.

> **Baking soda and powder.** Baking soda is sodium bicarbonate which, when heated, forms carbon dioxide gas, making your breads and cookies rise. Baking powder is basically baking soda with acid added. Shirley Corriher, in her great book *CookWise,* says that 1 teaspoon baking powder contains ¼ teaspoon baking soda. The other ¾ teaspoon contains the acid and cornstarch as filler.

> **If you don't bake frequently, it's important to check the expiration dates of your baking powder and soda before plowing ahead.** Or stir about ¼ teaspoon of baking powder into ½ cup of very hot water. The solution will immediately start to bubble if it's still good. To test baking soda, use the same method but add ¼ teaspoon of vinegar to the water before adding the soda. As before, if it bubbles up, your soda is fine to use.

> **Yeast.** We usually buy instant yeast and always double-check the expiration date before using, because once yeast is dead, it won't work at all. To test yeast's viability, mix it with the water or liquid called for in the recipe and add a pinch of sugar. Wait 5 minutes; the yeast should produce a bubbly foam. If you see this, the yeast is good to use. We like to store our yeast in the freezer, which keeps it reliably fresh.

> **Sugar and brown sugar.** We use white granulated sugar. We prefer dark brown sugar to light brown; the dark has deeper flavor.

ESSENTIAL FLAVOR BUILDERS

> **Vinegars.** Vinegar's complex tang is the secret ingredient in many recipes. We shake a bit of sherry vinegar into bean soup, and add rice vinegar to coleslaw dressings. If you had to choose just one vinegar, we'd recommend the mild rice vinegar, but we also keep balsamic, sherry, and cider vinegars on hand.

> **Anchovies.** A filet of anchovy blended into a marinade or dressing adds savory flavor without being too overtly fishy.

> **Chili paste.** We keep Korean chili paste or bottled Sriracha for drizzling over rice and adding to meat marinades.

> **Red pepper flakes.** Many dishes get better with a little kick from red pepper flakes!

> **Soy sauce.** Soy sauce is a way to add umami flavor and a little salt to dressings and soups.

ESSENTIAL FRIDGE STAPLES

If you looked in our refrigerators, here's what you would probably see:

> Yogurt. We're huge yogurt fans (plain, whole-milk, and as local as possible). Yogurt can go beyond the breakfast granola combo, too. Pour it into smoothies, or whisk it with eggs to bind together a light, casual pasta casserole with herbs and zucchini.

> Fresh herbs. Fresh herbs are perhaps the single greatest addition to your cooking. We throw handfuls into salads, marinades for meat, and roasted vegetables. Their fresh, vibrant flavor has no competitor.

> Fresh greens. We try to pick up a sheaf of greens like arugula, Swiss chard, or butter lettuce every other day at the market. We don't need a plan to use fresh greens. We make quick salads or throw the leaves into sautéed dishes.

> Citrus. Lemon and limes are always around. We squeeze them into cocktails or use them to make quick salad dressings.

> Eggs. We usually buy large eggs, and from the most local outfit we can find.

> Butter. Unsalted butter is a staple in our fridge (you can stock up and freeze the butter, too).

ESSENTIAL FREEZER STAPLES

Here are a few staples that we always have in the freezer, things that help us pull dinner out of a hat.

> Frozen greens and broccoli. On those days we've run out of fresh greens or want an easy addition to a casserole or pasta dish, frozen spinach or broccoli, lightly steamed, come to the rescue.

> Cooked chopped ham or carnitas. We like to freeze small portions of meat for adding to pasta or lunches.

> Frozen berries. A bag of frozen raspberries makes a quick and easy dessert, baked and topped with oat crumble or sugar cookie dough.

> Pancetta or bacon. Bacon freezes very well, and we usually have a packet in the freezer, waiting to be thawed for a last-minute stir-fry or breakfast.

> One emergency meal. Making a big batch of soup or pasta sauce? Pack one container into your freezer, to wait for that night you come home hungry from a long trip, or stagger home exhausted from work.

CHOOSING INGREDIENTS WISELY

Part of cooking well is choosing your ingredients wisely. It goes without saying these days that we're all concerned about the quality of the food we eat, especially meat. But there are no simple answers for shopping and eating responsibly, as food systems are complex and vary from one community to the next. Food is expensive, but many experts think it isn't expensive enough in the United States, and that America's food system is pushing down costs relentlessly at the expense of the quality of our food and our health. In the midst of that, how do you make good choices? This is a huge topic, but our quick philosophy is this: Do your own homework, and make your own judgments about the money you will spend on your food. There will always be compromises and trade-offs, and only you can consider the ones you want to make.

Establish relationships with your butcher, seafood provider, and growers at the farmer's market. It's rewarding to have conversations with the people who grow your food, and you will learn something from them, too. Building relationships transforms the process of shopping for food from passive consumerism into a positive experience that entails exploration and fulfills curiosity.

ORGANIC AND LOCAL CHOICES

We like to support local farmers, so we'll pay a little premium for fresh produce from the farmer's market, even when it's not officially organic. We also look out for organic produce when buying something off the "Dirty Dozen" list—the fruits and vegetables that have the highest pesticide residue. According to the Environmental Working Group's 2013 report, these include:

Apples	Peaches
Celery	Potatoes
Cherry tomatoes	Spinach
Cucumbers	Strawberries
Grapes	Sweet bell peppers
Hot peppers	Kale/collard greens
Nectarines (imported)	Summer squash

HOW WE THINK ABOUT MEAT

At The Kitchn we've always had a mix of dietary preferences among our contributors, and we're very aware and encouraging of vegetarian eating. But many of us also enjoy meat in reasonable quantities. For us, these meat choices go beyond beef, chicken, and pork to include lamb, goat, rabbit, and duck.

Our approach to meat is simple: Don't eat it a lot, and don't make it the centerpiece of every meal. Use meat for flavor; one chopped strip of bacon will add a lot of flavor to a pasta dish.

When judging how much to pay for meat, since well-raised, humanely butchered meat from local butchers often comes at a steep price, we make comparisons to restaurant eating. At a high-end restaurant, you may pay $40 to $80 for a really good steak meal. That's $30 to $60 a pound! But you can spend $15 to $30 for a truly excellent steak to cook at home—both a treat and a bargain.

We are very interested in some of the lesser-known cuts of meat and offal (Sarah Rae Trover's post on the wonders of beef heart is a classic), and we especially love goat, which is generally not too expensive and has a milder flavor than lamb. We look for darker meats in poultry, too; boneless skinless chicken thighs are very inexpensive and easy to cook, not to mention delicious.

SUSTAINABLE SEAFOOD

Fish is one of our favorite last-minute meals, since a pan-fried fish fillet can be cooked in a flash. However, seafood takes an extra measure of care and responsibility. Seafood's status is ever-changing; a fish that is fine to eat today may be endangered or overfished next year. We stay informed by using Monterey Bay Aquarium's Seafood Watch app on our smartphones to check the status of fish and other seafood while we are in the store. A good rule of thumb: the bigger the fish, the more likely that it's going to have both health problems and sustainability or bycatch problems.

PLANNING MEALS: *15 Simple Ways to Help Yourself Cook More Often*

Once your pantry is stocked, you can get down to business; you're equipped for dinner. Whether you are a planner or a spontaneous throw-it-together sort of cook, here are some ideas and tips, largely culled from our readers, of ways to get (and stay) inspired to cook well, and to do it more frequently. And yes, most of them revolve around planning ahead, as a little planning goes a long way in the kitchen.

GET INSPIRED

> **Spend time each week looking for recipes.** Carve out an hour on Saturday to sit down with a cup of coffee and recipe inspiration. This may feel like an indulgence, but just let yourself do it. Scan blogs and websites for recipes that look delicious. Pile up some cookbooks and reach for the sticky notes.

> **Save recipes in the simplest way that works for you.** Snip recipes and put them in a folder; bookmark them on your smartphone. Don't worry too much about your system; just use whatever works best and most easily. We've found that our readers love Pinterest because it's easy to visually browse what they save.

> **Ask your partner, family, or roommates what they like to eat.** This might sound obvious, but it's easy to get caught up in the week and forget to ask our households what they would like to eat. We get extra inspired, too, when we feel like we're cooking a meal as a gift—trying to delight the palate of someone we love.

> **Keep a meal journal.** One of our best inspirations is our own record of things we've cooked in the past. Start a journal and occasionally look back at what you were cooking a year ago, two years ago. It's a good way to remember things you used to cook, and still love. It can be even simpler, too: Emma Christensen, our recipe editor, keeps a running list with her husband on the refrigerator whiteboard called, "Stuff We Like to Eat." Even a simple list like this can remind you, in a pinch, that you love a baked egg over spinach for dinner.

"We have a list of meals that we love and are easy to cook hanging on our fridge. Those staples make it into the rotation frequently, and then I go through my Pinterest boards as well as cookbooks and magazines to find one to two new recipes to add into the rotation. Our staples list is getting longer and longer." —*Shelf81*

GET ORGANIZED

> **Start a calendar.** Now that you're gathering inspiration for what to eat, start a calendar of what you'd like to cook over the next few days or few weeks. It can be as organized as a Google calendar, with notes on each day for that day's menu. Or you can just jot notes to yourself in the corner of your laptop screen or weekly planner. The important thing is to write it down.

> **Create theme nights.** Some readers find it really helpful to have a theme night each week. Monday is pasta, Tuesday is fish, Wednesday is tacos. This doesn't work for everyone, but it may be especially helpful if you have kids. See if they want to get involved with planning their favorite tacos one week, or suggesting soups for the next month. Keeping the focus narrow will help you and your household make quick recipe decisions, too.

"I use a blank monthly calendar and plan the week's meals on the weekend, basing my grocery list on only those items. I now have a year and a half worth of meals to look back on—especially handy for ideas and to see what we were eating the same time a year ago." —*JenniferJulia*

> **Look for ingredient connections.** If you're thinking about cooking a pot of beans, look for other ways to put the rest of that pot to use. One night you stir some beans into soup, and then the next night you serve the rest with chicken on top. As you pick out recipes to make each week, look for ways to make your work do double-duty.

> **Plan for leftovers.** Most of us have at least some tolerance for leftovers. Faith regularly cooks one or two big healthy casseroles at the beginning of the week and eats them all week long for lunch. Some people can only eat leftovers for a single night. Either way, make a little extra of everything, and if you don't want it right away, freeze it.

"I use general guides like Soup Night, Pasta Night, beans to make it easier. I use grocery delivery Fresh Direct, and you can store shopping lists in there. I can simply dump the "Tomato Soup Week" list into my cart and I'll get everything I need for a typical week." —*CMCINNYC*

SHOP!

> **Choose a shopping day and make a list.** Successful meal planners look at their recipes and make a shopping list. Some online meal planning and recipe-saving services such as those from ZipList, Paprika, and Epicurious let you do this easily, extracting shopping lists from the recipes you have saved.

> **Shop what's on sale.** Some folks really like to organize their meals around sales. Is organic chicken a dollar off this week? Or canned chickpeas? Adjust your meal plan or shopping list based on the specials in your local grocery store and feel good about the savings.

GET IT DONE

> **Prep ingredients as soon as you get back from the grocery store.** Why wait until Monday night when you have less than 30 minutes to get dinner on the table? While unbagging groceries, wash and dry lettuce. Cut up fruit. Chop onions. Shred zucchini for quick stir-fries. Stack up glass containers of prepped ingredients in the refrigerator and bask in your own awesome preparedness.

> **Pre-cook components of your meals.** From-scratch meals don't have to be made in one night. Get some of the work done early, when you have the energy. For instance, start a batch of tomato sauce while you wash greens and prep squash. The sauce can go on pizza one night, and in lasagna the next.

> **Be strategic about freezing.** The freezer is your friend. Actually, it's the friend of future you. Make a double batch of that previously mentioned sauce and freeze half for later. Make a double batch of soup, stew, chicken cacciatore, cooked beans—then throw it in the freezer. A month later, those leftovers will look fresh and tasty!

> **Don't overstuff the refrigerator.** It's easy to get overwhelmed when your fridge is too full. Also, new items may get hidden in the back, forgotten behind the mustard. Don't let things go bad. Keep your fridge airy and light, with a sensible, realistic amount of food in it. Keep a list nearby of everything in the fridge, especially leftovers, as a visual reminder of what remains to be eaten.

> **Keep a well-stocked pantry.** Meals are easier and quicker to prepare if you keep your pantry well stocked. Don't run out of olive oil at inconvenient moments. Have spices ready to dress up chicken and beans quickly. Keep a lemon and a sheaf of fresh herbs in the fridge at all times.

FIND A COMMUNITY

If cooking is something you love and want to improve on, the final piece of advice we'd like to offer is this: find a food community. Whether that's a little pack of friends cooking through a new cookbook every month, or colleagues with an outsized passion for pizza, the real work of learning how to cook day in and day out is easier with encouragement from other folks. We hope that The Kitchn is a place for that, too; it's always been our aim to foster conversations every day that inspire you to cook and teach us all something new.

"I start with a blank index card. I list at least 7 meals that I will be interested in cooking for the next week. Usually this includes a composed salad of some sort, a soup, something with beans, a fish dish, a pasta dish or two, and what we call a "thunder bowl," which is usually whole grain plus greens and veggies plus eggs on top. Tonight it's bulgur, kale and broccoli, eggs, and maybe a bit of chorizo. The shopping list goes on the reverse of the index card. This goes to the store with me, and the meals are crossed off when eaten."

—PAMELA AT CLOCKWORKCROW

THE KITCHN'S COOKING SCHOOL

50 Essential Skills

There are many essential skills we use every day in the kitchen, skills that form the backbone of our cooking, enabling us to prepare food safely and quickly by habit, instinct, and with our senses. But not all cooking skills feel like Big Important Things to Know. Some of the most interesting discoveries lie in the smallest moments in the kitchen. From whisking eggs to measuring flour, many daily kitchen tasks are easy to take for granted.

At The Kitchn we've observed how much our fellow cooks enjoy discussing even the most minute aspects of their kitchen lives, sharing and examining the things they know and also learning something new in the process.

So let's talk techniques—the big and the small, the essential and the interesting. We spent some time walking through our kitchen habits and processes and came up with this list of 50 essential techniques and processes we depend on. Whether you're looking for a refresher or a beginner's course in the essential techniques of cooking, these are skills you'll want to know by heart.

PREPARATION TECHNIQUES

Lesson No. 1

HOW TO READ A RECIPE

Before cooking from a recipe, read it all the way through, asking yourself questions. Start with the obvious: Do you have all the ingredients? Look up unfamiliar terms. More questions to ask include:

> **Pan size.** Do you have the right pan?

> **Preheating.** Does the oven need to be heated first?

> **Does a rack in the oven need to be moved?** Do it before the oven is hot!

> **Do you need to soften or melt butter?**

> **Are there any ingredients divided in the recipe, or used twice?**

> **Are you dividing or multiplying the recipe?** If so, jot down notes on the final ingredient quantities, instead of adjusting them in your head on the fly.

Lesson No. 2

HOW TO PREPARE TO COOK

After you've read the recipe, what else should you do? On the one hand, there is the romantic ideal: a pristine workspace, with a scrubbed and empty sink. Small bowls laid out, with the ingredients chopped and prepped in each. Pans at the ready and a platter waiting for your finished dish. Candles on the table, children eager to eat. What luxury! That's why it's called an ideal.

In real life, what's truly essential before cooking is a clean cooking space. It's stressful and annoying when your worktop is cluttered. Even if (especially if) you have only one square foot of space, clear it and wipe it down.

Then look again at your recipe—grease any pans if needed. Make sure there's enough fridge or freezer space if you have to chill something. Begin with the end in mind, and think backward through each step of cooking. You don't need to create a TV-perfect setup, but you should do what it takes to feel comfortable in your kitchen before beginning.

TOOL SKILLS

Lesson No. 3

HOW TO MEASURE LIQUIDS

> **Liquid measuring cups versus dry.** Why use different kinds of cups for liquid and dry ingredients? Liquid measuring cups contain the same volume—they just give you a little breathing space above the top measuring mark. Measuring out 1 cup of water in a dry measuring cup means you need to fill it absolutely to the top (and you might spill a little!).

> **Measuring tips.** When measuring liquids, lift up the measuring cup or bend down and look at it from the side to make sure the liquid is level with the mark. When measuring sticky liquids like honey and molasses, measure them after adding oils so that they will pour out easily. (If you're not measuring any oils for your recipe, grease the inside of the measuring cup or measuring spoon first.)

Lesson No. 4

HOW TO MEASURE DRY INGREDIENTS FOR BAKING

The way you fill your measuring cup matters. If you plunge your measuring cup into the flour you will end up with more than if you spoon the ingredients into the cup. Pay attention to how a recipe tells you to measure your dry ingredients. Should the flour be leveled off lightly with the edge of a knife? Should the brown sugar be tightly or loosely packed? As always, the most accurate way to measure ingredients is by weight. Not all recipes have weight measures for ingredients, but when they do, it's wise to stick to them.

Lesson No. 5

HOW TO HOLD AND USE A CHEF'S KNIFE

> **How to choose a knife.** Searching for a knife that suits you is an important step in learning to cook well. It is best to try various knives at a cooking store like Sur La Table or another local shop with a good selection of cooking knives. Hold the knife. It should feel comfortable in your hand, and weighty enough to bring some force without being so heavy it tires your arm out. If the store is set up for it, try it out by cutting vegetables.

> **Holding a knife.** Grasp a chef's knife firmly and confidently. Choke up on the knife, by moving your hand to where the handle meets the blade and pinching the back end of the blade between your thumb and forefinger. (Don't lay your forefinger on the top of the blade.) The closer your hand is to the blade, the more control and leverage you'll have.

> **Protect your opposite hand.** "The Claw" is how we describe the position of your opposite hand while using a knife, the hand that is holding the onion or chicken breast or other piece of food. Hold the food down on the board, with your fingers in the shape of a claw, tucking in your thumb, and rest your wrist on the cutting board, knuckles out instead of fingertips. This way if your knife slips off an onion or piece of squash, you'll only scrape your knuckles, not gash your thumb.

> **Good knife skills.** To quickly cut up herbs or garlic, place the palm of your other hand on the tip end of the knife to rock the knife back and forth across the board. After chopping or mincing vegetables, when you want to scrape up pieces or clean your cutting surface, scrape with the back of your blade, not the sharp edge, so as not to dull your knife.

Lesson No. 6

HOW TO STABILIZE A CUTTING BOARD

A stable cutting board is an essential element of exercising good knife skills. It is very unsafe to cut on a board that is slipping out from under your knife, or rocking as you cut. The likelihood of cutting yourself rises, and the instability also slows down your work. It's nice to have a cutting board with rubber feet to keep it from rocking or sliding. If your cutting board doesn't have feet and tends to move around, here are two ways to keep it in place:

> **Use a wet towel.** Dampen a kitchen towel or a folded paper towel and lay it down under your board.

> **Put a foam shelf liner underneath.** Cut a piece of foam shelf liner (found at hardware stores) to the size and shape of your cutting board and lay it underneath.

COOKING SKILLS

Lesson No. 7

HOW TO BOIL AND SIMMER

Oh the cheek! We're going to tell you how to boil water because we don't think a cook is ever too old or too experienced to revisit this essential. The basics are basic: To boil water, place a pot with your desired volume of water over high heat on your biggest, strongest burner, and let it go. At a full rolling boil there will be large bubbles that make a lot of noise, a dull Niagara roar on the stove. A simmer is what you get when you turn the heat down after achieving a rolling boil. Occasional bubbles will pop up, or a stream of quieter, small bubbles. Turn the heat down even more and at a low simmer you'll have barely vibrating water and few bubbles if any.

Lesson No. 8

HOW TO HEAT A PAN

Many recipes begin with an instruction such as "Heat a pan on the stove." But how do you know a pan is hot enough? This depends on the recipe and the purpose of the hot pan. If you're heating a stainless-steel pan to sauté or sear, usually you will place the pan over medium to medium-high heat. Heating a pan takes a lot less time than you might think. A minute or two is usually enough to get it sufficiently hot.

If you're going to add oil, the oil should shimmer but not smoke after you pour it in the pan. Oil should never smoke. If the oil does smoke, remove the pan from the heat immediately and wipe out the oil, then let the pan cool down before trying again.

Simmer

Boil

HOW TO WHISK AND STIR

All right, we told you how to boil water, now we're talking about stirring and whisking. What's the difference? Stirring uses a spoon or spatula and is all in the elbow and shoulder. Whisking uses a whisk or fork, and the motion is in the wrist.

The goal of stirring, when you're assembling a salad, mixing pasta, or making anything else that involves lots of components, is to mix everything evenly and thoroughly. To do this, use a wide spatula or wooden spoon, and a bowl that is big enough to easily hold all your ingredients so that they won't spill out. Stir from the outside of the bowl toward the center, turning all the ingredients over.

When stirring a pot of something hot on the stove, like polenta, custard, or soup, remember one image: the figure eight. Stir with your long spoon touching the bottom of the pot, going around and around in a figure eight to make sure all areas and corners of the pot are covered.

When whisking, also remember the outside-in motion. Use your wrist to flip and tumble the liquid or batter, scraping the bottom of the bowl with the whisk on each turn.

HOW TO SAUTÉ

Sautéing is one of the most basic tasks in cooking. In French, to sauté means "to jump," since sautéing means constant stirring, tossing, and tumbling food in a pan over medium to high heat. You can act like a TV chef and flip your food in the air, but we aren't usually so daring! You'll get fine results simply using a spatula or spoon to keep the food in the pan moving as it cooks.

HOW TO DEGLAZE A PAN

While terribly fun with delicious results, plenty of fancy French techniques are not really weeknight routines. (Do you make a habit of demi-glace? Neither do we.) But deglazing is a radically simple and essential technique that will take your cooking to the next level. In fact, you should deglaze nearly every pot and skillet you use to sauté or braise food.

To deglaze simply means to pour liquid into a hot pan and to use that liquid to help scrape up any leftover bits of meat or grease that have formed a "glaze" or coating on the pan. This is the technique for making the simplest sauces and gravies. After you sear a steak and remove it from the pan, for instance, pour in a splash of any rich liquid, such as red wine or broth, and simmer it over low heat, scraping up all the delicious bits left behind by the meat. Easy sauce!

But even when you have no need for a sauce, always pour a cupful of warm water into your hot skillet when you're finished with it. Stir and scrape it for a moment over low heat, and presto—you'll have transformed your pan into a state of cleanliness, leaving almost nothing for the dishwasher to do.

HOW TO REDUCE A LIQUID

When reducing a liquid to intensify flavor or to make it thicker, bring it to a boil then lower the heat to a simmer. To check reduction, use the chopstick trick to see how far the liquid has reduced. Dip a chopstick into the liquid and note the liquid's height, rather like using a dipstick to check your car's oil reservoir! Knot a thin rubber band at that height on the chopstick. Bring the liquid to a simmer, and check how far it has reduced by dipping the chopstick in from time to time and comparing levels.

HOW TO DRY-ROAST SPICES

Roasting intensifies flavor, and one of our favorite ways to amplify flavor in a recipe is through dry-roasting spices. Try roasting a stick of cinnamon, then grinding it up to sprinkle on oatmeal, or roasting mustard seeds and cumin to add to a potato salad.

To roast spices, heat a dry skillet over medium heat. Add whole spices and toast them for about 60 seconds, shaking the skillet frequently, and take them off the heat as soon as they smell toasty. Pour onto a plate to cool.

Lesson No. 14

HOW TO SEPARATE AN EGG

Eggs separate better when they're cold; there is less chance of the yolk breaking. There are a couple of methods for cracking and separating an egg. Faith likes to separate an egg by breaking it into her hand, letting the egg white fall through her fingers and holding the yolk in her palm—messy, but effective. Sara Kate likes to pass the yolk back and forth between two shell halves. Choose whichever method works for you. Some people worry about salmonella getting passed into the egg from the outer shell when using this method, but we've never had a problem.

And since we're steeped in online media, we have to mention a video of a crazy trick involving a plastic bottle and an egg. Search "very cool way to separate yolk from egg white." Trust us.

If you get a bit of shell in the bowl, lift it out with another piece of shell. Also, the best way to clean up spilled egg whites is with a handful of salt. Throw it on the spill, let it congeal, then wipe up the mess.

Lesson No. 15

HOW TO THICKEN A SAUCE

If you have a sauce that didn't turn out as thick as you would like it, you have a few options. If it is a fruit or broth-based sauce, keep simmering it over low heat to reduce the sauce further.

You can also add a small pat of butter. This won't thicken the sauce substantially, but it will make it taste richer and give it a more luxurious texture.

Another option is to thicken the sauce with a roux (pronounced "roo"), which is a paste of equal amounts of butter and flour. If you've already got a sauce going in one pan, prepare the roux in a separate saucepan. Start with 1 or 2 tablespoons of butter for every cup of liquid you need to thicken (we generally start with 1 tablespoon of butter). If you are making a very thick sauce, start with 3 tablespoons of butter.

Melt the butter over medium heat in the separate saucepan. When it foams up, add an equal amount of flour. (For example, if you use 1 tablespoon of butter to thicken 1 cup of liquid, then add 1 tablespoon of flour.) The mixture will be clumpy at first, but whisk it vigorously into a smooth, thick paste. When the mixture begins to bubble, turn the heat down to low.

You only need to cook the roux for a minute or two; don't let it color. Add 1 cup of the liquid to the roux slowly, whisking constantly to avoid clumps and so the liquid is absorbed evenly. When the mixture is smooth, pour and whisk the roux back into your original pot of sauce. Simmer lightly for a couple minutes to help the sauce thicken.

Lesson No. 16

HOW TO COOK GRAINS

Each sort of rice and grain is cooked a little differently.

We usually consult the package instructions when cooking a new or unfamiliar grain, but we have provided a chart below with basic cooking times and liquid proportions for some of the most common grains and rice. When cooking grains, any clear liquid can be used, such as water, chicken stock, or vegetable broth. Avoid milk or dairy unless directed by a recipe, as more liquid may be needed for full absorption.

The basic method for cooking grains starts with bringing the liquid to a full boil. Stir in the grain and bring the pot back to a boil. Cover, if directed by the chart, and cook for the recommended time. If the grain is cooked covered, once it is cooked, after removing the pan from the heat, leave the lid on for at least 5 minutes, then remove the lid and fluff the grain or rice with a fork.

> **Rice varieties.** Long-grain rice will take more liquid than short-grain varieties, and brown rice also takes longer to cook than white rice. So don't swap one for the other willy-nilly.

> **Cooling grains.** When cooking rice or grains to be distinct, fluffy, and chewy for a salad, immediately spread them on a sheet pan after cooking, and gently stir in a drizzle of olive oil.

> **Measuring Cooked Grains.** To keep cooked rice or grains from sticking to a measuring cup, fill the cup with water and pour it out. Then measure the grains; they will slide out easily.

> **Freezing Grains.** Most rice and grains freeze very well. Spoon cooked, cooled grains into plastic freezer bags and smooth flat. Freeze in flat stacks, which are easier to store. Flattened sheets of cooked rice, straight from the freezer and peeled from their bags, reheat quickly in the microwave or in a saucepan without having to be thawed. (Bonus: The grains don't become mushy.) You can even use frozen rice for fried rice; add it straight to the pan, still frozen.

GRAIN	LIQUID NEEDED TO COOK 1 CUP OF GRAIN	COOKING TIME	COVERED?
White rice, long-grain	2 cups	18 minutes	Covered
White rice, short-grain	1½ cups	20 minutes	Covered
Brown rice, long-grain	2¼ cups	50 minutes	Covered
Brown rice, short-grain	2¼ cups	35–45 minutes	Covered
Quinoa	2 cups	15 minutes	Covered
Steel-cut oats	3½ cups	20–30 minutes	Uncovered
Wheat berries	3 cups	40–50 minutes	Covered
Farro	3 cups	30 minutes	Covered
Pearl barley	2½ cups	30 minutes	Covered
Millet	2 cups	15 minutes	Covered

HOW TO SEASON TO TASTE

Do you sometimes wish that a recipe would just tell you how much salt to use? Well, too bad. Salting to taste is one of the best ways to develop your palate as a cook.

Salt plays two very important roles in a dish. First, it reduces bitter flavors. Second, it allows the aromas and tastes of the other ingredients in the recipe to shine through. If you have a dish that tastes flat or bitter, a little salt may be the only fix you need. Before adding more spices or seasonings, try just a pinch or two of salt, depending on the number of servings. Taste again and see if the flavors have improved. Notice how much you added and file that info away for the next time you make a similar dish. Also, remember that salt adds texture as well, so leaving a dish a tiny bit short on salt leaves room for the person eating the dish to add finishing salt for a pleasant but subtle crunch to each bite.

Try to ignore the instinct to taste for saltiness. Usually we don't actually want the dish to taste salty. Instead, ask yourself how all the other flavors are coming through. Does this soup still taste muddy, or are the flavors bright? Can you taste the sweetness from the squash?

Taste your food throughout the cooking process—not just when you need to season it. Pay attention to how it tastes—do you notice something missing? It's best to err at first by salting too little; more salt can be added at the table if needed, but it's almost impossible to un-salt a dish.

And don't forget the acid—while many new cooks under-salt their food, salt isn't the only thing that makes a dish delicious. Acids such as vinegar and lemon also play a big part in answering that question: "What's missing?" A dash of vinegar in a soup or stew can brighten the dish's taste, as the acid makes savory flavors stand out more distinctly. But add it to the pot slowly; a teaspoon or less at a time for a recipe with 4 to 6 servings.

HOW TO ADAPT A RECIPE TO THE SLOW COOKER

If you love your slow cooker, we have some simple tips for adapting your favorite recipes to this handy tool. The best candidates are braised dishes such as meat stews, beans, and vegetables that need longer cooking and that cook in liquid. Read through a recipe and follow any steps that are done on the stovetop to develop flavor, like browning meat, sautéing onions and garlic, and folding in spices. Then watch for a transition word such as *simmer* or *bake*. Once your recipe moves into the long, low, and slow phase of cooking, toss it in the slow cooker. Here are some more tips:

> **Cut all ingredients the same size.** This ensures they'll cook at the same rate.

> **Use less liquid.** There is very little evaporation in the slow cooker. If you're adapting a stew, braise, or soup recipe, it's likely that you won't need to use all the liquid called for. Put all your ingredients in the slow cooker and then pour the broth over top. It should cover the vegetables by about ½ inch.

> **Place longer-cooking ingredients on the bottom.** Meats and root vegetables will take longer to become tender. Tuck them around the bottom and sides of the slow cooker, where they will have more direct contact with the slow cooker's heating element.

> **Choose a cooking time.** Recipes with meat, such as chili and pork shoulder, are best when cooked for 6 hours minimum on HIGH, or up to 10 hours on LOW. Vegetarian recipes are best cooked for around 4 hours on LOW, but they can cook for a minimum of 2 hours or a maximum of 6 hours (after which the vegetables start to get unpleasantly mushy).

> **Save these ingredients until the last hour of cooking:** Softer vegetables like peas, corn, bell peppers, and spinach, as well as seafood, cooked grains, or canned beans, dairy products, and coconut milk.

FRUIT AND VEGETABLE TECHNIQUES

Lesson No. 19

HOW TO STORE FRUITS AND VEGETABLES

Nothing is more frustrating than spending good money on produce and then having it rot. Never store fresh fruit with vegetables. Some fruits give off high levels of ethylene (a ripening agent) and can prematurely ripen and spoil surrounding vegetables. ("One bad apple" is a very real thing.)

Storing Vegetables

Before storing vegetables, remove ties and rubber bands and trim any leafy ends. Leave an inch of stem to keep the vegetable from drying out. Leafy greens can be washed before storing by soaking them in a sink full of water, while soft herbs like basil and cilantro and mushrooms should not be washed until right before they are used. Make sure the bag you store the veggies in has some puncture holes to allow for good air flow. Pack vegetables loosely in the refrigerator. The closer they are together, the more quickly they will rot.

Sturdy vegetables such as winter squash, turnips, potatoes, rutabaga, onions, and garlic can be left at room temperature, as long as they have plenty of airflow and ventilation, as in a wire or wicker basket.

Storing Fruits

Avocados, tomatoes, mangoes, melons, apples, pears, and stone fruits like plums and peaches, will continue to ripen if left sitting out on a countertop, while items like bell peppers, grapes, citrus fruits, and berries will only deteriorate and should be refrigerated. Bananas in particular ripen very quickly, and will also speed the ripening of any nearby fruits, so it is best to store them in a separate corner of the kitchen.

Lesson No. 20

HOW TO PREP SALAD GREENS

When you buy a whole head of lettuce or other greens, such as collards, you should wash them thoroughly. Separate the leaves gently and rinse them under lukewarm water. Shake the water off, then wrap them in a lint-free kitchen towel. Roll up the towel tight enough to absorb the water, then unroll the towel and let the greens air-dry. It's best to let salad greens get as dry as possible. Water on greens repels dressing.

HOW TO CUT VEGETABLES

You don't need to be a wizard with your knife, but if a recipe calls for matchstick potatoes, you should know what that means. Here's a quick guide to some of the common ways to cut up vegetables.

> **Cube.** The recipe should provide guidance on size, such as "small cubes," but cubed vegetables tend to be about 1 inch in size. If you're cubing a squash or root vegetable, slice off the top and bottom, then cut the vegetable in half lengthwise; lay the flat part on the cutting surface, then slice it into thick slices, which can be laid flat and cubed roughly.

> **Dice.** Dice are much smaller cubes. This cut is used especially with soft aromatics such as onions, bell peppers, and celery. Typical dice is about ½ inch.

> **Mince.** Minced vegetables are a lot finer than diced vegetables. Mincing is often used for garlic; rock the knife back and forth over chopped garlic, making it even finer. Add a pinch of salt to keep the garlic from sticking to the knife.

> **Slice/half-moon.** Sliced or half-moon vegetables (half-moon often applies to onions) are achieved by slicing vegetables in half lengthwise, then laying them on their flat side and thinly slicing them. Pay attention to the recipe, which should give you instructions on thickness.

> **Matchstick/julienne.** Either term, used interchangeably, means to cut a vegetable (most commonly carrots, zucchini, and peppers) into long, thin sticks.

> **Shred.** An even finer and thinner matchstick shape, shreds are short, thin ribbons created by running the vegetable through a food processor, on a mandoline, or by grating it on a box grater.

Lesson No. 22

HOW TO PREP GARLIC

To separate a head of garlic into cloves, press down quickly and sharply on the top of the head with the flat of a chef's knife. The quickest way to peel one or two garlic cloves is to lay them on a cutting board and smash them hard with the heel of your hand resting on the flat of your chef's knife. The papery skin will just fall away. To peel larger quantities, place separated cloves in a large metal bowl and invert a similarly sized bowl on top. Shake like crazy for 10 seconds, and then peek inside. The peels should have completely flaked away from the cloves (as seen in the gone-viral video from Saveur Magazine's test kitchens, How to Peel a Head of Garlic in Less Than 10 Seconds). One last tip: When mincing garlic, sprinkle it with a tiny pinch of salt to keep it from sticking to the knife.

Lesson No. 23

HOW TO CHOP GREENS INTO RIBBONS

When cooking greens, such as chard, spinach, and collards, it may be necessary to cut the greens into ribbons (also called "chiffonade"). To do this, fold the leaf in half and use the tip of your chef's knife to slice away any heavy rib in the center, like in collards or chard. Then stack several leaves or leaf halves on top of each other and roll them up starting with the short side into thick cigars. Slice the cigar in half lengthwise and slice the halves into thin ribbons. Wash the greens thoroughly to remove any grit.

Lesson No. 24

HOW TO PREP HERBS

For woody herbs like rosemary and thyme, often only the leaves are called for in a recipe. To remove the leaves, pinch your finger and thumb on the stem and slide upward, zipping the leaves away.

For tender herbs like basil, mint, and sage, pick the leaves off the stems and then finely chop. The quickest and easiest way to chop herbs is to put them in a tall cup, then use scissors to snip them into fine shreds right inside the glass.

Lesson No. 25

HOW TO BLANCH VEGETABLES

Blanching vegetables serves a couple of purposes. It preserves the crispness and color of green vegetables such as broccoli, spinach, and Brussels sprouts. It also helps to get rid of water in greens before baking. If you want to add spinach to a breakfast casserole, for instance, blanching the leaves then wringing them dry will help keep your casserole from getting soggy.

To blanch vegetables, have a bowl of ice water and a colander ready in the sink. Bring a large pot of water to a boil. Dump the vegetables into the hot water and then quickly drain them into the colander. Spinach should be in the water for 5 to 10 seconds at most; broccoli and cauliflower need a little less than a minute. Immediately empty the drained vegetables out into the ice bath to stop the cooking process.

Lesson No. 26

HOW TO STEAM VEGETABLES

To steam vegetables, cut them in small, evenly sized pieces. Bring an inch of water to a simmer in a deep pot. Put a steamer insert in the pot (a metal colander or strainer can do in a pinch). Add the vegetables, then cover the pot and steam the vegetables until they are tender to your taste. Steaming time varies widely by vegetable and the size of the pieces. Bite-sized broccoli florets will cook in 4 to 5 minutes.

Lesson No. 27

HOW TO ROAST VEGETABLES

Roasting at high heat makes nearly anything taste good! It caramelizes sugar and adds toasty flavor. This goes especially for vegetables—we love Brussels sprouts blitzed to a crisp in a hot oven, and cauliflower browned and golden.

To roast vegetables, cut them into evenly sized pieces. Softer vegetables like broccoli can be cut into pieces as large as 2 inches, but dense, crisp vegetables like winter squash and carrots should be around 1-inch cubed. Heat the oven very hot; we usually start at 425°F. Toss the vegetables lightly with olive oil and sprinkle generously with salt and pepper. Spread in a single layer on a heavy sheet pan. Depending on the vegetables and their size, cook for 10 to 60 minutes, until they are browned and tender. The more dense the vegetable, the longer it will take for them to cook. Beets will take up to an hour, while tender asparagus might be done in 5 to 8 minutes. It's best not to mix quick-cooking soft vegetables with long-cooking hard vegetables in the same batch.

HOW TO FREEZE FRUITS AND VEGETABLES

Many fresh fruits and vegetables can be frozen to take advantage of peak season flavor. Fresh berries, peaches, and plums freeze well, as do many vegetables. Cut the fruit or vegetables into similar shapes and sizes, place on an uncovered sheet pan, and freeze until solid. Then transfer to a freezer bag or sealed container for use later in crumbles and crisps, smoothies, or stir-fries.

Tomatoes can be stewed and canned or frozen. Butternut squash can be cooked in chunks or cooked and mashed and put into plastic bags to freeze.

HOW TO JUICE AND ZEST CITRUS

Citrus juice and zest are essentials in our kitchens. We couldn't cook without sneaking a lemon in somewhere! The zest of lemons and limes adds a lighter, more delicate flavor, while the juice is stronger and more acidic. We tend to use zest in baking, where the heat of the oven helps the aromatic oils bloom. Juices can be used in sauces, marinades, and dressings.

To zest a citrus fruit, rub it lightly on a fine grater such as a Microplane. Avoid rubbing off the white bitter pith below the outer skin. When measuring citrus zest, pack it very lightly into a measuring spoon.

For juicing, we like the handheld juicers, but you can also use a reamer or simply twist the tines of a fork inside half a lemon held over a cup. You'll get the seeds as well as the juice when using this method, so be sure to strain them out (or fish them out one by one!).

HOW TO CARAMELIZE ONIONS

Caramelized onions add intense flavor and a dark sweetness to soups, stews, sandwiches, meats, and more. To caramelize onions, slice a few onions thinly into even half-moons. (The slices should be the same thickness.) Melt butter or oil over medium heat in a dark pan like a cast-iron skillet or a heavy Dutch oven, to encourage browning. Add the onions along with a pinch of salt, which helps break down the onions' cell walls, causing them to release their

moisture. Stir frequently over low heat. The onions will steam off their moisture gradually, then shrink down and begin to brown. Turn down the heat if they scorch. Expect to cook a batch of caramelized onions for at least 30 minutes on the stovetop, letting them reach the color of mahogany brown.

You can also make caramelized onions in the oven. Heat the oven to 375°F. Melt butter or drizzle a generous quantity of olive oil into a heavy Dutch oven or pot, and stir in the sliced onion. Cover the pot and bake for 2 to 2½ hours, stirring every 15 to 20 minutes.

An even more hands-off option is to make caramelized onions in the slow cooker. Add sliced onions to the slow cooker with butter and a pinch of salt and cook on HIGH overnight, or for 8 to 10 hours.

Freeze leftover caramelized onions in small bags for use in last-minute dinners and sandwiches.

MEAT, POULTRY, AND SEAFOOD SKILLS

Lesson No. 31

HOW TO SAFELY THAW MEAT

When thawing frozen meat, it is best to leave it in the fridge overnight, well covered, in a bowl or container in case of packaging leakage, until it has thawed completely. You can cook some meat, such as ground beef, while partially frozen, but most frozen meat will cook too unevenly. If you need to thaw meat quickly, cut it into smaller pieces and seal it in a leak-proof bag. Submerge the bag in a bowl of cold water under a running tap for up to an hour or until completely thawed. You can also use the microwave on very low power to thaw meat. For the sake of flavor, you should immediately cook any meat that you've thawed in the microwave, because the microwaving will start the cooking process.

Lesson No. 32

HOW TO STORE MEAT

Keep all meat in its package until it's time to prepare it. If freezing meat in its original packaging for longer than two months, place a second layer of airtight wrapping, using either foil, plastic wrap, or a zippered plastic bag. While freezing meat will make it last indefinitely, its quality will degrade over time. In most cases, meat stays fresh and tasty in the refrigerator for only a few days and in the freezer for a few months. Here is a list of common storage times for meat, recommended by the United States Department of Agriculture:

MEAT	REFRIGERATOR	FREEZER
Hamburger & stew meats	1 to 2 days	3 to 4 months
Bacon	7 days	1 month
Sausage, raw, from pork, beef, chicken, or turkey	1 to 2 days	1 to 2 months
Steaks	3 to 5 days	6 to 12 months
Cooked meat & meat dishes	3 to 4 days	2 to 3 months
Chicken or turkey, whole	1 to 2 days	1 year
Chicken or turkey, parts	1 to 2 days	9 months

Lesson No. 33

HOW TO SEAR MEAT

Get over any trepidation you may have about searing meat. When starting a stew or a braise, you build flavor by browning the meat until it is dark brown, crusted, and on the edge of burnt. This is where the flavor of the dish comes from (despite the widespread belief, searing doesn't actually "lock in" moisture).

To sear meat, heat a skillet over high heat. Pat the meat very dry with a paper towel. Place the meat in the skillet, but don't crowd the skillet, and don't move the meat for the first few minutes. Flip it gently, and don't poke it with a fork. Let the meat get darker than you might expect, especially if it will be cooked low and slow afterward.

You also might consider grilling meat to develop flavor. Faith loves to grill a pork roast to get that smoky flavor before putting it in the slow cooker to make carnitas.

Lesson No. 34

HOW TO BROWN GROUND MEAT

To brown ground beef, add it to a preheated pan and cook it over medium-high heat, stirring frequently, breaking up the crumbles, until the meat is browned and crisped on the edges.

Lesson No. 35

HOW TO DRAIN FAT

For the sake of your plumbing, don't pour liquid fat down the drain. We usually pour off the fat into a mug or empty can saved just for this purpose. If it's extra tasty fat, like the fat from duck breast or thick bacon, pour it into a sealable container and stash it in the fridge or freezer for use later when roasting vegetables. For fatty dishes, like short ribs or stew, cook it a day ahead, refrigerate it, then scrape the solidified fat off the top before reheating the dish.

Lesson No. 36

HOW TO USE A MEAT THERMOMETER

To check the temperature of meat or seafood, insert a probe thermometer in the thickest part of the meat or fish. For poultry, this means the thickest part of the thigh (avoid the bone and the breast cavity). To see if your meat thermometer is calibrated properly, insert the probe in a pot of boiling water. If it reads 210°F, then it's right on target. (For more information on safe cooking temperatures, see page 290 in the Resources.)

Lesson No. 37

HOW TO CUT MEAT

Cutting up raw meat can be messy and tedious, but we have a tip to make it easier: Freeze uncooked meat for about an hour before cutting it.

If it's already cooked, cut meat and poultry against the grain. It is easier to cut this way, and it also produces a bite that is easier to chew.

HOW TO CUT UP A CHICKEN

This method will work for a roasted chicken, as well as preparing a raw chicken for cooking or making stock.

If you're carving a cooked chicken, let the roast chicken rest, well covered, for about 10 minutes to let the juices recirculate. Stabilize a large cutting board. Have paper towels or a rag on hand to wipe your hands as you go.

Now move on to the wings. You are probably sensing the pattern here: Cut away a little of the skin and meat, where the wing meets the body, and rotate the joint until it pops out. You can also do the same to the lower joint of the wings (the tips) and cut them away. These have very little meat on them anyway, and unless you really like them, they are best reserved for the stockpot.

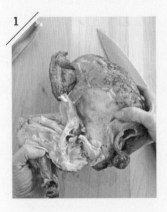

Place the chicken breast-side-down on the cutting board. Using the tip of your chef's knife, slit the skin where the leg is joined to the body. Cut a small slit in the meat as well, exposing the joint; then once the joint has been exposed, rotate and bend the leg away from the body so the joint pops out. Use the knife to sever the joint, pressing down hard through the remaining skin
and cartilage. If you encounter a complete block, you probably hit bone instead of the joint. If this happens, move a quarter inch closer to the joint and try again. You should hear a crunch and feel the leg separate. Repeat with the other leg.

To remove the breasts, cut a slit down the middle, between the breasts, to expose the breastbone, and then keep cutting down on one side until you hit the ribs. Once there, just run the knife along the ribs (almost parallel to the ribs) to cut off the breast meat. Repeat on the other side.

If desired, you can separate the thigh from the drumstick; the process is similar to separating the leg from the body. Cut through the skin and make a shallow slit in the meat. Rotate the joint so that it pops out, and then remove the thigh from the drumstick by cutting straight down through the remaining cartilage and skin.

Now you are left with a nice platter of chicken pieces and a carcass. If the chicken has been cooked, pick off any remaining meat and refrigerate or freeze it for soups, sandwiches, or tossing with pasta. Cooked or uncooked, the carcass can be used to make chicken stock and soup (for chicken stock instructions see page 188).

Lesson No. 39

HOW TO BRINE MEAT & POULTRY

Brining is an excellent technique for tenderizing tougher, drier cuts of meat by infusing the meat with salt and helping it retain moisture. Ideal candidates for brining include pork chops and other lean cuts of pork, chicken breasts, and Thanksgiving turkey.

The basic ratio of salt to water for brine is 1 tablespoon salt per cup of water (or 1 cup salt to 1 gallon of water). Warm the water and stir the salt to help it dissolve. If desired, add aromatics like black peppercorns, bay leaf, juniper berries, or fresh herbs like rosemary. Place the meat in a large container, and pour in enough brine to cover. Always cover the container and refrigerate immediately.

Brining time will vary depending on the size of the meat. A turkey ideally needs to brine overnight or at least 12 hours. We like to do this in a clean plastic bucket. Smaller cuts like pork chops or chicken breast take far less time and are typically ready to be cooked in ½ hour to an hour, although you can brine them overnight as well.

Lesson No. 40

HOW TO BRAISE MEAT AND VEGETABLES

Braising is a two-step cooking process. First, meat or vegetables are browned to develop flavor (see How to Sear Meat, page 120). Then they are cooked slowly until tender, with a small amount of liquid such as stock or wine (usually enough to cover the meat by ½). The long, slow stage of braising can happen on the stovetop, in the oven, or in a slow cooker, and the length of time will vary depending on the cut of meat and the size of the pieces. Beef goulash might cook on low for 2 hours, while carnitas could spend 5 hours in the oven.

This process creates especially melt-in-your-mouth results in fatty cuts of meat, like pot roast, since it helps break down tough muscles and melt collagen slowly.

BAKING SKILLS

Lesson No. 41

HOW TO PREHEAT THE OVEN

Most baked goods, especially biscuits, cakes, and cookies, depend on the oven's heat to help them rise right away, so it's important to have the oven thoroughly heated. Aim to preheat your oven at least 20 minutes before baking, especially if you're making something finicky like a sponge cake or soufflé.

Some recipes will ask you to put the dish in a preheated oven, then lower the temperature immediately or after a few minutes. Be on the lookout for instructions like these.

Lesson No. 42

HOW TO CHECK OVEN TEMPERATURE

We recommend keeping an oven thermometer in your oven because most home ovens cycle through a range of temperatures. Ovens rarely hold a precise temperature. In fact, *New York Times* food columnist Mark Bittman advises against worrying too much about oven temperatures. Instead, think of them as a range: "Really low (under 275°F degrees); moderate (between 275°F and 350°F); high (over 350°F but under 425°F); and maximum." If you want precision, use the oven thermometer for peace of mind. Every oven is different, too, so learn the hot spots in your oven, and keep an oven thermometer in there to double-check that it's holding the temperature you want.

HOW TO GREASE AND FLOUR A PAN

When greasing a pan, we like to use the paper wrapper from a stick of butter (save them and freeze them in baggies as you work through a pound of butter). Wipe the wrapper thoroughly over the inside of the pan, leaving a light layer of butter. You can also grease a pan with a light layer of olive oil, wiped on gently with a paper towel.

Some recipes, like those for cakes, recommend flouring the pan as well, which makes for a smooth and even release. To flour a pan, grease it, and then tap in a tablespoon or so of flour. Shake and rotate the pan to move the flour evenly over its bottom and side surfaces, then turn the pan over and tap the rest out into the trash or sink. If you are baking a chocolate cake, dust the pan with cocoa powder instead of flour so as not to leave a white residue on the dark cake.

Lesson No. 44

HOW TO CREAM BUTTER AND SUGAR

When creaming butter and sugar, as you would for making a cake or cookies, the butter shouldn't start off rock hard or greasy soft, nor should you throw in the whole stick at once. Cut the butter up into chunks. If using a modern stand mixer, add the sugar immediately and blend with the paddle attachment until the mixture is uniform and smooth, whipped and creamy—which usually takes at least several minutes at high speed. If you are using lower-powered hand beaters, add the sugar gradually until it is fully incorporated.

Lesson No. 45

HOW TO CUT IN BUTTER

To "cut in butter" means to work cold butter into a flour mixture, without softening or melting it first. Many recipes, like biscuits, pie dough, and shortbread, depend on cold butter—because it gives a puffy and flaky result, instead of producing something flat and greasy. When cutting in butter, be careful if using a food processor—it can blend the mixture to a fine meal too fast. It's best to use a pastry blender, or hold a knife in each hand and cut the butter in a crisscross fashion until it mixes with the flour to create nubs the size of small peas.

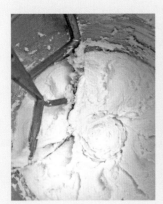

Lesson No. 46

HOW TO SOFTEN BUTTER

Many recipes call for softened butter. The best way to soften butter is to leave it out on the countertop for a few hours, so that it softens evenly and without melting. But if, like us, you don't always heed our advice to read the recipe ahead of time and you miss the need for soft butter until the last minute, then the microwave is your friend. Every microwave is different, and you want to avoid melting your butter into a pool. Cut the butter into small pieces, place it in a bowl, and start slow and low. Try short bursts of 10 seconds at 40 percent and 50 percent power, until the butter is soft but not greasy. Alternately, cut or grate the butter into small pieces and put it in a sealable plastic bag. Pound and press the bag with a rolling pin until the butter has softened.

Lesson No. 47

HOW TO FOLD A BATTER

When "folding" ingredients into a batter, try not to deflate or overmix the batter while adding one last ingredient, such as flour or mix-ins like chocolate chips. Sprinkle the ingredients on top of the batter, and then use a broad spatula or wooden spoon to stir from the bottom of the bowl to the top, turning over the batter like a cement mixer, until the ingredients are just incorporated.

Lesson No. 48

HOW TO KNEAD DOUGH

The goal of kneading yeast dough is to develop the gluten, the stretchy protein found in wheat. Well-developed gluten gives bread its spring and elasticity. To do this, turn out a lump of dough onto a lightly floured board or countertop. Press into the dough with the heels of your hands, and then fold half of the dough over, like closing a book. Rotate the dough toward you and press and fold again.

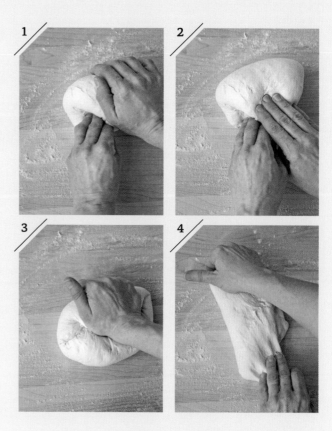

Continue kneading as directed by the recipe or until the dough passes the "windowpane" test. Holding a small lump in both hands, use your thumbs and forefingers to stretch it four ways. If the dough stretches enough that you can see light through it without it immediately breaking, then it's ready.

You can also knead dough in a stand mixer or food processor, using the dough hook attachment. Be careful not to overknead dough when using a (tireless) mechanical helper. Depending on the recipe, we usually knead dough in the mixer for 5 to 8 minutes.

HOW TO WHIP EGG WHITES AND CREAM

Whipping egg whites into soft, firm, or stiff peaks causes a lot of anxiety among home cooks, probably because older cookbooks have issued dire warnings about using slightly greasy bowls or how a dab of egg yolk in the whites can cause abject failure. Don't listen to this. Modern hand mixers and powerful stand mixers speed right by a bit of contaminating oil. It's still best to separate your egg whites and yolks carefully, but don't get yourself in a froth in the process.

The stages of whipping egg whites and cream are quite similar. Both egg whites and cream start out liquid in the bowl. A few minutes of mixing on medium speed creates some foam. Eventually the whites or cream begin to thicken. Egg whites will turn opaque. Eventually, after you turn up the mixer speed, the foam will reach the soft-peak stage, form-ing little peaks with tips that slump over. Usually, with cream, this is where you stop. It's the most deli-cious stage of whipped cream, and if you go on you risk turning the cream into butter. With egg whites, depending on the recipe, you can keep beating them until they are extremely stiff and glossy. If you tip the bowl over they won't slide out, and their tips stay in firm and spiky peaks.

Lesson No. 50

HOW TO TOAST NUTS

Toasted nuts are about 300 percent more delicious than untoasted nuts, especially in salads and desserts, where a raw bitterness can distract the palate from sweet flavors. To toast nuts, preheat the oven to 350°F. Spread the nuts in an even layer on a baking sheet or in a cake pan. To encourage even browning, drizzle a small amount of oil over the nuts and toss to coat evenly (this is optional). Place the pan in the oven and roast the nuts for 5 minutes. Stir or shake the pan.

Continued on next page

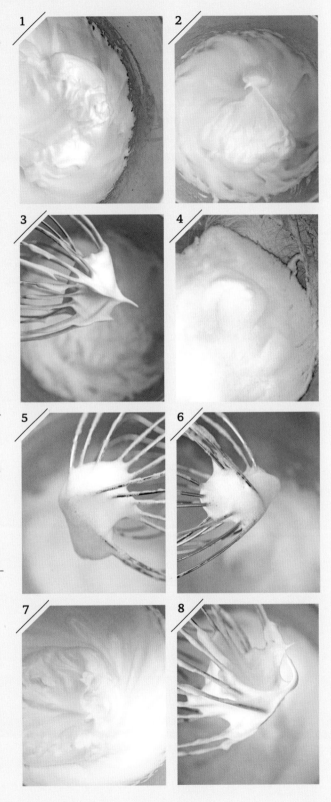

Check for doneness; the nuts should look dark, and start to smell nutty. You may hear them crackling. Return them to the oven and check again in 3 minutes. Nuts usually take 8 to 12 minutes to roast, and no longer than 15 minutes. Remove the pan from the oven and immediately transfer the nuts to a plate or another baking sheet. Do not cool the nuts on the baking sheet you just pulled from the oven, or you will risk scorching them. Cool completely, then store in an airtight container.

MORE TIPS AND BASIC COOKING LESSONS

Many of our recipes include basic and valuable lessons that have other applications in the kitchen. Here's a guide and index to some of the most helpful cooking lessons embedded in the recipe section.

For dozens more cooking lessons from The Kitchn, visit our ever-growing collection of How-To posts at www.thekitchn.com/categories/how_to. We'll help you master every home cooking skill imaginable, from How to Cut a Mango to Cleaning a Cast-Iron Skillet.

THE RECIPES

Here's the real heart of the matter: food. With thousands of recipes in our archive, we decided to give you some perennial favorites of our readers, and then develop a bunch more that would help round out a collection of recipes that will get you cooking any meal of the day, any time of the year. After all, we see recipes as road maps to a surefire dish, gentle suggestions of something to cook, and everything in between. One simple recipe will serve all levels of cooks.

If you've never cooked before, here are more than 100 recipes that you can follow step-by-step and find success. There's nothing too esoteric here, and nothing that will set you back financially.

If you are an experienced cook, think of these as a hint that might inspire you. The point is, use this section with gusto. Stain it, splatter it, mark it up. No matter what type of cook you are, this is your playground.

A recipe can be everything from a few thoughts scrawled on a scrap of paper to a very formal list of ingredients and step-by-step directions. It can be spoken or written, memorized or consulted in a book. It can even be made up as you go along, an improvisation, a spontaneous whipping up of this or that.

Depending on who we are, some of us love recipes for their guidance and reassurance, and some of us hate them for their restrictions and bossiness. Some of us prefer just to read them but not actually cook them, and others like nothing more than to tinker around and put our own unique stamp on them. Some will share their recipes with abandon, and (sadly) others will guard them closely, changing an important herb or omitting a step before they finally pass them on.

Like road maps, we need recipes to help guide us and to offer us assurance. They remind us that someone has been here before us and this is how they made it work. In that sense, a recipe is a communication, a conversation even. Recipes are written records of the time and place in which we live, the food and ingredients available to us, and what we value.

But in the end, it's not the recipe that will make the cake, or the soup, or the casserole. It's you, and all that you bring to that endeavor. If you're distracted and sloppy, the recipe will not save you, nor can you give the recipe credit the time it turned out even better than ever. That was you. And it's you who will slice the cake and serve it, clean up after making it, and send the neighbors home with a piece. It's you who will eat what's left for breakfast the next morning and who will, it is hoped, enjoy that indulgence without too much guilt.

Just as sheet music doesn't sing and a map doesn't make a left turn at the intersection, a recipe is only an idea, a suggestion, until you pick it up and make it yours.

TWO-EGG FRENCH OMELET

MAKES 1 OMELET

"Don't let yourself be frightened at the prospect of making an omelet," said Judith Jones, when Sara Kate interviewed her in her home kitchen. This is good advice coming from the person who edited Julia Child's cookbooks and who is a fantastic cook in her own right. When you're cooking for just yourself, a simple two-egg omelet is the perfect meal: minimum fuss, ready in a flash, and easily filled with any tasty scraps of vegetables or cheese.

We describe in some detail here the basic technique of an omelet, but mastery comes with practice as you learn how to control the heat of your particular stove. The basic idea of an omelet is to cook eggs into a flat pancake so you can fold it over your filling. It shouldn't take more than 2 minutes, tops. A nonstick skillet does help, and this is one of the few times we recommend using one. If your pan is larger than 8 inches, double the recipe, which will make an omelet large enough to feed you and a friend.

2	large eggs
	Salt and freshly ground black pepper
2 to 3	tablespoons shredded cheese (optional)
¼ to ½	cup cooked filling, warmed (optional, see variations)
2	teaspoons unsalted butter

Whisk together the eggs in a small bowl with a pinch of salt and pepper, if desired, until the whites and yolks are completely combined and slightly frothy. Place the bowl of whisked eggs together with the shredded cheese, warmed filling, and a plate for serving next to the stove.

Melt the butter in an 8-inch nonstick skillet over medium-high heat. Swirl the pan to completely coat the bottom. When the butter is no longer sizzling, the pan is hot enough to cook the omelet.

Pour the eggs into the center of the skillet and immediately tilt the pan in all directions to completely cover the bottom. The eggs should sizzle gently (if they don't, warm your pan a little longer next time). With a heat-proof spatula, gently drag and push the cooked portions of the eggs from the edges toward the middle of the pan to form waves in the omelet as it sets, and to create space

around the edges of the pan. Tilt the skillet so that the uncooked egg flows from the top of the omelet toward the edges and under the omelet.

The omelet is finished when there is no more liquid egg. The top will look very uncooked and wet, but no longer runny (residual heat will continue cooking the omelet after it is folded). The bottom should be set and the edges should look crisp. From the time you pour in the eggs, the whole process should take about 1 to 2 minutes.

Take the pan off the heat. Sprinkle the cheese down the center of the omelet and top with the filling, then fold the omelet in thirds. With your spatula, lift the edge of the omelet furthest from you (opposite the skillet's handle) over the filling. Fold the other edge over the top. Tilt the skillet to slide the omelet toward the edge and carefully transfer the omelet to your plate. Eat immediately.

OMELET FILLING SUGGESTIONS

▼

CHEESE: ½ cup of any shredded or finely chopped cheese, such as Cheddar, fontina, chevre, or Swiss. Fills 2 omelets.

SOUTHWESTERN: ½ diced onion, sautéed, plus 1 diced roasted red pepper, and 1 finely diced sausage link, with ½ teaspoon chili powder and shredded smoked Cheddar. Fills 2 omelets.

MUSHROOM: 1 cup thinly sliced mushrooms, sautéed in butter or olive oil until tender and seasoned with fresh thyme and sprinkled with Parmesan. Fills 2 omelets.

GREENS & GOAT CHEESE: 2 cups sliced (into ribbons) kale, chard, or spinach, sautéed in olive oil until tender, and topped with crumbles of goat cheese. Fills 2 omelets.

MORNING EGG BAKE *with* TURKEY, RED PEPPERS, *and* SPINACH

SERVES 6

This is a favorite in Faith's house, since it takes barely 10 minutes to assemble before baking and leftovers make excellent meals on the go. It's morning protein, the easy way. Consider this recipe a template, and then experiment with the ingredients you have on hand. No turkey? Diced ham works just as well. Want to go meat-free? No problem. Add an extra cup or two of vegetables—any fresh greens or cooked leftovers will play nicely here.

Olive oil

10 large eggs

1 cup whole or 2% milk

1 teaspoon salt

Freshly ground black pepper

1¼ cups finely grated Parmesan cheese

4 ounces goat cheese, crumbled (about 1 cup)

6 ounces baby spinach, roughly chopped (about 4 cups)

1 12-ounce jar roasted red peppers in oil, drained and chopped (about 1½ cups)

10 ounces roasted turkey breast, chopped (about 2 cups)

Preheat the oven to 350°F. Lightly grease a 9 × 13-inch baking dish with olive oil.

In a large bowl beat the eggs thoroughly, then whisk in the milk, salt, and a generous quantity of black pepper. Whisk in 1 cup of Parmesan cheese and the goat cheese.

Spread the spinach in the prepared baking dish and distribute the red peppers and turkey breast on top. Pour in the egg mixture and sprinkle with the remaining ¼ cup Parmesan cheese and drizzle lightly with olive oil. (At this point the egg bake may be covered and refrigerated overnight, if desired.)

Bake for 45 minutes, or until the top is puffed and slightly golden and a knife inserted in the middle comes out clean. Let cool for 10 minutes before serving. Serve with fresh fruit and toast.

KALE *and* GRUYÈRE BREAKFAST STRATA *with* SMOKY TOMATO SAUCE

SERVES 6

In 2012 we published a few holiday brunch recipes from Southern cookbook author Sheri Castle. All of her recipes were spectacularly enticing (check out her recipe for Fresh Grape Cake on our site), but Faith's imagination was spiked by Sheri's recipe for savory bread pudding with a smoky red pepper sauce. Here's a twist on that recipe, a hearty, somewhat lighter strata made of good bread, eggs, garlicky kale, and Gruyère, with a smoky tomato sauce to drizzle on top. Whether served on Christmas morning or when hosting the in-laws for brunch, this savory bread pudding will rise to the occasion.

Olive oil or butter, for greasing the pan, and more oil if needed
6 large eggs
1½ cups whole milk
1 cup heavy cream
1½ teaspoons salt
1 teaspoon smoked paprika
½ teaspoon ground black pepper
12 ounces day-old Italian or French bread, cut into 1-inch cubes (about 6 to 8 cups)
4 ounces (about 3 slices) bacon or turkey bacon, chopped
6 garlic cloves, minced
6 to 8 ounces curly kale, ribs removed and leaves chopped (about 8 cups)
¼ cup white wine
4 ounces Gruyère cheese, finely grated (2 to 2½ cups)
Smoky Tomato Sauce, for serving (recipe follows)

Heat the oven to 350°F. Lightly grease a 9 × 13-inch baking dish with olive oil or butter.

Beat the eggs in a large bowl, then whisk in the milk, cream, salt, paprika, and black pepper. Stir the bread cubes into the egg and milk mixture and set aside.

Cook the bacon in a wide, deep skillet over medium heat for about 10 minutes or until the fat has rendered and the bacon is beginning to turn crispy. Add the garlic and cook for 2 to 3 minutes, or until it turns golden. Add the kale in handfuls, stirring to coat with the bacon and garlic. (If you use low-fat turkey bacon, you may find the pan is too dry. Add a drizzle of olive oil to help coat the greens.) When the kale has been incorporated and is slightly wilted, pour in the white wine and scrape up any dark brown bits on the bottom of the pan. Cook for about 2 minutes, or until the kale is wilted.

Fold the cooked kale, bacon, and garlic into the bread and egg mixture. Fold in about three-quarters of the

grated Gruyère. Spread the bread and egg mixture in the prepared baking dish and sprinkle the remaining cheese over the top. At this point the strata can be covered and refrigerated overnight.

Bake for 50 minutes or until the pudding is slightly puffed and golden. It should be firm and dry in the center and browned around the edges. Cool for 10 minutes before serving. Serve topped with warm Smoky Tomato Sauce (recipe follows).

Smoky Tomato Sauce
MAKES ABOUT 2 CUPS

This smoky sauce is tangy, sweet, and piquant. It takes this breakfast casserole from simply delicious to utterly memorable.

¼ cup unsalted butter
1 tablespoon tomato paste
1 large yellow onion, diced
4 garlic cloves, minced
1 14.5-ounce can plum tomatoes, drained
2 teaspoons smoked paprika
Juice of 1 lemon (about 3 tablespoons)
1 tablespoon (packed) dark brown sugar
½ cup (loosely packed) chopped fresh flat-leaf parsley
Salt and freshly ground black pepper, to taste

Heat the butter in a 2-quart saucepan over medium heat. When it is melted, add the tomato paste, onion, and garlic and cook, stirring often, until the onion and garlic are soft and golden, about 10 minutes. Add the tomatoes and cook for another 15 minutes or until the tomatoes soften and release their juices. Turn off the heat and stir in the paprika, lemon juice, sugar, and parsley.

Transfer the sauce to a blender and puree until smooth. Be careful when blending hot liquids: Hold the lid down firmly with a folded towel, because the hot liquid will try to shoot out the top! You may also puree the sauce directly in the pan using an immersion blender. Taste the sauce and season with salt and pepper.

Serve slightly warm or at room temperature. Store covered and refrigerated for up to one week.

MINI QUICHES
in PROSCIUTTO CUPS

MAKES 12 MINI QUICHES

Egg cups are another excellent make-ahead breakfast, hearty with protein. A lining of prosciutto helps hold the quiches together and allows them to slide right out. (Prosciutto just happens to be awfully tasty, too.) Make these quiches ahead of time and grab them in the morning for a quick and satisfying breakfast. They are good cold, but they can also be warmed in a few seconds in the microwave.

- 1 tablespoon olive oil, plus more to grease the pan
- 6 ounces thinly sliced prosciutto, at least 12 slices
- 2 garlic cloves, minced
- 2 cups chopped Swiss chard leaves
- 8 large eggs
- ¼ cup cream
- ½ cup finely grated Parmesan cheese
- ¼ teaspoon smoked paprika
- ¼ teaspoon salt
  Freshly ground black pepper

Preheat the oven to 375°F. Lightly grease the 12 wells of a muffin pan with olive oil. Cut each slice of prosciutto crosswise, and press each half into a muffin cup so it completely lines the cup. Repeat for each cup.

Heat the olive oil over medium heat in a wide sauté pan. Add the garlic and cook for 2 to 3 minutes or until golden and fragrant. Add the Swiss chard and cook for 3 to 4 minutes or until wilted. Remove from the heat.

Beat the eggs thoroughly in a large bowl, and whisk in the cream, Parmesan cheese, paprika, salt, and a generous amount of black pepper. Fold in the chard. Divide the egg batter evenly among the prosciutto-lined muffin pan cups.

Bake for 25 minutes or until the quiches are puffed and golden brown and the edges are pulling away from the muffin cups. Let cool for 10 minutes on a cooling rack then remove the egg cups by tugging gently on the edge of the prosciutto.

Serve warm or refrigerate in a covered container for up to 5 days. To reheat, warm on low in the microwave, or for 5 to 7 minutes in a 325°F oven.

BREAKFAST TACOS

MAKES 4 TACOS

Ask a Texan about breakfast tacos and you'll get a real earful. The fact is, a fresh tortilla wrapped around some excellent eggs, with perhaps some potatoes and roasted salsa, pretty much hits the spot every time. If you decide you're going to become one of those breakfast taco people—Texan or not— make the extra effort to find great tortillas, bright and fresh eggs, and then leave the rest to the condiments.

- 6 large eggs
- ½ teaspoon coarse kosher salt
- 2 tablespoons corn oil
- 1 12-ounce russet potato, peeled and cut into ¼-inch to ½-inch dice
- ¼ cup chopped onion, from about ½ medium onion
- ¼ teaspoon freshly cracked black pepper
- 4 8-inch flour tortillas

FOR SERVING
  Sliced green onions
  Sliced avocado
  Pickled jalapeño peppers
  Guacamole (page 154)
  Roasted Tomatillo Salsa (page 153)

In a small mixing bowl, beat the eggs with ¼ teaspoon of the salt.

In a large skillet, heat the oil over medium heat. Add the potatoes with the remaining ¼ teaspoon salt. Sauté the potato chunks, stirring occasionally to prevent burning, but browning them on all sides. After 5 minutes, add the onion and continue to sauté, stirring occasionally. Sprinkle with the pepper and sauté for 3 to 4 more minutes, or until the potatoes are tender.

Pour the beaten eggs into the pan and allow them to coat the bottom of the pan. Turn the mixture a few times until the eggs are almost set, about 1 minute.

Heat the tortillas in a clean, dry skillet over medium heat, about 30 seconds on each side. Place warm tortillas on plates and divide the egg and potato mixture among the four tortillas. Serve immediately with accompaniments.

EVERYDAY GRANOLA

MAKES ABOUT 6 CUPS

If you know how to make a fine batch of granola, you will bring joy and light to everyone around you. You'll have an easy backup when the holiday shopping list doesn't quite match your budget, a great gift for your pals who invite you to their weekend houses, and a totally hippy-tastic breakfast to offer your family each morning. Serve it drowned in milk, rained over yogurt, mixed with chopped fresh peaches in the summer, or baked on top of apples and pears in the dark months.

3 cups old-fashioned rolled oats (not instant)
1 cup chopped nuts, such as almonds, walnuts, or pecans
1 cup dried, shredded, unsweetened coconut
½ cup seeds, such as sesame or pumpkin
½ cup (lightly packed) light brown sugar
1½ teaspoons salt
¼ teaspoon ground cinnamon
½ cup oil, such as olive or walnut
½ cup liquid sweetener, such as honey or maple syrup
¾ teaspoon pure vanilla extract
2 egg whites, lightly beaten
¾ cup chopped dried fruits, such as cherries or apricots, or whole currants or blueberries

Preheat the oven to 300°F.

In a large bowl, mix the oats, nuts, coconut, seeds, sugar, salt, and cinnamon.

In a small bowl, whisk together the oil, liquid sweetener, and vanilla. Pour the liquid mixture into the dry mixture and stir to combine. Add the egg whites and combine thoroughly.

Scrape the mixture out onto a half sheet pan (18 × 13 inches) and bake for about 45 to 50 minutes, or until the mixture is light brown and toasty. Stir after 20 minutes, moving the crispy bits from the perimeter into the center and distributing the granola in the center out toward the edge of the pan.

Remove the pan from the oven and add the dried fruit. Using a spatula, stir to combine the mixture and let the granola cool. The mixture may be sticky, but it will harden as it cools. Transfer to an airtight container.

Granola will stay fresh for 7 to 10 days. For a longer shelf life, store in an airtight container in the refrigerator for up to two weeks.

FRUIT-ON-THE-BOTTOM YOGURT CUPS

SERVES 6

Ever since the very beginning at The Kitchn we've been all about figuring out fun DIY projects for traditionally store-bought foods. Yogurt cups are one easy project, and they are the winner hands-down compared to their store-bought counterparts. They are inexpensive, since a big tub of plain yogurt is cheaper (and less processed) than the equivalent number of individual fruit-on-the-bottom yogurt cups. They can also be lower in sugar and more tailored to your tastes. If you take a few minutes at the beginning of the week you can put together a batch of these cups in Mason jars, and you'll have scrumptious yogurts to take to work or to tuck into your child's lunchbox.

¾ to 1 cup fruit jam, slightly warmed

3 cups plain whole-milk, Greek, or low-fat yogurt

3 cups fresh fruit, such as blueberries, sliced strawberries, bananas, or kiwi fruit

1 to 1¼ cups toasted nuts or granola (page 139)

Add 2 tablespoons of fruit jam to the bottom of a half-pint jar. Spoon in ¼ cup yogurt and top with ½ cup fresh fruit. Spoon in another ¼ cup yogurt, and top with 2 to 3 tablespoons of nuts or granola. Screw the jar lid on and repeat with five more half-pint jars. Refrigerate until ready to eat. The cups are best eaten within one week.

FIG *and* ALMOND QUINOA BREAKFAST PORRIDGE

SERVES 4

We've seen a meteoric rise in the popularity of quinoa over the last several years, and we're not surprised. It has a fluffy texture, an appealingly nutty taste, and its high protein content is satisfying. We've been throwing it into our lunchboxes and onto the dinner plate, but it also has a place in the breakfast bowl. This warm, dairy-free quinoa porridge was inspired by reader luvthesnow who told us: "I made breakfast quinoa with a touch of brown sugar, figs, orange zest, and cinnamon. It was supposed to last for 3 days, but it's already gone!"

1 cup golden quinoa

2½ cups almond milk, plus extra for serving

¼ cup maple syrup, plus extra for serving

½ teaspoon ground ginger

¼ teaspoon ground cinnamon

Zest and juice of 1 small orange (about ¼ cup orange juice)

½ cup finely chopped dried figs

1 teaspoon pure vanilla extract

½ teaspoon salt

½ cup sliced roasted almonds

Toasted coconut, for serving

Place the quinoa in a fine-mesh strainer and rinse for 2 to 3 minutes under running water. Drain. Stir the quinoa together with the almond milk, maple syrup, ginger, cinnamon, and orange zest in a 2-quart saucepan. Bring to a boil over medium-high heat, then lower to a simmer and cook, stirring frequently, for 20 minutes, or until the quinoa is tender and the porridge has reduced slightly and is creamy. You will notice that the germ will spring out from the quinoa seed, like a tiny curl. This is a good way to tell by sight if the quinoa is fully cooked.

Meanwhile, heat the orange juice to boiling in a small saucepan or in the microwave and stir in the dried figs. Remove from the heat and set aside.

When the quinoa is cooked, stir in the vanilla, salt, and plumped-up figs with the juice. Stir in the sliced almonds and serve with additional maple syrup and almond milk if desired.

The porridge can be refrigerated for up to 3 days and reheated in the microwave or on the stovetop. Stir in extra almond milk to thin it when reheating, since the quinoa will thicken considerably after it cools.

SWEET GREEN SMOOTHIE

MAKES 2 CUPS

We like to encourage you to sit down and savor every one of your meals. We founded The Kitchn on that premise. But we know that some mornings you have to hop on your feet quickly and get out the door, and we'd rather you "cook" than grab a doughnut on the corner. That's where smoothies come in. This formula, using greens and nut-based protein, is what Sara Kate drinks to get through an intense period of work. Now go on, fill the blender with hot soapy water and get out the door. You can wash up when you get home.

1 large handful roughly chopped kale, spinach, collards, or a combination
2 tablespoons natural (unsweetened) almond or peanut butter
1 cup pure unsweetened coconut water
1 tablespoon flax oil (optional)
1 frozen peeled banana, cut into several pieces
⅛ teaspoon ground cinnamon

Place all ingredients in a blender and puree until completely uniform in color and all the bits of green are pulverized. Serve immediately.

SAUCY BEAN *and* SAUSAGE SKILLET

SERVES 4

Some breakfast dishes neatly straddle the divide between morning and evening, breakfast and dinner. This is one of those meals, a skillet full of smoky sausage cooked with tangy tomatoes and tender beans. Crack an egg on top for yet one more layer of morning cheer.

12 ounces smoked andouille or spicy chicken sausage, sliced into ½-inch coins
2 stalks celery, diced
1 large onion, diced
2 garlic cloves, minced

1 14.5-ounce can roasted diced tomatoes, with juices
1 15-ounce can pinto beans, with their liquid
1 bay leaf
1 packed tablespoon dark brown sugar
1 tablespoon sherry vinegar
1 teaspoon ground cumin
  Salt and freshly ground black pepper
4 scallions (green tops only), finely chopped
4 large eggs (optional)
  Crisp toast, for serving

Heat a deep, 10-inch, heavy skillet over medium-high heat and sear the sausage until browned and beginning to crisp, flipping after a few minutes. Stir in the celery, onion, and garlic and turn the heat down to medium. Cook, stirring frequently, for about 5 minutes, or until the vegetables are soft and fragrant. By this point there will probably be a dark brown crust forming.

Stir in the diced tomatoes, and bring to a simmer, stirring and scraping up the brown bits on the bottom of the pan. Stir in the beans with their liquid. Add the bay leaf, brown sugar, sherry vinegar, and cumin. Bring to a boil and lower the heat. Simmer gently until the liquid is slightly reduced and the mixture is hot, about 10 minutes. Taste and season, if necessary, with salt and pepper. (At this point the mixture can be cooled and refrigerated for up to 3 days. Before serving, reheat in a skillet.) Sprinkle with the scallions when serving.

If you would like to serve this dish with eggs, make 4 wells in the beans with the back of a spoon and crack one egg into each. Season with salt and pepper. Put a lid on the pan and cook over medium-low heat until the whites are set. Remove and serve immediately, piled on crisp toast, if desired.

SWEET POTATO *and* CARAMELIZED ONION HASH *with* BAKED EGGS

SERVES 4 TO 6

We take a particular pleasure in helping you conquer breakfast, as the accomplishment of a hot breakfast on a busy morning ranks up there with achieving an empty e-mail inbox. The best breakfasts are the ones you make ahead of time, like this one. There's some labor involved in putting together the savory, garlicky hash of sweet potatoes and caramelized onions, but once you've done that, it's there, waiting for you in the fridge. Plop a poached or baked egg on top for a healthy, substantial meal that will carry you through the whole morning.

2	tablespoons unsalted butter
2 to 3	large yellow onions (about 2 pounds), halved, thinly sliced, then halved again
	Coarse kosher salt and freshly ground black pepper
3	large sweet potatoes (about 3 pounds), skin intact, chopped into ¼- to ½-inch cubes
¼	cup olive oil
1½	teaspoons salt
1½	teaspoons smoked paprika
	Freshly ground black pepper
2	tablespoons (packed) finely minced fresh rosemary or oregano leaves
4 to 6	large eggs
	Parmesan cheese, for serving (optional)

Move an oven rack to the middle of the oven. Preheat the oven to 450°F. Line a large baking sheet with foil or parchment paper.

Melt the butter in a cast-iron or other heavy skillet over medium-high heat. When it foams up, add the onions and sprinkle lightly with salt and pepper. (Don't worry if they are crammed into the pan; they will rapidly cook down.) Lower the heat slightly and cook the onions, stirring occasionally, and lowering the heat if they seem to be burning. Cook the onions until they are dark brown, about 20 to 30 minutes.

While the onions are caramelizing, toss the sweet potatoes in a large bowl with the olive oil, 1½ teaspoons salt, smoked paprika, a generous helping of black pepper, and the minced rosemary or oregano. When the caramelized onions are done, stir them into the sweet potatoes.

Spread the mixture in one layer on the prepared baking sheet and roast for 25 to 40 minutes, stirring every 10 to 15 minutes, until the sweet potatoes are soft and browned. Let the hash cool and store it in a covered container in the refrigerator for up to 5 days.

To serve, heat the oven to 425°F. Spread a relatively thin layer of the cooked sweet potato hash in a baking dish, such as a cast-iron skillet or a 9 × 13-inch baking dish. You can also bake the hash in individual ramekins. Make small wells in the sweet potatoes and crack in the eggs. Sprinkle lightly with salt and pepper.

Bake for 10 to 20 minutes, or until the sweet potatoes are hot and the eggs are baked to your preference. (Test the eggs by prodding them with a fork to check the firmness of the white and to see how runny the yolk is; baked eggs are deceptive in that the white often looks much less cooked than it really is.)

Serve immediately, with shavings of Parmesan cheese, if desired.

VARIATIONS

Before roasting, fold in smoked turkey, roasted chicken, or cooked breakfast sausage, if desired.

BREAKFAST PIZZA

MAKES TWO 10-INCH PIZZAS

Here's the ultimate upgrade on your early adulthood bad habit: pizza for breakfast. Serve it proudly, instead of eating it with shame at the open fridge. Throw together the dough on Saturday night and serve pizza for brunch on Sunday.

- 2 rounds Pizza Dough (see page 207)
- 1 cup Fresh Tomato Pizza Sauce (recipe follows)
- 1 cup whole-milk ricotta
- ⅔ cup freshly grated Parmesan cheese
  Toppings of your choice (see suggestions that follow)
  Flaked sea salt and freshly ground black pepper
- 4 to 6 large eggs

SUGGESTED TOPPINGS

Prosciutto, salami, thinly sliced parboiled potatoes, chopped fresh herbs, fresh spinach (sprinkled on after baking)

Place a pizza stone or an upside-down baking sheet on the bottom rack of the oven. Heat the oven as high as it will go, at least 500°F.

Using the heel of your hand, gently press and stretch the first ball of dough on a well-floured surface into an 11- to 12-inch circle, about ¼ inch thick, and lay it on a sheet of parchment.

Using the back of a ladle, spread out ½ cup of pizza sauce to within ½ inch of the edges of the dough. Dot the pizza with 6 to 8 rounded tablespoons of ricotta, sprinkle with ⅓ cup Parmesan, and scatter any other toppings (except the eggs) evenly across the top of the pizza.

Crack each egg into an individual ramekin. Pull the rack out halfway and slide the pizza onto the stone. Carefully slip 2 to 3 eggs out of their cups and onto the pizza. Sprinkle on a little salt and pepper. Carefully slide the rack into the oven and bake for 5 to 7 minutes or until the whites and yolk are just barely set.

Take the pizza out of the oven and sprinkle more Parmesan on top. Let cool for five minutes before serving.

Repeat with the second ball of dough and the remaining toppings.

Fresh Tomato Pizza Sauce

MAKES ABOUT 1 CUP, ENOUGH FOR TWO 10-INCH PIZZAS

- 1 cup canned whole, diced, or crushed tomatoes with juices
- 2 garlic cloves, roughly chopped
- ½ teaspoon balsamic vinegar
- 1 teaspoon olive oil
- 1 teaspoon freshly grated lemon zest
  A few leaves of fresh basil
  Salt and freshly ground black pepper to taste

Combine all of the ingredients in the bowl of a blender or food processor and process until they have reached the desired consistency.

The sauce will keep for up to a week in the fridge, or 2 months frozen. Freeze the sauce in individual bags in portions of ½ cup each. When you want to use the sauce, defrost it overnight, snip off a corner of the bag, and squeeze out the sauce.

QUICK DROP BISCUITS
with QUICK BERRY JAM

MAKES 9 BISCUITS

This recipe comes from a strong memory Sara Kate has of her parents making breakfast. Mom would make Bisquick drop biscuits in her family's cast-iron skillet, and her dad would make a "special drink," a very 1970s blender creation involving raw eggs and instant coffee. She has lived to tell the tale, but she has decided to share only the biscuits with you, in a from-scratch version. To evoke Mama Gillingham's touch, dust the tops with cinnamon sugar just before popping them in the oven. While you're waiting, make yourself a batch of the quickest berry jam ever.

- 8 tablespoons (1 stick) cold unsalted butter, plus 1 tablespoon
- 2 cups unbleached all-purpose flour
- 1 tablespoon baking powder
- 1 teaspoon salt
- ¾ to 1 cup whole milk

BISCUIT TOPPINGS

- 4 tablespoons (½ stick) unsalted butter, melted (optional)
- ½ teaspoon sugar (optional)
- ¼ teaspoon ground cinnamon (optional)
  Quick Berry Jam (recipe follows)
  Salted butter, for serving

Heat the oven to 450°F. Grease a cast-iron skillet or round cake pan with 1 tablespoon of the unsalted butter.

Sift the flour, baking powder, and salt into a large mixing bowl. Transfer to the bowl of a food processor and pulse in the remaining ½ cup of cold butter, or in the same mixing bowl cut in the butter using a pastry cutter or two knives. Add the milk and mix gently until a soft dough forms.

Drop the dough by large spoonfuls into the greased pan, nestling the biscuits close together. If desired, pour the melted butter over the top, mix together the sugar and cinnamon, and sprinkle it over the butter.

Bake for about 12 minutes, or until the tops are lightly browned. Serve hot with butter and jam. These biscuits

will keep in an airtight container for 2 days. To reheat, wrap biscuits in foil and heat in a 300°F oven or toaster oven for 5 minutes.

Quick Berry Jam
MAKES 1 CUP

- 1 pint berries, sliced (about 2½ cups)
- ¾ cup sugar
- 1 teaspoon lemon juice

Combine the berries, sugar, and lemon juice in a heavy saucepan. Cook over medium heat, mashing down the fruit with the back of a wooden spoon. Bring the mixture to a rolling boil then lower the heat to medium and cook, stirring often, for 15 minutes more, occasionally skimming any foam from the surface with a metal spoon.

Carefully transfer the jam into clean jars and let cool. Screw on the lids and refrigerate. The jam will keep for 2 to 3 weeks.

LOFTY BUTTERMILK PANCAKES

MAKES 18 TO 24 THREE-INCH PANCAKES

We are fervently grateful to Dana Velden for introducing us to these practically perfect pancakes. They are golden and crisp on the outside, and tender and tangy inside, thanks to buttermilk and a trick with the eggs. Stirring in the egg whites separately gives these pancakes their superb texture, and the buttermilk adds airiness and zip.

If you don't have buttermilk on hand, you still have options! Thin ⅔ cup plain yogurt with milk until it reaches the 1 cup mark. Or substitute 1 cup milk for 1 cup buttermilk, adding 1 tablespoon white vinegar to the milk and letting it stand for 5 minutes until thick and foamy.

2½	cups all-purpose flour
2	tablespoons sugar
1½	teaspoons salt
1	teaspoon baking powder
1	teaspoon baking soda
2	large eggs, separated
2	cups buttermilk
½	cup milk
10	tablespoons unsalted butter, melted and cooled
	Neutral oil with a high smoke point, such as canola or peanut oil, for frying

Heat the oven to 225°F and prepare a large baking sheet by setting a steel cooling rack inside. Place the baking sheet in the oven.

Whisk the flour, sugar, salt, baking powder, and baking soda together in a large bowl. In a separate, smaller bowl, whisk together the egg yolks, buttermilk, and milk. Add the melted butter and whisk until well combined.

Pour the milk mixture into the flour mixture and stir with a wooden spoon until barely combined. Add the egg whites and stir just until a thick batter is formed. Set aside for 5 minutes.

Heat a large skillet over medium-high heat. When hot, coat the skillet with ½ teaspoon of oil. After about 30 seconds, when the oil shimmers but is not smoking, lower the heat to medium-low, and using a ¼ cup measure, drop the pancake batter onto the skillet. The batter will spread into a pancake about 3 inches wide. Cook for about 2½ minutes. (If the pancake scorches or the oil smokes, lower the heat.)

When the bubbles that form on the edges of the pancakes look dry and airy, use a thin spatula to gently lift one side of each pancake and peek underneath. If the pancake is golden brown, flip it and cook on the other side for 2 to 2½ minutes, or until the bottom of the pancake is golden brown.

Remove the pancakes from the skillet and transfer them onto the baking sheet in the oven. Scrape any stray crumbs or scraps out of the skillet, add a little more oil, and cook the remaining batter in batches.

Serve as soon as possible, with butter and warm maple syrup.

SPICED APPLE CRANBERRY MUFFINS

MAKES 1 DOZEN JUMBO MUFFINS OR 1½ DOZEN REGULAR-SIZE MUFFINS

Everything about these muffins is right: They're sweet but not too sweet; they'll clear out those frozen cranberries languishing in your freezer; they're great warmed up and slathered with butter and tucked into your weekend morning when you are lazing about; and, best of all, you can make them on Saturday night and reheat them the next morning while reading the Sunday paper.

  3 cups all-purpose flour
  1 cup sugar
  1 tablespoon baking powder
  1 teaspoon ground cinnamon
  ½ teaspoon baking soda
  ½ teaspoon salt
  2 large eggs, at room temperature
1½ cups whole or low-fat plain yogurt
  8 tablespoons (1 stick) unsalted butter, melted and cooled, plus additional for greasing the pan
  1 teaspoon pure vanilla extract
  1 medium tart apple (such as Granny Smith), cored (not peeled) and cut into ¼-inch cubes
  1 cup (4 ounces) fresh or frozen cranberries

Place an oven rack at the center position. Preheat the oven to 350°F. Grease or insert liners into 12 jumbo muffin cups or 18 regular muffin cups.

Into a medium mixing bowl, sift the flour, sugar, baking powder, cinnamon, baking soda, and salt.

In a large mixing bowl, whisk the eggs to break up the yolks. Use the whisk to stir in the yogurt, melted butter, and vanilla.

Gradually add the dry ingredients to the wet, stirring gently with a wooden spoon until the batter is barely combined. Add the apple and cranberries and stir gently until there is no trace of flour left.

Scoop the batter into the muffin tin cups, filling them almost to the top. Divide the batter evenly among the muffin cups.

Place the muffin tin in the oven and bake the muffins for 30 to 35 minutes, rotating the pan about halfway through the baking time. The muffins are done when they are golden brown and a toothpick inserted into the center of a muffin comes out clean.

Remove the muffin pan from the oven and place it on a wire rack. Allow the muffins to rest for a few minutes in the tin, until they're cool enough to touch, then remove them from the tin and serve warm. The muffins will stay fresh in an airtight zippered plastic bag in the refrigerator for up to 3 days. They may also be wrapped individually in plastic wrap, placed in an airtight zippered plastic bag, and frozen for up to two months. To serve leftover muffins, wrap them in foil and reheat in a 350°F oven for 5 minutes; if the muffins are frozen, reheat for 15 minutes.

COCONUT BANANA BREAD

MAKES ONE 9-INCH LOAF

What exactly do you do with all those brown bananas that inevitably pile up? Sure, you can make smoothies, Magic One-Ingredient Ice Cream (page 257), or food for the baby in the house. But without a banana bread recipe in your back pocket, admit it, you're a little lost. Here's one that gives a nod to the tropics with shredded coconut, coconut oil, rum, and Jamaican allspice.

    Nonstick cooking spray or butter, for greasing
 ⅓ cup dried, shredded, unsweetened coconut
  3 tablespoons dark rum or orange juice
  2 cups unbleached all-purpose flour
  1 teaspoon baking soda
  1 teaspoon Jamaican allspice
  ½ teaspoon fine salt
  4 ripe bananas, mashed (about 1½ cups)
  1 teaspoon pure vanilla extract
  2 large eggs, lightly beaten
  ½ cup coconut oil (liquefied)
 ⅔ cup (lightly packed) dark brown sugar
 ⅓ cup roughly chopped and lightly toasted walnuts

Preheat the oven to 350°F. Grease a 9 × 5-inch loaf pan then line it with parchment paper on the bottom and up the long sides, overhanging the top of the pan by 1 inch on each side. Grease the parchment paper.

On a baking sheet, arrange the coconut in an even layer. Toast it in the oven for 2 to 3 minutes, shaking the pan occasionally. Be sure to keep an eye on your coconut because it can burn quickly. Remove from the oven and set aside.

Place the rum in a small saucepan set over medium heat. Bring to a simmer then toss in the coconut flakes and turn off the heat. Cover the pot and set aside.

In a medium mixing bowl, sift together the flour, baking soda, allspice, and salt. In a large mixing bowl, mash the bananas with the vanilla, using the back of a fork, leaving the mixture slightly chunky. Stir in the eggs, coconut oil, and brown sugar. Add the dry ingredients to the banana mixture, then add the coconut and rum. Stir until just combined. Gently fold in the nuts.

Pour the mixture into the prepared pan and bake for about 45 minutes, until a cake tester or wooden skewer comes out clean. Set the pan on a wire rack, and turn out the loaf onto a rack when the pan is cool enough to handle.

The bread will keep in the freezer wrapped tightly in plastic wrap for up to a month.

Tip from The Kitchn

For a more tropical banana bread, add ⅓ cup finely chopped dried pineapple to the rum and coconut mixture and replace the walnuts with an equal amount of chopped and toasted macadamia nuts.

OVERNIGHT (NO-KNEAD) BREAD

MAKES 1 LOAF

In this riff on Jim Lahey's incredible no-knead bread, we incorporate all the tips and tricks we've picked up in the years since we first made it. If you're pressed for time, add a little more yeast to cut the rising time in half. Or follow the recipe as it is, but throw the dough in the fridge until you're ready to bake it.

This recipe is truly versatile and has become a staple for us. Ingredients such as minced herbs, ground spices, chopped olives, shredded cheese, and toasted nuts also make great mix-ins.

- 1½ cups water
- ¼ teaspoon active dry or instant yeast
- 3 cups all-purpose flour
- 1¼ teaspoons salt

Mix the water and yeast in a large bowl and allow to stand until the yeast is dissolved, about 5 minutes. Add the flour and salt. Stir to form a very wet, shaggy dough. Make sure all the flour has been incorporated; the dough should feel sticky to the touch.

Cover the bowl and set it somewhere warm and away from kitchen traffic for 12 to 18 hours. At this point, the dough can be refrigerated for up to three days if you don't have time to bake it right away.

Turn the dough out onto a lightly floured surface. Dust your hands with flour. Starting with the edge nearest you, lift up the dough and fold it over on itself. Next, pick up the edge farthest from you and fold it over the dough as well. Repeat with the edges to the left and right. The dough should hold together in a neat package. Sprinkle the top generously with flour and cover with a clean cotton dishtowel. Let the dough rise until doubled, about 2 hours (slightly longer if chilled from the fridge).

When you see that the dough has almost finished rising, place a 3½-quart (or larger) Dutch oven or heavy pot with an ovenproof lid in the oven and heat the oven to 475°F.

To bake the bread, remove the pot from the oven and remove the lid. Dust your hands with flour and scoop the dough from the counter. It's okay if it sticks; a bench

scraper can be used to transfer the dough. Drop the dough, seam side down, into the Dutch oven.

Cover the pot and return it to the oven. Bake the loaf for 30 minutes. Remove the lid and continue baking for another 15 to 30 minutes, until the loaf turns a deep golden brown. Don't be afraid to let it get really deep brown in spots. If you're unsure if it has finished baking, you can check that the internal temperature is 200°F using an instant read thermometer.

Remove the loaf from the Dutch oven with heatproof spatulas and potholders. Transfer to a wire rack to finish cooling. Wait until the loaf has cooled to room temperature before slicing it.

VARIATION

For a whole-wheat version of this recipe, replace 1 cup of all-purpose flour with 1 cup whole wheat flour or other whole-grain flour.

STICKY LEMON ROLLS *with* LEMON CREAM CHEESE GLAZE

MAKES 12 LARGE BREAKFAST ROLLS

One of the pleasures of writing for an Internet audience is getting nearly instant feedback on the things that satisfy our readers, and we've heard loud and clear that this recipe has made many folks happy. These rolls are what you turn to when you graduate from cinnamon rolls; they're fresh yet gooey, yeasty and tender, oozing with lemon sugar and a creamy glaze. A happy morning all round.

>   3 large lemons, at room temperature
> ¾ cup milk, warmed to about 100°F (warm but not
>   hot on your wrist)
> 2½ teaspoons active dry yeast
> ½ cup unsalted butter, very soft
> ¼ cup sugar
>   2 teaspoons pure vanilla extract
> 4 to 4½ cups all-purpose flour
> ½ teaspoon salt
> ½ teaspoon freshly grated nutmeg
>   2 large eggs

FOR THE STICKY LEMON FILLING

>   1 cup sugar
> ¼ teaspoon freshly grated nutmeg
>   3 tablespoons unsalted butter, very soft

FOR THE LEMON CREAM CHEESE GLAZE

>   4 ounces cream cheese, softened
>   1 cup confectioners' sugar

Zest and juice the lemons. Divide the zest into three equal parts and set aside. Set the juice aside.

Pour the warmed milk into the bowl of a stand mixer. Sprinkle the yeast over it and let the mixture sit for a few minutes or until foamy. Using the mixer paddle, stir the softened butter, sugar, vanilla, and 1 cup of the flour into the milk and yeast mixture. Stir in the salt, nutmeg, and ⅓ of the lemon zest. Stir in the eggs. Slowly add enough of the remaining flour until a soft yet sticky dough forms. Switch to the dough hook and knead for about 5 minutes, or until the dough is elastic and pliable.

If you do not have a stand mixer, stir together the ingredients by hand, then turn the soft dough out onto a lightly floured countertop. Knead the dough by hand for 5 to 7 minutes, or until the dough is smooth, pliable, and stretchy.

Clean out the mixing bowl then lightly grease it with oil. Form the dough into a ball and turn it around in the bowl to coat it all over with oil. Cover the bowl with a towel and let the dough rise in a warm place (75–80°F is ideal) for 1 hour or until puffy and doubled in size.

While the dough is rising, make the filling. In a small bowl, mix the sugar with the nutmeg, then work in the second third of the lemon zest with the tips of your fingers until the sugar resembles soft sand. Slowly drizzle in a few tablespoons of the lemon juice, stirring. Stop when the sugar and lemon juice form a thick, clumpy mixture like wet sand. (You may use as much as half of the lemon juice, but you will probably stop before adding that much, depending on how much juice you got from your lemons.) Set the filling aside.

To assemble the rolls, lightly grease a 9 × 13-inch baking dish with baking spray or butter.

On a floured surface pat the dough out into a large yet still thick rectangle—about 10 by 15 inches. Spread the dough evenly with the 3 tablespoons of butter, then spread the lemon-sugar mixture over the top. Roll the dough up tightly, starting from the top and rolling toward you. Stretch and pull the dough taut as you roll, to keep the lemon sugar firmly inside. Pinch the roll tightly shut. Cut the rolled up dough into 12 rolls. Pinch the cut side on the bottom of each roll closed to help keep the lemon sugar inside, and place each roll, one of the cut sides up, in the prepared baking dish.

Cover the rolls with a towel and let them rise for 1 hour or until puffy and nearly doubled in size. (You can also refrigerate the rolls at this point. Cover the pan tightly with plastic wrap or a towel, and place it in the refrigerator for up to 24 hours. When you are ready to bake the rolls, remove the pan from the fridge, and let the rolls rise for 60 to 90 minutes before proceeding with baking.)

Heat the oven to 350°F. Place the rolls in the oven and bake for 35 minutes, or until firm and golden on top.

While the rolls are baking, prepare the glaze. In a small food processor (or with a mixer or a sturdy whisk), whip the cream cheese until light and fluffy. Add ¼ cup of the remaining lemon juice and blend until well combined.

Add the confectioners' sugar and blend until smooth and creamy.

When the rolls finish baking, smear them with the cream cheese glaze, and sprinkle the final third of lemon zest over the top of each roll to garnish. Let the rolls cool for at least 10 minutes before serving, but serve while still warm.

MONKEY BREAD *with* BOURBON CRÈME ANGLAISE

SERVES 8 TO 10

This recipe comes from our resident Southern writer, Nealey Dozier. We buzzed over how something so decadent could get slipped so slickly into the site's breakfast category. Nealey originally fell for a monkey bread with a creamy peach glaze in Atlanta, but her recipe called for a bourbon dipping sauce, "because bourbon is always in season." This is a recipe for when you want jaws to drop and those around you to insist, for years to come, that you make your famous Monkey Bread.

FOR THE DOUGH

¼ cup warm water (105–110°F)

1 envelope (2¼ teaspoons) active dry yeast

1¼ cups whole milk

2 tablespoons (¼ stick) unsalted butter, plus more for greasing the bowl and Bundt pan

1 large egg, lightly beaten

¼ cup granulated sugar

1 teaspoon salt

4½ cups all-purpose flour, plus more as needed

FOR THE CARAMEL COATING

1 cup (lightly packed) dark brown sugar

2 teaspoons ground cinnamon

½ cup (1 stick) unsalted butter, melted

FOR THE BOURBON CRÈME ANGLAISE

1 cup heavy cream

1 cup whole milk

6 large egg yolks

⅓ cup granulated sugar

Pinch of kosher salt

½ teaspoon pure vanilla extract

2 tablespoons bourbon

To make the dough: Pour the warm water into a small bowl or measuring cup. Sprinkle the yeast and a pinch of sugar over the warm water and let the mixture sit until it becomes foamy, about 10 minutes.

Meanwhile, in a deep and heavy saucepan, heat the milk and butter over medium-low heat until the butter is just melted. Turn off the heat and cool the mixture (to approximately 105°F–110°F). Stir in the egg, sugar, and salt, followed by the yeast mixture.

In the bowl of a stand mixer fitted with a dough hook, or directly in the saucepan, add 2 cups of flour to the milk mixture and mix until the flour is absorbed and the dough is sticky. Add another 2 cups of flour and continue to mix on medium-low speed until the dough is shiny and smooth, about 6 to 8 minutes. (If you're making the dough by hand, stir in the 2 cups of flour using a wooden spoon and then knead the dough on a floured coun-tertop for 6 minutes.) Add more flour, tablespoon by tablespoon, if the dough is too sticky. The dough should remove easily from the sides of the bowl, or be stretchy and tacky yet smooth if you're kneading it by hand.

Transfer the dough to a large, well-greased mixing bowl, cover with plastic wrap, and let it rest in a warm, draft-free place for 1 hour, or until it has doubled in size.

Turn out the dough onto a lightly floured surface and pat into a rough, flat square, about ½ inch thick. Using a pastry cutter or knife, cut the dough into small pieces, about 1 inch in size, and roll each one in the palm of your hands to form a smooth ball.

TO MAKE THE CARAMEL COATING

Combine the sugar and cinnamon in a medium bowl. Have the melted butter ready in a separate bowl. Dunk each ball of dough into melted butter, then roll it in the cinnamon-sugar mixture until coated evenly.

Layer the balls in a well-greased Bundt pan, stagger-ing the rows as you build. Cover the pan tightly with plastic wrap and set it in a warm, dry place for 1 hour until doubled in size, or refrigerate it overnight then bring to room temperature and let it rise until doubled in size.

TO PREPARE THE BOURBON CRÈME ANGLAISE

Heat the cream in a heavy saucepan over medium-low heat until a ring of bubbles begins to form around the edges. In a separate bowl, whisk together the milk, eggs, sugar, and salt.

Pour about ¼ of the hot cream into the egg mixture, whisking vigorously to prevent the eggs from scrambling. Slowly pour the warmed egg mixture into the remaining cream in the saucepan, whisking constantly. Cook over medium-low heat, stirring constantly, until the sauce thickens and coats the back of a wooden spoon (about 10 minutes).

Whisk in the vanilla and bourbon. Strain the sauce through a fine mesh sieve and chill, covered, until ready to serve.

Preheat the oven to 350°F. Remove the plastic wrap from the Bundt pan and bake the monkey bread for 30 to 35 minutes, until the top is a deep golden brown and the caramel is bubbling. Cool the bread in the pan for 5 minutes, then turn it out onto a serving platter. Serve immediately with bourbon crème anglaise dipping sauce.

SMALL BITES

BAKED CHIPS, TOMATILLO SALSA, *and* GUACAMOLE

SERVES 4 TO 6

Put out homemade tortilla chips, guacamole, and salsa and we promise, guests will swoon. Perhaps nowhere else does the value of homemade offerings shine through more than with chips and dips. Do a side-by-side comparison with the store-bought stuff and see for yourself. This salsa's unique flavor comes from the smoky chipotle pepper. If you are unable to find chipotle, try dried ancho, guajillo, or pasilla chiles. A comal is a round, flat, griddle much like a cast-iron griddle, and a molcajete is a type of Mexican mortar and pestle, so if you don't have these traditional Mexican kitchen tools, you can toast your chilies on a griddle and mash your guacamole using a mortar and pestle, or a bowl and a fork.

Oven-Baked Tortilla Chips
MAKES 60 CHIPS

10	6-inch corn tortillas (fresh and handmade, if possible)
2	tablespoons neutral vegetable oil, such as grapeseed oil
1	teaspoon flaked sea salt

Preheat the oven to 350°F.

Brush both sides of each tortilla with oil. Make two stacks of five tortillas. Using a large, sharp knife, cut the first tortilla stack in half using one firm chop, if possible. Cut each of the halves in thirds, forming 6 stacks of 5 wedges. Repeat with the second stack of 5 whole tortillas.

Arrange the tortilla wedges in a single layer on two half sheet pans (18 × 13 inches). Sprinkle salt evenly over the tortilla wedges.

Place the trays in the oven and bake the tortilla chips until they are golden brown and crisp, about 12 to 15 minutes, rotating the pans after 7 minutes. The chips will still be slightly flexible in the middle, but will crisp further as they cool.

Remove the trays from the oven and let cool slightly. As they cool, the tortilla chips will continue to crisp all the way through. Test one and if it isn't as crisp as you would like, return the trays to the oven for another 2 or 3 minutes.

Once the tortilla chips are fairly cool, remove them from the tray and serve. Store in an airtight plastic bag or container if you won't be eating them right away. Homemade tortilla chips are especially susceptible to getting stale, so be sure to bag them up as soon as possible.

The tortilla chips can be stored at room temperature in an airtight container for up to 5 days.

Roasted Tomatillo Salsa
MAKES 1 CUP

1	pound tomatillos (10 to 12), husked and rinsed
½	yellow onion, quartered
4	dried chipotle chilies, stemmed
10 to 12	garlic cloves, peeled
1	teaspoon kosher salt

Position the broiler rack about 8 inches from the heat source and set the oven to broil. Line a baking sheet with foil.

Arrange the tomatillos and onion wedges on the pan and roast, turning them over once halfway through, for 20 to 30 minutes, until their tops and bottoms have blackened and the tomatillos are a khaki-green color. Remove the pan from the oven and cool the vegetables to room temperature.

Meanwhile, heat a comal, griddle, or heavy skillet over medium-low heat and toast the chilies and roast the garlic on the comal until the chipotle peppers have puffed up and are blistered in spots, 3 to 5 minutes. Remove the peppers and continue roasting the garlic cloves for 8 to 10 minutes, turning them over frequently, until they are tender and golden brown with some blackened spots.

Blend the roasted tomatillos, onions, chilies, garlic, and salt in a blender or food processor until smooth.

The salsa will keep in the refrigerator, covered tightly, for up to 5 days.

Continued on next page

Guacamole

MAKES 1½ TO 2 CUPS

3	ripe avocados
¼	cup finely chopped red onion (about ½ an onion)
½	jalapeño pepper, minced (more or less, to taste)
¼	cup chopped cilantro leaves and upper stems
	Pinch of flaked sea salt, or to taste
	Juice of 1 lime (about 1½ to 2 tablespoons)

Cut the avocados in half and remove the pit. Spoon the flesh of the avocados into a molcajete, a Mexican mortar and pestle, or a mixing bowl. Add the onion, jalapeño, cilantro, and salt and combine. Add the lime juice and stir gently, so as not to crush the ingredients too aggressively. The guacamole will be slightly chunky.

Serve immediately, or place one of the avocado pits in the mixture, cover the container tightly with plastic wrap pressed directly on the surface of the guacamole, and store in the refrigerator for up to 2 days. To serve, add a squirt of lime and stir.

POTATO CHIPS TWO WAYS: DEEP-FRIED *and* BAKED

Everyone should try frying their own potato chips at least once in their life. Transforming raw potatoes into actual, honest-to-goodness potato chips feels like nothing short of a culinary miracle. Don't be intimidated by the idea of heating a pot of oil on your stove—you actually need only about an inch of oil to make potato chips, and an instant read thermometer will help you keep track of the temperature. Do it. It's worth it.

That said, the baked potato chip also deserves some love. Brushed with olive oil and sprinkled with salt, the thin slices of potatoes become crisp and very snackable in the heat of the oven. Baked chips have a more toasted flavor than their deep-fried cousins, but they perform just as well when scooping up dip at a party.

Deep-Fried Potato Chips

SERVES 4 TO 6

1 to 2	large russet or yellow potatoes (about 6 ounces each)
	Peanut oil or any cooking oil with a smoke point higher than 375°F
	Coarse kosher salt

Scrub the potatoes clean and slice them into ⅟₁₆- to ⅛-inch-thick rounds on a mandoline. Place them in a bowl and cover with cold water. Drain and refill the bowl several times until the water is clear of starch. Lay the slices in a single layer on a clean dishcloth and pat them completely dry with a second dishcloth.

Preheat the oven to 200°F. Line a large baking sheet with paper towels and set aside.

Set a large skillet over medium-high heat and fill it with about an inch of oil. Heat the oil to 350°F, checking the temperature frequently with an instant read thermometer.

When the oil is hot, lower slices of potatoes into the hot oil in a single layer. Use two metal dinner forks to flip the slices occasionally. Fry the slices until they just start to turn golden brown and the edges begin to curl, roughly 2 to 5 minutes. The slices will cook at different rates depending on size, thickness, moisture content, and potato variety; as they finish cooking, simply lift the cooked potatoes from the oil with your forks and set them aside on the prepared baking sheet. Sprinkle the fried chips with salt while they're still warm.

Allow the oil to come back up to temperature between batches and repeat until all the chips are cooked. Monitor the temperature with your thermometer and lower the heat if the oil starts to become too hot (the temperature will dip when you first add the potatoes). Remove the pan from heat if you see or smell smoke at any time.

When finished, let the oil cool, then strain it to remove any food particles, and use a funnel to pour it back into a storage container. Frying oil can be reused a few times; strain out any debris before reusing, and discard it once it turns dark or smells off.

Fried potato chips are best eaten the same day, but will last in an airtight container for up to a week.

Baked Potato Chips

SERVES 4 TO 6

1 to 2 large russet or yellow potatoes
          (about 6 ounces each)
   ½ cup olive oil
       Kosher salt

Heat the oven to 450°F. Arrange two racks in the oven, spaced evenly apart, dividing the oven into thirds. Line several dinner plates with paper towels and set them near the oven.

Scrub the potatoes clean and slice them into ⅟₁₆- to ⅛-inch-thick rounds on a mandoline. Place them in a bowl and cover with cold water. Drain and refill the bowl several times until the water is clear of starch. Lay the slices in a single layer on a clean dishcloth and pat them completely dry with a second dishcloth.

Line two baking sheets with parchment and brush the parchment with olive oil. Arrange the potato slices in a single layer in the pan. Do not let the chips touch or overlap or they will stick while baking; bake in batches if necessary. Brush the tops of the chips with olive oil and sprinkle evenly with salt.

Bake for 10 minutes. Flip the potato slices and rotate the pans in the oven. Reduce the oven temperature to 350°F, and bake for another 5 minutes. Flip the chips and rotate the pans again. Remove any chips that have turned golden brown and place them on the prepared dinner plates. Sprinkle the chips with a second dose of salt while they are still warm from the oven.

Continue baking and flipping the chips every 5 minutes, removing the potatoes that are done, until all the chips have finished baking. This will take 15 to 20 minutes total for thinner chips and 20 to 25 minutes total for thicker chips. Repeat with any remaining potato slices.

Baked chips are best eaten within a day or two but will keep in an airtight container for up to a week.

CHEESE SAVORIES

MAKES ABOUT 80 CRACKERS

Homemade crackers come together quickly in the food processor and can be made days ahead, so when it's time to serve the crackers, all you need to do is bake them for 15 minutes. These cookie-like crackers are the perfect partner to your cheese plate, or you can stuff a handful in your pocket for an afternoon hike.

   ½ cup almond flour (almond meal)
  1¼ cups unbleached all-purpose flour
  1¼ teaspoons kosher salt
   ¾ teaspoon freshly ground black pepper
    4 tablespoons (½ stick) cold unsalted butter
  1½ cups Gruyère cheese, grated (about 6 ounces)
    1 large egg, at room temperature
    2 tablespoons heavy cream
       Flaked sea salt

In a food processor fitted with the metal blade, pulse the flours, kosher salt, and pepper. Add the butter and cheese; pulse until fully blended. Add the egg and cream and blend for about 20 seconds, until ingredients are fully mixed, evenly moist, and form a cohesive ball.

Divide the dough in half. Using plastic wrap, form each half into a log, about 5 inches long and 1½ inches wide. Freeze the logs for 45 minutes to an hour, or until thoroughly chilled. The logs of dough will keep frozen for up to two months. Thaw the dough slightly before slicing.

Preheat the oven to 375°F. Line a baking sheet with parchment paper.

Using a sharp knife and even, downward pressure, slice the dough into circles, about ⅛ inch thick. If the dough breaks when you try to slice it, let it warm up a bit more. Turn the log one quarter turn after each cut so that it keeps its shape. Place the cut circles on the baking sheet. Using a pastry brush, lightly brush each circle with water and sprinkle with sea salt.

Bake for 15 to 18 minutes, until crisp and golden around the edges. Remove the pan from the oven, let the crackers cool for a minute in the pan, then transfer them to cool completely on a wire rack. The crackers will keep in an airtight container for up to 4 days.

SEEDED SEMOLINA CRACKERS

MAKES ABOUT 3 DOZEN CRACKERS

Making your own crackers isn't about saving the $2 or $8 or whatever it is that you might spend on them. Take a little time and find out how much pleasure you can find in an evening spent with some dough, a rolling pin, and some seeds. Learn the method and then elaborate; swap out the seeds for chopped rosemary and freshly grated Parmesan cheese, or go for the cracker version of an everything bagel and add dried onion and garlic flakes.

- 2 teaspoons sesame seeds
- 2 teaspoons poppy seeds
- 1 teaspoons fennel seeds
- ½ teaspoon flaked sea salt
- 1 cup semolina flour or unbleached all-purpose flour, plus more for rolling
- ⅓ cup whole-wheat flour
- 1 teaspoon sugar
- 1 teaspoon kosher salt
- 2 tablespoons extra-virgin olive oil
- ¼ cup water, plus more for brushing

Position a rack in the lower third of the oven and preheat the oven to 450°F. Lightly flour two baking sheets.

In a small bowl, combine the sesame seeds, poppy seeds, fennel seeds, and sea salt. Fill a separate small bowl with water.

In a large bowl, whisk the semolina flour, whole-wheat flour, sugar, and kosher salt. Add the olive oil and ¼ cup water to the flour mixture and stir gently until a soft ball of dough forms. If needed, add more water 1 tablespoon at a time to reach the desired consistency.

Set the dough on a lightly floured work surface and divide it in half. Pat each half into a square. Set one square aside and cover with a clean, slightly damp towel. Using a rolling pin, roll out the first square of dough on the floured surface into a rectangle about ¹⁄₁₆ inch thick.

With a pastry brush, brush the dough lightly with water and sprinkle half of the seed mix evenly over the surface. With a dough scraper, pizza cutter, or sharp knife, cut the dough into 1 × 2-inch rectangles, or any shape you wish.

Using a metal spatula, transfer enough crackers to fill one of the prepared baking sheets, leaving ½ inch of space in between. Poke each cracker with the tines of a fork to prevent puffing. Repeat with the remaining dough. Bake the crackers for 10 to 12 minutes, until they are nicely browned.

Transfer the crackers onto a cooling rack and let the crackers cool completely. They will crisp up as they cool. Store the cooled crackers in a zippered plastic bag or other tightly sealed container. The crackers will keep for up to a week at room temperature.

QUICK SWEET *and* SPICY PICKLES

MAKES TWO 1-PINT JARS

These pickles come together quickly and are a great thing to stash in the fridge for a week's worth of snacks or to put out at a party. For the brine, it really depends on what flavors you like and how sweet you like your pickle juice. Sara Kate has fond memories of her grandparents always having bread and butter pickles in their fridge. In this recipe, we trigger that memory, but turn down the sweetness just a bit and add some spice.

1 pound kirby cucumbers, sliced into ¼-inch-thick rounds (about 4 cups)

½ large yellow onion, thinly sliced (about 1 cup)

2 garlic cloves, minced

2 tablespoons kosher salt

1¼ cups cider vinegar

⅓ cup sugar

2 teaspoons whole mustard seeds

1 teaspoon ground turmeric

½ teaspoon crushed red pepper flakes

½ teaspoon celery seeds

Pinch teaspoon ground cloves

In a large bowl, mix together the cucumbers, onion, garlic, and salt. Lay plastic wrap over the surface of the vegetables and weigh them down with another bowl (preferably a heavier or weighted bowl). Let them rest for approximately 3 hours and then drain off the liquid.

In a large saucepan, combine the vinegar, sugar, mustard seeds, turmeric, crushed red pepper flakes, celery seeds, and ground cloves. Bring the mixture to a boil.

Stir the drained cucumber mixture into the boiling vinegar mixture. Remove the pan from the heat. Using a slotted spoon, transfer the pickles to sterile containers, and then divide the remaining liquid among the containers. Seal and chill in the refrigerator.

The pickles will keep in the refrigerator in a tightly sealed container for 2 weeks.

THE ESSENTIAL KALE CHIP

SERVES 4 TO 6 AS A SNACK

Sara Kate once joked on The Kitchn that making a batch of kale chips meant she could consume an entire bunch of kale in one sitting. It's true. These chips are the perfect snack to serve while dinner is on the stove, or to get you through a movie marathon. Experiment with different oils such as sesame and coconut, or just go with olive oil and a simple sprinkle of sea salt. These days it is easy to find many varieties of kale, such as lacinato (dinosaur kale), curly, and Red Russian. We prefer lacinato because of its more uniform texture, but all varieties will be delicious!

1 bunch (about 8 ounces) kale

2 to 3 tablespoons sesame oil, coconut oil (liquefied), or other flavored oils

Sea salt, to taste

Preheat the oven to 275°F. Rinse and dry the kale, then remove the stems and tough center ribs. Cut the leaves into large bite-size pieces, toss them in a bowl with 2 tablespoons of oil, and rub the oil into the leaves. If, after you toss it well, the kale still seems dry in spots, add another tablespoon of oil and massage it into the leaves. Sprinkle the kale with salt.

Arrange the leaves in a single layer on a large baking sheet or two 9 × 13-inch sheets. The baking time can vary widely depending on the variety of kale, the size of the spine, the moisture level, and the size of the chips, but in general, bake the chips for 15 to 20 minutes, or until crisp but not browned. Place the baking sheet on a rack to cool. Serve within one day.

BABA GHANOUSH
(SMOKY EGGPLANT DIP)

MAKES 1 TO 1½ CUPS

Baba ghanoush was Faith's gateway eggplant dish—the first thing that really showed her how silky and delicious eggplant can be. This creamy (yet vegan!) dip is made from eggplant that is roasted until very soft and charred. The more roasted the eggplant, the smokier (and tastier) the dip will be. Try grilling it over a medium flame on a covered grill. Baba ghanoush is also delicious in pita wraps with fresh vegetables, or in a grilled cheese sandwich made with fresh mozzarella and basil.

1 large eggplant (1¼ to 1½ pounds)
Extra-virgin olive oil
Kosher salt
2 garlic cloves, smashed
Juice of 1 lemon (about 3 tablespoons)
¼ cup tahini
Freshly ground black pepper
Ground sumac, for garnish

Preheat the oven to 425°F. Cut the eggplant in half lengthwise. Rub the cut side lightly with olive oil and sprinkle generously with kosher salt. Roast, cut side up, for 50 to 60 minutes, or until very soft and blackened around the edges. The eggplant halves will be puffy and expanded but will collapse as they cool. Let the eggplant cool for 1 hour.

Scoop the flesh from the skin, place it in a colander, and press out and drain any juice. Discard the skin. Transfer the eggplant to a mortar or food processor. Add the garlic, lemon juice, tahini, and black pepper and blend thoroughly until very smooth. Taste and add additional olive oil, lemon juice, salt, and pepper as needed.

Refrigerate for at least 1 hour to let the flavors blend. Before serving, dust lightly with ground sumac. Serve with warm pita bread, baked pita chips, or chopped raw vegetables.

Refrigerate any leftovers in a covered container for up to 5 days.

ROASTED GARLIC
and LEMON HUMMUS

MAKES ABOUT 2½ CUPS

If there's one thing to start making at home instead of buying it at the store, it's hummus. It's incredibly easy to make, and it tastes far better than the grocery-store version. This recipe takes a little extra time because of roasting the garlic, but it's worth the effort. Make a double batch to keep in the fridge all week or as a please-all appetizer (it's vegan, lactose-free, and gluten-free!) for a party.

8 large garlic cloves, peel intact
3 tablespoons extra-virgin olive oil, plus more for garnish
1 15-ounce can chickpeas
¼ cup tahini
¼ cup freshly squeezed lemon juice (from 1 to 1½ lemons)
½ teaspoon salt
¼ teaspoon paprika, plus more for garnish
⅛ teaspoon ground cumin

Preheat the oven to 400°F.

In a small bowl, toss the garlic cloves with 1 tablespoon of the olive oil. Place the garlic in a piece of foil and loosely seal. Roast for 30 minutes or until the garlic is soft. Allow the garlic to cool then squeeze the pulp out of the skins into a small bowl.

Drain and rinse the chickpeas thoroughly.

Place the remaining olive oil, roasted garlic pulp, chickpeas, tahini, lemon juice, salt, paprika, and cumin in a food processor or blender and puree until very smooth. Add more lemon juice or some warm water if the hummus is too stiff.

Serve in a bowl, garnished with a drizzle of olive oil and a sprinkle of paprika. The hummus will keep in a tightly sealed container in the refrigerator for up to 5 days.

ROASTED CHICKPEAS
with **DUKKAH**

MAKES ABOUT 1¼ CUPS

When you want to sneak something with more protein onto the snack table, mine the secret snack power of chickpeas. When you roast garbanzo beans in the oven, they morph into crunchy, toasty little nuggets, like popcorn or wasabi peas—tiny and easy to eat by the handful. Flavor them in any way you like; we like our roasted chickpeas simply seasoned with olive oil and salt, or tossed with aromatic spice mixes such as garam masala. Here we offer them with a healthy shake of dukkah (DOO-kah), the Egyptian blend of nuts and spices that is practically a snack in its own right (try it sprinkled on dips, homemade pita chips, flatbreads, and meat).

2 15-ounce cans chickpeas
2 tablespoons extra-virgin olive oil
½ cup dukkah (recipe follows)
1 teaspoon flaked sea salt, or to taste

Rinse and drain the chickpeas and dry them thoroughly in a salad spinner. Or spread them in a single layer in a baking dish and air-dry them overnight in a cold oven. The drier the chickpeas, the more effective the roasting process will be.

Preheat the oven to 425°F. Spread the chickpeas in a single layer on a large rimmed baking sheet. Roast for 10 minutes and then stir. Roast for an additional 10 minutes and check for doneness. The chickpeas will not completely crisp while warm; they will be firm on the outside but still a little soft inside. Don't let them turn dark brown, which means they have scorched.

Remove the chickpeas from the oven and toss them with the olive oil, dukkah, and salt in a large bowl. Return them to the baking sheet and bake for an additional 5 minutes, then remove them from the oven and let them cool for 15 minutes. Serve warm, or let them cool completely and store them in an airtight container. The roasted chickpeas are best served within 3 days, but they can be stored for up to 2 weeks.

Dukkah (Egyptian Nut and Spice Blend)
MAKES ABOUT ½ CUP

¼ cup toasted nuts, such as almonds or hazelnuts
2 tablespoons toasted sesame seeds
2 tablespoons toasted coriander seeds
1 tablespoon toasted cumin seeds
½ teaspoon sea salt
   Freshly ground black pepper

Combine all ingredients in a food processor and pulse briefly, or grind together in a food chopper or mortar and pestle. Grind until the mixture is coarsely chopped but stop before it becomes a paste.

Store in an airtight container in the refrigerator for up to 2 weeks.

SRIRACHA-HONEY POPCORN CLUSTERS

MAKES 10 TO 16 CUPS
DEPENDING ON VARIETY; SERVES 8 TO 12

Party appetizer? Afternoon snack? Clandestine midnight nibble? All we know is that when a batch of this crunchy spicy-sweet popcorn is around, we're completely unable to stop eating it. There's just enough spice that you don't notice it until you're about two handfuls in, but even then, the slow and steady burn is the perfect counterpoint to the sweetness of the honey. Other hot sauces also work well in this recipe, although Sriracha's tangy heat makes it our pick here (not to mention a cult favorite). For a spiced-up version of Cracker Jacks, throw in a few handfuls of cashews or peanuts.

½ cup unpopped corn kernels
1 tablespoon vegetable oil
¾ cup (1½ sticks) unsalted butter
¾ cup honey
2 to 3 tablespoons Sriracha hot sauce
1 teaspoon kosher salt
1 teaspoon pure vanilla extract
¼ teaspoon baking soda

Preheat the oven to 250°F. Line two baking sheets with parchment or aluminum foil and set aside.

Warm 3 corn kernels and the oil in a 4-quart or larger heavy pot over medium heat. When the kernels pop, add the rest of the corn kernels to the pan, shake to coat with oil, and put a lid on the pot. Pop the corn, shaking the pan occasionally, until the popping slows. Empty the popped corn immediately into a large heatproof bowl.

Melt the butter in a 2-quart saucepan over medium heat. Add the honey and increase the heat to medium-high. Bring to a rolling boil and cook for 4 minutes, stirring constantly as the mixture foams. Remove the pan from the heat.

Add the Sriracha (2 tablespoons for mild; 3 tablespoons for spicy), salt, vanilla, and baking soda to the pan of honey-butter sauce. Stir to combine; the syrup will bubble and foam. Pour the hot syrup over the popcorn immediately, stirring the popcorn as you slowly pour.

Once you've poured all the syrup over the popcorn, continue stirring until the popcorn is evenly coated.

Divide the popcorn between the baking sheets and spread into an even layer. Place the baking sheets in the oven. Bake for one hour, stirring the popcorn every 15 minutes. The finished popcorn will be a slightly darker shade, and will turn dry and crunchy once completely cooled.

Wait a few minutes until the popcorn is cool enough to handle and then quickly press the popcorn into clusters with your hands. If the popcorn cools too much and won't stick, put the pan back in the oven for a few minutes until the popcorn is warm again. Let the clusters cool completely. (The popcorn can also be cooled as is, without clustering, and eaten by the handful like regular popcorn.)

These popcorn clusters are best eaten within a day or two but will keep well in a sealed container at room temperature for up to a week.

SMOKED SALMON DEVILED EGGS
with **CRISPY CAPERS**

MAKES 2 DOZEN

Deviled eggs may seem like a 1950s housewife convention, but the fact is everybody loves them, so you may as well learn how to make them. Whether it's your first time or you're already an expert, try this fresh combination of flavors. This recipe features everything that's good about an egg bagel with smoked salmon and capers, and you won't have to fill up on bread. If medium eggs aren't available, go for the standard large size. The advantage with the medium eggs is that they're easier to get down in one gulp.

- 12 medium eggs
- 1 tablespoon olive oil
- 2 tablespoons drained and roughly chopped capers, patted dry
- 2 ounces sliced smoked salmon, chopped very fine (about ½ cup)
- ⅓ cup plus 2 tablespoons crème fraîche or sour cream
- 1 tablespoon Dijon mustard
- 1 tablespoon freshly squeezed lemon juice (from about ½ lemon)
- ½ teaspoon freshly grated lemon zest
- ¼ teaspoon freshly ground black pepper
-    Pinch of fine sea salt
- 1 teaspoon chopped fresh flat-leaf parsley, for garnish

Hard-boil the eggs (see Tip). Peel each egg and slice it in half lengthwise.

Heat a small skillet over medium heat and add the olive oil. Add the capers and fry until crispy, about 2 minutes. Remove the capers from the pan and drain on paper towels.

Scoop out the egg yolks and place them in a mixing bowl. Add all of the salmon but 2 tablespoons, and also add the crème fraîche, mustard, lemon juice, lemon zest, pepper, and salt. Mash the yolks with a fork, and spoon the mixture back into the egg whites.

Top each egg with some fried capers, a pinch of chopped parsley, and a few pieces of the remaining salmon.

Tip from The Kitchn

The fresher the egg, the harder it is to peel. Try to plan for hard-boiled eggs well in advance. We like to use eggs that are at least a week old.

FOR PERFECTLY HARD-BOILED EGGS
▼

Place room-temperature eggs in a single layer in a saucepan and add enough cold water to cover by 1 inch. Add 1 tablespoon vinegar and ½ teaspoon salt to the water to help prevent the shells from cracking and the whites from running should the shells crack. Bring the water to a boil over high heat. Once the water boils, turn off the heat, cover the pot, and let it stand for 10 minutes. Remove the eggs with a slotted spoon and gently place them in an ice bath.

Peel and use hard-boiled eggs or store the unpeeled eggs in a covered container in the refrigerator for up to 5 days.

THREE TUSCAN CROSTINI

EACH VARIATION SERVES 8 TO 10

It goes without saying that you can slather just about anything on a little piece of toasted baguette, but a few Italian toppings wouldn't hurt. Here are a few crostini toppings we have cobbled together from our various trips to the heart of Italy. Start with a fresh baguette and toast it just barely with a smear of olive oil. Then pick the freshest ingredients for the toppings. A platter of these three crostini will more than wow your dinner guests.

FOR THE CROSTINI

- 1 small (14- to 16-inch-long) baguette, cut crosswise into ½-inch-thick slices
  Olive oil

Preheat the oven to 375°F.

Brush the baguette slices with olive oil. Arrange on a rimmed baking sheet. Toast in the oven until golden, about 7 minutes. Cool. At this point the crostini are ready for the toppings that follow. (The crostini can be prepared a day ahead and stored in an airtight container at room temperature.)

Mushrooms with Thyme and Ricotta
MAKES 1 CUP; TO TOP ABOUT 24 CROSTINI

- 1 tablespoon olive oil
- 2 shallots, finely chopped (about ¼ cup)
- ½ teaspoon salt, plus more to taste
- 8 ounces mixed wild mushrooms, chopped fine (about 3 cups)
- 2 garlic cloves, minced
- 1 teaspoon chopped fresh thyme
- ½ teaspoon freshly grated lemon zest
  Freshly ground black pepper
- 1 cup ricotta cheese
  Chopped fresh flat-leaf parsley, for garnish

Heat the oil in a large skillet over medium-high heat. Add the shallots and salt; sauté for 1 minute. Add the mushrooms; sauté until they begin to brown, about

6 minutes. Stir in the garlic; sauté for 1 minute. Remove from the heat. Stir in the thyme and lemon zest. Season with additional salt and pepper to taste. Cool. Can be made 2 days ahead of time. Cover and refrigerate.

To serve, spread a spoonful of ricotta on each crostini, top with a spoonful of mushrooms, and garnish with parsley. Serve.

Olive Tapenade with Orange Zest
MAKES ABOUT 1 CUP; TO TOP ABOUT 24 CROSTINI

- 8 ounces pitted kalamata olives, drained, halved, and rinsed
- 1 anchovy fillet
- 1 garlic clove, minced
- 2 tablespoons finely chopped toasted pine nuts
- 2 tablespoons chopped fresh flat-leaf parsley leaves
- 1 tablespoon freshly squeezed lemon juice (from about ½ lemon)
- 1 tablespoon extra-virgin olive oil
- 1 tablespoon orange zest
  Freshly ground black pepper to taste

Place all ingredients in a food processor. Pulse several times until the mixture is combined and the olives appear very finely minced, but the mixture is not blended into a paste. To serve, smear on crostini rounds. The tapenade will keep well in the refrigerator for up to 5 days.

Fig, Mint, and Prosciutto
MAKES ABOUT 1 CUP, TO TOP ABOUT 24 CROSTINI

- 12 slices prosciutto, sliced in half crosswise (about ½ pound)
- 12 ripe figs, halved
- 2 tablespoons balsamic vinegar
- 3 tablespoons fresh mint leaves, cut in chiffonade
- 2 tablespoons flaked sea salt

Arrange a piece of prosciutto on each crostini so that the meat doesn't hang over. Place a smashed fig half on top. Top with a few drops of balsamic vinegar, a small pinch of mint, and a few flakes of sea salt. Serve immediately.

CHICKEN LIVER PÂTÉ *with* SAGE, APPLE, *and* THYME

MAKES ABOUT 2½ CUPS

We are always on the lookout for make-ahead appetizers that are a little different from the usual spread of cheeses, meats, and crudités. Chicken liver pâté doesn't enjoy the popularity it had when Julia Child was culinary queen, but this elegant yet economical hors d'oeuvre is due for a comeback. In this recipe, our editor Anjali Prasertong cooks apple, shallots, fresh herbs, and brandy with the lowly liver, transforming it into an umami-rich spread that can be made up to one week ahead and will tempt even the most liver-hesitant to reach for more.

1 pound chicken livers

6 tablespoons unsalted butter, at room temperature

2 slices bacon, chopped

1 cup chopped shallots (about 4 shallots)

1 garlic clove, chopped

1 large Granny Smith apple, peeled, cored, and chopped into ½-inch cubes

1 tablespoon chopped fresh sage leaves

1½ teaspoons fresh thyme leaves

¼ cup apple brandy or bourbon

1 teaspoon salt

Freshly ground black pepper to taste

2 tablespoons to ¼ cup clarified butter, melted (optional, recipe follows)

Fresh thyme and sage sprigs (optional)

Sliced baguette, crackers, or mini toasts, for serving

Trim the livers of any excess fat and tough connective tissue; set aside.

In a large skillet over medium heat, melt 2 tablespoons of the butter. Add the bacon and cook, stirring occasionally, until the edges are just beginning to brown. Add the shallots and garlic and cook, stirring occasionally, until the shallots are soft and browning at the edges. Add the livers, apple, sage, and thyme and cook, stirring occasionally, until the livers are just barely pink inside when cut and the apple pieces are soft.

Transfer the liver mixture to the bowl of a food processor. Pour the brandy into the skillet and bring to a boil over low heat, while scraping up the browned bits from the bottom of the pan. Boil for about 1 minute to reduce slightly, and then pour over the liver mixture. Add the salt. Process until the mixture is very smooth, scraping down the sides of the bowl as needed.

Transfer the mixture to a bowl and mix thoroughly with the remaining 4 tablespoons of softened butter. Add pepper to taste. Pack into small ramekins or jars and smooth the top of the pâté with a spatula or knife. Cover with plastic wrap, pressing the wrap against the surface of the pâté.

For longer storage, pour in enough clarified butter to cover the top of the pâté in each ramekin or jar and add a decorative herb sprig. Chill until the butter is firm and cover with another thin layer of melted clarified butter, then cover with plastic wrap or a lid. For the best flavor, refrigerate at least overnight before serving.

To serve, let the pâté soften at room temperature for about 30 minutes and set out some crackers or baguette slices. Pâté will keep refrigerated for up to 1 week, or up to 2 weeks if sealed with clarified butter.

Clarified Butter

MAKES ABOUT ¼ CUP

6 tablespoons unsalted butter

Melt the butter in a heavy saucepan over very low heat. Simmer it gently until the foam rises to the top. Once the foam stops rising to the surface, after about 5 to 8 minutes, remove the pan from the heat and skim off the foam with a spoon. (Don't worry about skimming every last bit of foam; the remaining foam can be strained later.) You may notice some solids at the bottom of the pan.

Place a strainer over a heatproof bowl and line the strainer with cheesecloth or a coffee filter. Carefully pour the warm butter through the cheesecloth-lined strainer and into the bowl, leaving any solids in the bottom of the pan.

Once the butter has cooled a bit, pour it into a jar. Clarified butter will keep for up to 3 months in the refrigerator or 6 months in the freezer.

THREE-CHEESE TOMATO TART

SERVES 6 TO 8

Here's a simple summer recipe that comes together in a snap. Puff pastry makes a delicious base for summer's gorgeous garden gems. Try using a variety of tomatoes, such as dark and striped heirlooms, or a mixture of cherry tomatoes such as Sungolds and grape tomatoes.

    1 sheet frozen puff pastry, slightly softened
    2 medium tomatoes or 1 pint cherry tomatoes,
       cut into ¼-inch slices
    ½ cup shredded fontina cheese
    ½ cup goat cheese
       Flaked sea salt and freshly ground black pepper
       Freshly grated Parmesan cheese, to taste
    1 teaspoon freshly grated lemon zest
    2 tablespoons finely chopped fresh basil

Preheat the oven to 425°F. Line a rectangular baking sheet with parchment paper.

Unfold the puff pastry onto the baking sheet, pinching any holes in the seams closed. Using a fork, prick the dough all over to prevent it from puffing up during baking. Return it to the refrigerator.

Lay out the tomato slices on a large sheet of paper towel. Cover with more paper towels and allow to drain for approximately 30 minutes (this is crucial to avoiding a watery tart).

Remove the pastry from the refrigerator and sprinkle it evenly with shredded fontina and small spoonfuls of goat cheese. Arrange the tomato slices over the cheese. Season generously with salt and pepper. Sprinkle a generous amount of Parmesan cheese on top and distribute the lemon zest over the tart.

Bake for 20 to 25 minutes, until the pastry is golden brown and the cheese is melted. Remove the pastry from the baking sheet and let it cool on a wire rack for 5 minutes. Garnish with basil.

Cut into desired square or rectangle pieces and serve immediately.

BAKED BRIE
with BLACKBERRIES *and* SAGE

SERVES 4

We like appetizers that draw guests into the kitchen, around a delicious plate of food meant to be shared. Baked Brie is such a dish: a crowd-pleasing starter that never fails to prompt requests for the recipe. The secret is that it couldn't be easier; it's just a wheel of cheese baked until it's hot and gooey, with a heap of sweet fruit on top.

    8 ounces fresh blackberries (about 1½ cups)
    8 small fresh sage leaves, finely chopped
       (about 1 tablespoon)
    3 tablespoons (packed) dark brown sugar
    1 8-ounce wheel Brie cheese
       Freshly ground black pepper

Preheat the oven to 450°F. Toss the blackberries, sage, and brown sugar in a shallow pie plate. Roast for 10 minutes, or until the blackberries are soft and the juices are bubbling.

Meanwhile, slice away the very top of the Brie wheel, removing just the rind. Place the Brie in a small oven-proof dish or another pie plate. Spoon the hot blackberries on top of the Brie, and pour the syrup over it. Bake for 8 to 12 minutes, or until the Brie is very hot and soft but has not collapsed.

Remove from the oven; season with black pepper. If desired, carefully use a broad spatula to move the Brie from the baking dish to a plate. Serve immediately with rye or whole-wheat crackers.

BACON-WRAPPED POTATO BITES
with SPICY SOUR CREAM DIPPING SAUCE

MAKES ABOUT 3 DOZEN

This recipe falls into the category of knock-it-out-of-the-park crowd pleaser! Elizabeth Passarella's Bacon-Wrapped Potato Bites have enjoyed massive popularity—especially during football tailgating season. These hot, tender potatoes wrapped in crispy bacon can make a casual appetizer spread more robust and filling. Once you've mastered the recipe, try using other firm and colorful vegetables, such as sweet potatoes and butternut squash.

1	pound small or medium red potatoes, chopped into about 36 ¾-inch pieces
1½	teaspoons salt, plus more as needed
1½	teaspoons minced fresh rosemary
1	tablespoon olive oil
	Freshly ground black pepper
12	pieces thick-cut bacon
1	cup (8 ounces) sour cream
1 to 3	teaspoons hot sauce, such as Sriracha or Texas Pete

Preheat the oven to 400°F. Line a baking sheet with parchment paper or foil.

Put the potatoes in a medium pot, cover with cold water, and bring to a boil. Season the water with 1 teaspoon of salt. Boil the potatoes for 3 to 4 minutes, until you can stick a fork into them without too much resistance. You want the potatoes to be almost but not fully cooked through so they won't fall apart during the next steps.

Drain the potatoes and put them in a large bowl. Add the rosemary, olive oil, the remaining ½ teaspoon of salt, and a few grinds of pepper, and toss gently until the potatoes are evenly coated.

Cut the strips of bacon crosswise into thirds. Wrap each potato bite in a piece of bacon, securing it with a toothpick. This recipe can be prepped up to this point the day before you plan to serve the potato bites.

Place the potato bites on the baking sheet, spaced an inch or two apart. You may need to bake the potato bites in two batches.

Cook the potato bites for 15 minutes and then flip each piece. Cook for another 15 to 20 minutes, until the bacon is cooked through and as crisp as you like it.

Mix the sour cream and hot sauce in a small bowl. Season with salt and pepper. Pile the hot potato bites on a plate and serve with the dip.

LETTUCE CUPS
with RED PEPPER LENTILS

SERVES 6 TO 10

These intensely delicious lettuce cups are based on the Turkish dish mercimek köftesi, *which came to our attention through a reader who rhapsodized over lentil balls full of smoky red pepper flavor, with a tangy pomegranate sauce, rolled up in crisp, fresh lettuce leaves. Our version turned out to be one of the best snacks or appetizers that we know. It takes a little time to put these together, but everything can be done ahead of time.*

FOR THE LENTIL BALLS

- 1 tablespoon olive oil
- ½ red onion, finely chopped (about ½ cup)
- 4 garlic cloves, minced
- ½ cup store-bought or homemade Quick Red Pepper Paste (recipe follows)
- 1 teaspoon ground cumin
- 1 teaspoon sweet paprika
- 1½ cups red lentils
- 1 to 2 teaspoons salt
- ¾ cup bulgur wheat
- ½ cup finely chopped scallions, green parts only (from 1 to 2 scallions)
- 1 cup finely chopped fresh cilantro (from 1 bunch)
- 3 tablespoons freshly squeezed lemon juice (from about 1 lemon)
  Freshly ground black pepper

FOR THE POMEGRANATE SAUCE

- ¼ cup pomegranate molasses, warmed
- ½ cup store-bought or homemade Quick Red Pepper Paste (recipe follows)

FOR ASSEMBLING THE LETTUCE CUPS

- 2 small heads butter lettuce, separated into leaves

To make the lentil balls: In a 2-quart or larger saucepan, heat the olive oil and cook the red onion and garlic over medium heat for 5 minutes, or until soft and fragrant. Add ¼ cup of the red pepper paste, the cumin, and paprika, and sauté for 30 seconds.

Stir in the red lentils and pour in 3 cups water and 1 teaspoon salt. Bring to a boil, then simmer for 10 minutes or until the lentils have softened. Stir in the bulgur wheat. Remove from the heat and cover the pan. Let the lentils and bulgur rest for 20 minutes, or until the mixture is thick and soft. Stir in the remaining ¼ cup red pepper paste, as well as the scallions, cilantro, lemon juice, and a generous quantity of black pepper. Taste and add more salt and pepper if desired. Set aside to cool.

To make the pomegranate sauce: In a small bowl, whisk together the warmed pomegranate molasses and red pepper paste until well combined. Taste and add more red pepper paste or salt and pepper if desired.

To assemble the lettuce cups: When the lentil mixture has cooled, form it into walnut-sized balls or stubby cigar shapes, or don't shape the lentil mixture if you'd rather not. Place one or two lentil balls or a dollop of lentil mixture in the center of a lettuce leaf, drizzle with sauce, and roll up the lettuce or pinch it closed like a taco to eat. Eat immediately or refrigerate the lentil mixture for up to 3 days.

Tip from The Kitchn

Pomegranate molasses is pomegranate juice, without added sugar, that has been reduced into a rich, tangy syrup. It can be found in Mediterranean grocery stores and online, and we've even seen it in the international section of our large local grocery store.

Quick Red Pepper Paste
MAKES ABOUT 1½ CUPS

- 1 12-ounce jar roasted red peppers, drained
- 1 teaspoon smoked paprika
- ½ teaspoon red pepper flakes
- 2 tablespoons olive oil

In a small food processor, blend the red peppers with the smoked paprika, red pepper flakes, and olive oil until it forms a thin paste or sauce. Leftover paste may be refrigerated in a covered container for up to 1 week.

ROASTED SHRIMP *with* HORSERADISH KETCHUP

SERVES 6

We have an unabashed love for a big bowl of shrimp, but we have freshened up the old steakhouse classic, shrimp cocktail, by roasting the shrimp and serving them with a homemade sauce. Whip up your own sassy ketchup spiked with fresh horseradish. This ketchup recipe makes plenty of extra sauce, so there will be some left over for slathering on burgers or hot dogs.

2 pounds uncooked extra-jumbo shrimp (16 to 20 shrimp per pound) with tails on, peeled and deveined
  Olive oil
  Salt and freshly ground black pepper
  Horseradish Ketchup, for serving (recipe follows)

Place the broiler shelf on the lowest level and preheat the oven to broil. Pat each shrimp dry and spread them out in one layer on a large baking sheet. Drizzle with olive oil, salt, and pepper and shake to coat well. Broil for 5 to 6 minutes or until pink and cooked through. Cool for at least 10 minutes before serving.

Pile the shrimp in a pretty pie dish or shallow bowl, arranged around a dipping bowl of Horseradish Ketchup (recipe follows). Don't forget to set out another small bowl for the discarded tails.

Horseradish Ketchup
MAKES ABOUT 1¼ CUPS

The amount of horseradish you use in this recipe is very much up to you. We like to feel a tingle of heat shoot straight up to the brain, but maybe you want something milder—or even more electrifying. For the hottest horseradish flavor, use freshly grated horseradish root.

1 tablespoon olive oil
4 garlic cloves, minced
1 cup chopped yellow onion (from about ½ large onion)
2 14.5-ounce cans diced tomatoes, drained
¼ cup cider vinegar
1 teaspoon salt
½ teaspoon freshly ground black pepper
½ teaspoon ground paprika
⅛ teaspoon ground cloves
⅛ teaspoon ground ginger
⅛ teaspoon ground cinnamon
2 tablespoons (packed) dark brown sugar
1 tablespoon molasses
3 to 5 tablespoons prepared horseradish, or to taste

Heat the olive oil over medium heat in a 2-quart or larger heavy saucepan. Add the garlic and onion and cook for 2 minutes, stirring frequently. Add the tomatoes, vinegar, salt, pepper, paprika, cloves, ginger, and cinnamon and cook until the tomato pieces fall apart, about 20 minutes.

Puree in a blender, holding the lid down very tightly with a folded towel. (The lid will try to shoot off, so be careful!). Alternately, use a handheld immersion blender right in the pan. Puree until the mixture is smooth and then strain it through a fine-mesh strainer. Whisk in the brown sugar and molasses, return the mixture to the stove, and continue to cook over medium heat, stirring often, until the sauce has the consistency of ketchup. Whisk in the horseradish and taste for seasoning.

Let the ketchup cool to room temperature then refrigerate in a tightly covered container. The ketchup will keep refrigerated for up to 2 weeks.

MINTY SUMMER ROLLS
with SPICY PEANUT SAUCE

MAKES 8 ROLLS

Here is one of our favorite snacks for a warm evening. Heaps of fresh mint, shaved colorful vegetables, and light rice noodles neatly wrap up, ready for a spicy, tangy peanut sauce. For vegetarians, a mixture of ½ teaspoon light soy sauce, ½ teaspoon lime juice, and ¼ teaspoon sugar can be substituted for the fish sauce.

FOR THE SPICY PEANUT SAUCE

- 2 tablespoons creamy natural peanut butter
- 2 tablespoons rice vinegar
- 1 tablespoon soy sauce
- 1 teaspoon sugar
- ½ teaspoon red pepper flakes

FOR THE NOODLE FILLING

- 2 ounces cellophane noodles (also called bean threads or glass noodles; about 1 cup cooked)
- 1 teaspoon sesame oil
- Crushed red pepper flakes, to taste

FOR THE VEGETABLE FILLING

- ⅓ seedless cucumber
- ½ medium carrot, peeled
- ½ red bell pepper, seeded
- 2 to 3 medium radishes
- 1 scallion, chopped (green and light green parts only)

FOR DRESSING THE VEGETABLE FILLING

- 1½ teaspoons rice vinegar
- ½ teaspoon sugar
- 1 teaspoon fish sauce
- 1 tablespoon freshly squeezed lime juice (from about ½ lime)

FOR ASSEMBLING THE ROLLS

- 8 8½-inch rice paper spring roll wrappers
- 2 tablespoons roughly chopped cilantro leaves
- 16–24 fresh mint leaves

To make the spicy peanut sauce: Whisk together all the ingredients until smooth and creamy. Set aside.

To make the noodle filling: If the cellophane noodles are very long, break them into smaller bits. Cook the noodles according to the package directions. Drain the noodles, place them in a bowl, and toss with the sesame oil and red pepper flakes.

To make the vegetable filling: Using a mandoline or box grater, slice the cucumber, carrot, and red pepper and radishes into very thin strips, or julienne by hand (see page 116).

Whisk together the rice vinegar, sugar, fish sauce, and lime juice in a large bowl. Add the vegetable filling and the scallion and toss to coat.

To prepare the wrappers: Fill a 9-inch round (or larger) cake pan halfway with hot water (not so hot that you can't touch it). Immerse the wrappers one at a time in the hot water bath. Watch for the wrapper to begin curling, then immediately flip it over, and continue flipping until it is just softened, about 30 seconds total. Be careful not to oversoak the wrappers; otherwise they will tear.

To assemble the rolls: Use both hands to pull the wrapper out of the water, being careful so it won't collapse on itself. Spread it immediately on a plate and begin the assembly process.

To fill the softened wrapper, lay about 3 to 4 mint leaves down the center of the wrapper from left to right. Then add 1 to 2 tablespoons of the noodle filling. On top of the noodles, add an eighth of the veggie mixture. Top with a sprinkle of cilantro and a few mint leaves. Whatever is resting directly against the wrapper will be visible through the translucent wrappers.

To complete the roll, first fold the left and right edges of the wrapper over the filling, and then fold the bottom edge toward the center. Continue rolling the filled wrapper away from you until it is closed and snug. Continue the process of filling the remaining wrappers. Partway through you may need to change the hot water you use for soaking the wrappers. As you finish each roll, place it on a cookie sheet and cover the rolls with a damp towel.

Serve immediately, by slicing each roll in half with a sharp knife and serving the peanut sauce on the side.

DRINKS

EL PRESIDENTE

This rum cocktail is a Prohibition classic from Havana, Cuba, where expats would go to drink and dance the nights away while America was sunk in a liquor-free decade. Rum drinks are due for a comeback, thanks to the underground culture of tiki bars and the availability of better rum. (We're fans of Pusser's, a deeply flavorful yet affordable bottle.) This cocktail is easy to drink, and simple to multiply into a pitcher drink for a crowd, who will appreciate its smooth sweetness and the spark of orange from the curaçao.

This drink is usually stirred, but we find that grenadine, especially the homemade sort, sometimes seizes up in a stirred drink. Shaking the drink briefly helps the flavors mix completely.

1½ ounces (3 tablespoons) aged rum
1 ounce (2 tablespoons) white vermouth, such as Dolin
½ ounce (1 tablespoon) orange curaçao
1 teaspoon grenadine
   Thinly cut orange peel, for garnish

Combine all ingredients in a shaker with ice. Shake for about 10 seconds, or until well combined and chilled. Strain the mixture into a chilled cocktail glass or Champagne coupe and garnish with an orange peel.

Tip from The Kitchn

We mentioned that Pusser's is one of our favorite rums, and we also want to recommend Pierre Ferrand Dry Curaçao Ancienne Méthode, an excellent orange curaçao that was formulated in part by David Wondrich, the cocktail expert. Because it's formulated without artificial flavoring to be drier and truer to the original spirit of curaçao, it makes any drink more complex and interesting.

PURE MEXICAN MARGARITA

Joanne Weir, a San Francisco chef, tequila expert, and the subject of one of our early kitchen tours on the site, makes a margarita at her Bay Area restaurant Copita that is known as one of the best in the region. She says—and we agree wholeheartedly—that the biggest mistake people make with their margaritas is that they use too many ingredients such as Triple Sec, Grand Marnier, and Cointreau. Perfection in a margarita is all about balancing sweet and tart. This is what we are doing in this stripped-down recipe: 100 percent agave tequila (Weir prefers blanco), freshly squeezed lime juice, and agave nectar.

2 ounces (¼ cup) tequila
2 tablespoons freshly squeezed lime juice (from 1 to 2 limes)
¾ ounce (1 tablespoon plus 1½ teaspoons) agave nectar or ½ ounce (1 tablespoon) Simple Syrup (page 185)
¾ ounce (1 tablespoon plus 1½ teaspoons) cold water
1 lime slice, sliced crosswise into a wheel

Shake the tequila, lime juice, agave nectar, and water vigorously in a cocktail shaker or lidded jar with a handful of ice and strain into a chilled rocks glass filled with ice. Garnish with the wheel of lime.

Optional garnish: Before filling the glass with ice, moisten the rim and dip it in a dish of Lime-Chili Rim Salt (page 185).

MICHELADA ESPECIAL

page 183

SOUTHSIDE GIN COOLER

page 183

RHUBARB-VANILLA SODA

page 181

COCONUT BOURBON NOG

MAKES 1 QUART, ABOUT 4 TO 5 SERVINGS

Tone down the sweetness of eggnog with coconut milk and booze it up with bourbon and you have the kind of eggnog we always crave but never get at holiday parties. Give yourself the option of a holiday slushie by freezing this nog for a few hours and spooning it into glasses, or freezing it in an ice cream maker to produce a freshly churned, creamy ice cream with a kick. Leave out the bourbon for a virgin nog.

 2 large egg yolks
 2 cups whole milk
 ¾ cup coconut milk, stirred
 6 ounces (¾ cup) bourbon
 ½ cup confectioners' sugar, sifted, plus more as needed
 2 teaspoons pure vanilla extract
 ½ teaspoon ground cinnamon
   Freshly grated nutmeg, for garnish

Whisk the egg yolks and 1 cup of the whole milk in a small metal bowl set over a small pot of water. Bring the water to a simmer. Stir the mixture until it thickens enough to coat a wooden spoon and the temperature reaches 160°F. Pour the mixture into a blender with the remaining ingredients and blend until frothy. Taste and add more sugar if desired. Pour the nog into a glass pitcher and refrigerate until well chilled. Serve within a day, stirring or blending again before serving.

BEEKEEPER'S BALM COCKTAIL

MAKES 1 DRINK

When our cocktail writer Maureen Petrosky loses her voice, she mixes up this elixir: a wonderful combination of rum, honey, lemon, and lemon balm, a citrusy herb in the mint family. If you can't find lemon balm, substitute mint or basil. Whether you're run down from being sick or tired at the end of a long day, the fresh herbaceous flavor, not to mention the rum, can give your system a needed lift. Once you're on the

mend, you might want to serve this cocktail to friends, so we've included a scaled-up recipe for a crowd.

 1 tablespoon honey
 1 tablespoon boiling water
 2 ounces (¼ cup) light rum
 1½ tablespoons freshly squeezed lemon juice
   (from about ½ lemon)
 4 to 6 leaves fresh lemon balm, mint, or basil leaves
 4 ounces (½ cup) club soda
   Lemon slices, for garnish

Stir the honey and hot water in a tall heatproof glass until the honey is dissolved. Add the rum and lemon juice. Add the lemon balm or other herbs, and muddle them with the back of a wooden spoon.

Fill a 12-ounce glass halfway with ice. Pour in the cocktail and top with club soda. Garnish with lemon slices and serve.

Beekeeper's Balm for a Crowd
SERVES 8 TO 10

 8 tablespoons honey
 ½ cup boiling water
 2 cups light rum
 ¾ cup freshly squeezed lemon juice
   (from 4 to 5 lemons)
 1 cup (loosely packed) fresh lemon balm, mint, or
   basil leaves
 1 liter club soda
 ½ cup dark rum (optional)
   Lemon slices, for garnish

Stir the honey and hot water together in a pitcher until the honey is dissolved. Add the rum and lemon juice. Add the lemon balm or other herbs, and muddle them with the back of a wooden spoon.

Fill 8 to 10 canning jars or glasses halfway with ice. Divide the cocktail evenly among the glasses. Top with club soda. For a stronger drink, top each glass with ½ ounce (1 tablespoon) of dark rum as a floater. Garnish with lemon slices and serve.

Coconut Bourbon Nog

TO MAKE THE SLUSHIE VERSION:
Freeze the nog until it is slushy,
which will take 3 to 4 hours, but
you can leave it in the freezer for
up to a day. Stir before serving it in
chilled glasses, finished with a few
gratings of fresh nutmeg.

TO MAKE THE ICE CREAM:
Freeze the Coconut Bourbon Nog
in an ice cream maker according
to manufacturer's instructions.
Store in an airtight container in
the freezer with a sheet of plastic
wrap touching the surface.

RYE *and* GINGER HOT TODDY

MAKES 1 DRINK

This drink could just as easily be called "the cure for what ails you," especially if you've come down with a sniffly winter cold. Ever since our resident cocktail expert, Maureen Petrosky, shared this recipe with us, its components have been mainstays of our winter cupboard. Even when we're not under the weather, a mug of this toddy and a good book before bed is the perfect end to a long, chilly day.

    1 cup cold water
2 to 3 thin slices peeled ginger
   1½ ounces (3 tablespoons) rye whiskey
    2 teaspoons honey
      Lemon wedge

Combine the water and ginger in a small saucepan over medium-high heat and bring to a boil. Pour the liquid into a mug, straining out the ginger. (Leave the ginger to steep for a stronger, spicier flavor.) Add the whiskey and honey, and squeeze in the juice of the lemon wedge. Stir to melt the honey and serve immediately.

WHISKEY OLD FASHIONED *with* BLOOD ORANGE

MAKES 1 DRINK

In this version of an old fashioned we put an orange spin on the classic formula with a fat slice of orange peel and orange bitters instead of the usual angostura bitters. We like to make this drink with rye instead of the traditional bourbon, because rye is extremely smooth, often with hints of vanilla and warm spices, perfect for pairing with orange essence. Temper the drink with a splash of club soda if the straight liquor is too intense for you.

1 sugar cube or 1 teaspoon sugar
2 dashes orange bitters
   Juice from 1 wedge of a large blood orange
2 strips blood orange peel
2 ounces (¼ cup) rye whiskey, or bourbon
   Club soda (optional)

Place the sugar cube in the bottom of an old fashioned glass. Pour the orange bitters and the blood orange juice directly onto the sugar so that the sugar absorbs the juices. Squeeze one of the strips of orange peel to express the oils, run it around the rim of the glass, and, using the back of a spoon, muddle it with the bitters and sugar.

    Add the whiskey and one or two large ice cubes. Stir gently and garnish with the second strip of orange peel. Top with a splash of club soda, if you wish.

Tip from The Kitchn

If you cannot find a blood orange, feel free to use a navel or Valencia orange.

IRISH COFFEE

It seems Americans are always asking for instructions on making an Irish coffee. When Sara Kate traveled to Ireland, most of the people she met said that Irish coffee isn't that Irish at all. Irish folks argue it was invented in America, while others say it was created for some ragged American tourists by an Irish chef one cold night. Either way, folks around the world enjoy a little whiskey in their coffee now and then, and this is a fine way to serve it. This drink is best if you don't stir the whipped cream into the Irish coffee; instead just drink the coffee through the whipped cream.

 6 ounces (¾ cup) hot, fresh brewed coffee
 1 teaspoon (packed) brown sugar
 1½ ounces (3 tablespoons) Irish whiskey, or more to taste
 ¼ cup freshly whipped cream (see page 125)

Pour hot water into a mug or glass to take the chill off. Pour out the water. (This will also prevent the glass from cracking.) Fill the mug about three-quarters full with the coffee. Add the sugar and stir until it is fully dissolved.

Add the Irish whiskey and top with the whipped cream. Serve immediately.

RHUBARB-VANILLA SODA

Homemade soda is a beautiful thing, especially when it happens to be bright pink and popping with fresh sweet-tart flavors. And it's so easy to make! Just simmer down a few cups of diced rhubarb with sugar and a vanilla bean, strain the syrup, and mix with sparkling water. We love serving this soda or a variation at spring brunches and baby showers. Try mixing it into cocktails, too—rhubarb gin spritzers, anyone?

 2 pounds rhubarb, roughly chopped
 1 cup sugar
 1 whole vanilla bean
    Sparkling water

Combine the rhubarb and the sugar in a medium saucepan. Split the vanilla bean down its length, scrape out the seeds, and add both the seeds and the pod to the pan. Stir in 2 cups of tap water.

Bring to a boil over medium heat, then lower to a simmer and cook until the rhubarb has completely broken down into a thick, jam-like mash, about 15 minutes. Remove the pan from the heat and let the rhubarb cool until it is no longer steaming. Strain through a fine-mesh strainer, pressing down on the fruit to extract as much juice as possible. (You should have between 3 and 4 cups of syrup.)

Let the syrup cool completely. Store the cooled syrup in a sealed container in the refrigerator. The syrup will keep refrigerated for about 2 weeks.

To serve, combine ⅓ to ½ cup of chilled syrup with 1 cup of sparkling water.

VARIATIONS

Rhubarb-Ginger Soda

Replace the vanilla bean with 5 thinly sliced coins of peeled ginger.

Rhubarb-Mint Soda

Omit the vanilla bean. After removing the rhubarb from the heat, stir ¼ cup (loosely packed) mint leaves into the mashed rhubarb.

Strawberry-Rhubarb Soda

Replace half the rhubarb with hulled and sliced strawberries.

SPIKED STRAWBERRY LIMEADE

We're disappointed when lemonade or limeade isn't punchy enough, but weak, with barely a hint of citrus, and mostly sugar. This limeade is all lime, with just enough sugar to keep it from puckering the mouth. It's punchy in another way, too— spiked and boozy with vodka. This is your summer pitcher drink, pretty as a picture, delicate pink from the strawberries, and easy to whip up. It will bring the guests back, glasses held out for another. Keep the nondrinkers happy, too, with the nonalcoholic version, which is just as tasty.

    1   cup freshly squeezed lime juice (from
        6 to 10 limes)
    ¾   cup sugar
    1   pound fresh strawberries, hulled and sliced
        lengthwise
    12 mint leaves
    12 ounces (1½ cups) vodka
 3 to 4 cups chilled flat (noncarbonated) or sparkling water

Stir the lime juice with the sugar in a small saucepan and bring to a simmer over medium heat. Lower the heat and cook, stirring frequently, for about 5 minutes or until the sugar is completely dissolved. Remove the pan from the heat.

Drop the strawberries into a 2-quart pitcher. Gently crumple the mint leaves between your fingers to help release their oils, and mix them with the strawberries using a long-handled spoon. Pour in the vodka, then add the lime syrup. Refrigerate overnight, or for at least 4 hours.

To serve, mix in the chilled flat or sparkling water. Taste before serving, and if it's too sweet (or boozy) for you, top it off with a little more water.

NONALCOHOLIC VARIATION

Omit the vodka and make the drink entirely with chilled flat or sparkling water.

SPARKLING PEACH SANGRIA

Here's another smash hit for the crowd from Maureen Petrosky, our cocktail columnist with a knack for the pitcher drink. Pitcher drinks are easy on the host and the guests—no last-minute mixing, and no waiting at the bar for a pour. This sangria is most suited to high summer, when peaches are at their sweetest. It's best when made a few hours ahead of time so that the juices can mingle, but it is perfectly terrific made at the last minute (we speak from experience).

    1   pound yellow peaches (about 2 large), pitted, sliced,
        plus more for garnish
    1   cup peach or apricot brandy
    1   750-milliliter bottle Moscato wine, chilled
    1   liter sparkling water or club soda, chilled

Place the peaches in a large glass pitcher and pour in the brandy. Muddle gently with a spoon to help release the juices. Pour in the Moscato and seltzer water. Stir with a wooden spoon to mix.

Chill, or serve immediately, pouring it into ice-filled glasses. Garnish each glass with a fresh peach slice.

Tip from The Kitchn

Moscato is a sweet, spritzy wine with a very low alcohol content. (Moscato and Moscato d'Asti can come in as low as 5–6% abv). The wine often has peachy or apricot notes, which makes it a perfect base for this drink. Look for an inexpensive Moscato ($10 or less) from California or Italy for this pitcher drink. If you prefer a less sweet drink, substitute a dry Prosecco or spritzy dry Riesling instead.

MICHELADA ESPECIAL

SERVES 1

Sara Kate's friend Pati Jinich is the one who debunked her belief that a good Michelada has tomato juice in it. It's more of a "dressed up beer," says Pati, a cook, author, and television personality who lives in DC, but who is often found in her native Mexico City sipping this very drink. She calls hers a Michelada Especial, and tints it red with hot sauce. We love this drink with plenty of lime juice, a good dose of spice, and salt from a dash of soy sauce (or even Braggs Liquid Aminos!).

1	chilled beer mug or pint glass
¼	lime wedge
	Lime-Chili Rim Salt (page 185)
	Ice cubes (optional)
3	tablespoons freshly squeezed lime juice (from 1 to 2 limes)
1 to 2	teaspoons spicy sauce, such as Tabasco or Cholula, to taste
	A dash of soy sauce or Worcestershire sauce
1	chilled Mexican beer, such as Pacifico, Negra Modelo, Corona, or Bohemia

Rub the rim of the chilled beer mug with the lime wedge and dip the rim gently into a bowl of Lime-Chili Rim Salt to cover. If you're using ice cubes, put them into the glass. Pour in the lime juice, hot sauce, and soy sauce. Fill the glass with beer. Stir well and serve immediately.

SOUTHSIDE GIN COOLER

MAKES 1 DRINK

Crisp gin and tonics signal the beginning of summer in many households, but at Faith's place, the Southside is the drink to sip on the back deck in June. It's a gin and tonic livened up with a bit more lime and a handful of sweet summer mint.

2	ounces (¼ cup) gin
1	ounce (2 tablespoons) Simple Syrup (see page 185)
	Freshly squeezed juice of ½ lime (about 1 tablespoon)
6 to 8	fresh mint leaves, plus more for garnish
	Chilled club soda
	Lime wedge, for garnish

Fill a cocktail shaker halfway with ice and add the gin, simple syrup, lime juice, and mint leaves. Shake vigorously until chilled. Fill a 12-ounce Collins or highball glass halfway with ice. Strain the gin mixture into the glass.

Top off with chilled club soda to taste. Stir briefly. Garnish with mint leaves and a lime wedge.

COCKTAIL ESSENTIALS

Flavored simple syrups are a fast way to a good drink, even if you're not adding alcohol. A little basil simple syrup mixed with sparkling water is a summer cocktail the whole family will love. Or swap out the water for tonic and add a splash of gin.

Simple Syrup
MAKES 8 OUNCES

1 cup water
1 cup sugar

In a small saucepan over medium heat, bring the water and sugar to a simmer, then lower the heat to low and cook, stirring often, until the sugar is completely dissolved. Remove the pan from the heat and let the mixture cool for about 30 minutes. Pour the syrup into a glass container and store tightly sealed in the refrigerator. It will keep for up to a month.

Herbed Simple Syrup

Add ¼ cup finely chopped fresh herbs, such as basil, rosemary, lemongrass, mint, or lavender to the water and sugar. Continue to prepare as described above. When finished, pass the mixture through a fine-mesh strainer, pressing the aromatics against the screen to extract the maximum amount of flavor. Pour the syrup into a glass container and store it tightly sealed in the refrigerator. It will keep for up to a month.

Grenadine
MAKES 8 OUNCES

¾ cup unsweetened pomegranate juice
¾ cup sugar
1 teaspoon orange blossom water (available at specialty grocery stores and online) (optional)
¼ teaspoon freshly squeezed lemon juice

In a small saucepan, heat the pomegranate juice and sugar over medium-low heat until just barely bubbling, about

5 minutes. Do not allow the mixture to boil. Remove the pan from the heat and continue stirring until the sugar is completely dissolved. Stir in the orange blossom water and lemon juice and let the syrup cool to room temperature. Pour the syrup into a glass container with a tight-fitting lid and refrigerate. It will keep for up to a month.

Boozy Cherries
MAKES 1 QUART

These little gems are perfect for any cocktail calling for a maraschino cherry, from adults-only Shirley Temples to Manhattans.

6 ounces (¾ cup) bourbon
½ cup unsweetened cherry juice
½ cup sugar
1 pound large sweet cherries, pitted
1 tablespoon freshly squeezed lemon juice

In a small saucepan over medium-low heat, bring the bourbon, cherry juice, and sugar to a simmer. Stir in the cherries and lemon juice and remove from the heat. Set aside to cool. Pour the mixture into a jar, cover, and refrigerate for at least 3 days before using, or longer for a more intense flavor. The cherries will keep for up to 3 weeks refrigerated.

Lime-Chili Rim Salt
MAKES ABOUT ½ CUP

½ cup kosher salt
1 teaspoon dried chili powder (such as ancho, chipotle, or cayenne)
1 tablespoon freshly grated lime zest (from about 2 limes)

In a small bowl, stir together the salt and chili powder, then work the zest into the mixture with your fingertips. Store in a covered container at room temperature. Use this salt mixture to rim glasses for margaritas (page 175), Micheladas (page 183), shots of tequila, and other Mexican cocktails.

SKILLET-ROASTED WHOLE CHICKEN

SERVES 4

All of us at The Kitchn adore this method for making a roasted chicken; we borrow it from the much-missed chef Judy Rodgers of Zuni Café in San Francisco. The important things to note are to use a hot skillet, cast iron if possible, and to start with a very dry bird. Have paper towels at the ready to pat her down like a baby coming out of a pool. A small chicken takes only about an hour to cook, so we can easily make this chicken for weeknight meals. Prep it the night before, put it in the oven when you get home from work, and let it cook while you wind down from the day. It's that simple.

1 tablespoon coarse salt
1 teaspoon freshly ground black pepper
Zest of 1 lemon
1 tablespoon (packed) dark brown sugar
One 3- to 4-pound fresh whole chicken
Olive oil or butter
Lemon halves, garlic cloves, fresh herbs (such as thyme, rosemary, or sage), for stuffing the cavity of the bird (optional)

Place a 10- to 12-inch skillet, preferably cast iron, on the middle rack of the oven and heat it to 475°F.

In a small bowl, mix the salt, pepper, lemon zest, and brown sugar. Set aside.

Remove any packaging from the chicken and drain out any juices or blood trapped in the plastic. Reach inside the chicken's body cavity and remove the bag of giblets. The giblets can be discarded, saved for stock, or used to make gravy later on.

Pat the chicken very thoroughly with paper towels or a kitchen rag, making sure to absorb any liquid behind the wings or legs and inside the body cavity, too.

Massage the outside of the chicken with olive oil or butter, and then coat it with the spice rub. If desired, stuff the inside of the chicken with halved lemons, whole cloves of garlic, or herbs. Again, gently pat the chicken dry with paper towels or a kitchen towel reserved for handling raw meat.

Carefully remove the hot skillet from the oven and place it on top of the stove. Place the chicken, breast side up, in the skillet. You should hear it sizzle. Transfer the skillet back into the oven and roast for 20 minutes.

After 20 minutes, check the chicken; the skin should have started to bubble and blister. If the chicken appears to be burning or smoking, reduce the oven temperature by 25 degrees before returning the chicken to the oven.

After 10 minutes, remove the skillet from the oven and place it on a burner. Carefully turn the chicken over onto its back, taking care not to tear the skin. This is best achieved with two wide, flat wooden spoons or spatulas.

Return the chicken to the oven and roast for another 10 to 20 minutes, depending on the size of the bird. Finally, turn it back breast side up and roast for another 5 to 10 minutes to crisp the skin.

Check the chicken for doneness by inserting a meat thermometer into the meatiest part of the breast. It should register at least 165°F. If the chicken is not quite done, it will have to roast a while longer. But if the skin is already browned, cover the chicken with foil before returning it to the oven.

When the chicken is done, transfer it from the skillet to a plate and tent with foil. Pour off the clear fat from the skillet and reserve it for another use. To make a sauce from the pan drippings, add a few spoonfuls of water, stock, or white wine and put the skillet on a burner over low heat, using the back of a spoon to scrape up any crusty brown bits from the bottom of the pan.

Let the chicken rest for 10 to 15 minutes. Carve the chicken (page 121) and serve with the pan drippings sauce.

The cooked chicken will keep in the refrigerator, tightly wrapped, for up to 3 days.

Tip from The Kitchn

Make sure you measure out the ingredients and prep the spice rub before handling the raw chicken so you don't have to worry about cross-contamination.

Continued on next page

Easy Homemade Chicken Stock
MAKES ABOUT 1 QUART STOCK

After you enjoy your delicious roast chicken, pop its carcass in a pot and make homemade chicken stock, perhaps the ultimate kitchen conjunction of frugality and luxury. Making your own chicken stock is a snap. You can make it right away or throw the carcass in the freezer and do it later. You can add all the vegetables we suggest below, for a classic stock, or just a handful of peppercorns. No matter what, it's guaranteed to beat anything you buy at the store!

Bones and carcass from one roasted chicken
2 onions, quartered
3 to 4 stalks of celery, chopped
1 to 2 carrots, unpeeled and roughly chopped
2 bay leaves
4 to 5 sprigs fresh thyme
6 to 8 parsley stems

OPTIONAL EXTRAS

Whole garlic cloves
Fennel fronds
Leek tops
1 teaspoon whole peppercorns

Pull the chicken carcass into a few pieces that will fit into a 4-quart (or larger) pot.

Put the chicken bones, vegetables, and herbs in the pot and cover them with water by about an inch. Bring to a boil then reduce the heat and cook on very low heat for 2 to 3 hours. You should just see a few bubbles here and there, a little movement in the liquid, and bit of steam over the pot. Add more water if the bones start to become exposed. The ideal temperature is between 180° and 190° for the liquid.

Skim off any foam or film that floats to the top of the stock. This isn't strictly necessary, but it will make your stock look and taste more clean.

Strain the stock into a large bowl. Discard the solids. (If you'd like a clearer broth, strain it again through cheesecloth.) Cool the stock quickly by placing the bowl in a large pan of ice and stirring frequently. When cool, separate into portion-sized containers or bags. Refrigerate stock for up to a week or freeze it indefinitely.

ALTERNATIVE METHODS
▼

> **Oven Method.** Alternatively, you can cover the pot and put it in a 225°F oven for 4 to 6 hours.

> **Slow Cooker Method.** You can also cook the stock for 6 to 8 hours in a slow cooker on the LOW setting.

> **Pressure Cooker Method.** We're huge fans of making stock in the pressure cooker, which speeds the process up to about 45 minutes. Refer to your appliance's manual for specific instructions.

Tips from The Kitchn

> **Be Flexible.** We'll say it again: the amount and kinds of vegetables given in this recipe are just a guideline. Use what you have and your stock will still be great.

> If it fits in your pot, you can cook the stock inside the pasta strainer insert. This makes the job of separating the solids a cinch.

> You can double or triple the recipe depending on how many chicken carcasses you have.

> You can also make this using turkey or duck carcasses.

ITALIAN CHICKEN SALAD SANDWICHES

MAKES 6 SANDWICHES

Recently we went looking for a chicken salad recipe that would suit a mayonnaise hater. We came upon a recipe we liked so much, and made it so frequently, that we tweaked and created our own version. This has crunch from bits of fried pancetta, color from roasted red pepper, and tang from the Dijon dressing. Of course, no one says you have to use this for sandwiches. Eat it with a spoon or spoon it over some lettuce and eat it as a salad.

FOR THE CHICKEN SALAD

 4 ounces pancetta, cubed
4 to 5 cups shredded roasted chicken (page 187)
 ⅓ cup thinly sliced red onion (about ¼ medium onion)
 ½ cup diced celery (1 large stalk)
 ¼ cup chopped celery leaves
 ½ cup thinly sliced roasted red pepper, drained (about 1 whole red pepper)
 Handful of chopped fresh flat-leaf parsley
 Flaked sea salt and freshly ground black pepper

FOR THE VINAIGRETTE

 2 tablespoons red wine vinegar
 1 teaspoon Dijon mustard
 ½ teaspoon salt
 Freshly ground black pepper
 1 teaspoon sugar
 ¼ cup olive oil

FOR SERVING

12 slices hearty Italian or peasant bread
 Lettuce leaves
 Tomato slices

To make the chicken salad: In a small skillet set over medium heat, fry the pancetta cubes, stirring constantly until browned, about 2 minutes. Drain on paper towels.

In a large bowl, combine the shredded chicken, onion, celery, celery leaves, red pepper, parsley, and cooked pancetta. Season with sea salt and black pepper.

To make the vinaigrette: Whisk together the vinegar, mustard, salt, pepper, and sugar in a small bowl. Slowly stream in the olive oil, whisking vigorously, until well combined. Pour the vinaigrette over the chicken mixture and toss to coat. Adjust the seasoning to taste.

Assemble each sandwich by spooning ¾ to 1 cup of the chicken mixture onto a slice of bread, adding lettuce and tomato, then topping it with another slice of bread.

The chicken salad will keep in an airtight container in the refrigerator for 3 days.

SLOW COOKER LEMON GARLIC CHICKEN

SERVES 4

Slow cooker recipes are some of our most popular at The Kitchn, and this garlicky, lemon-scented chicken is the most popular of them all. Simply pop a chicken in the slow cooker with a few lemons, a handful of garlic, and some herbs, and then you're free to read the paper, run errands, play in the park, or go wherever your weekend adventures take you. Come dinnertime, your house will smell amazing and you will have a chicken dinner ready to eat. Press the garlic cloves out of the skins and spread them on baguette slices for an extra treat.

 One 4- to 5-pound whole chicken or the equivalent in chicken parts
 1 head of garlic, separated into cloves
 6 sprigs fresh thyme
 1 tablespoon olive oil
 1 teaspoon salt
 2 lemons
 2 tablespoons soy sauce
 ¼ cup store-bought or homemade low-sodium chicken stock (see page 188)

FOR THE GRAVY

 2 cups low-sodium chicken stock
 ¼ cup all-purpose flour
 Salt and freshly ground black pepper

Remove the bag of giblets from the chicken and discard (or reserve for stock). Pat the chicken dry with paper towels.

Peel 3 of the garlic cloves and mince them. Strip the leaves from 2 sprigs of the thyme. Mix the minced garlic, thyme leaves, olive oil, and salt in a small bowl.

Gently work your fingers under the chicken's skin covering the breast meat and slide them back and forth to separate the skin from the meat without tearing it. Scoop up a dollop of the garlic-thyme mix and work it under the skin, covering both breasts. Rub any remaining seasoning over the drumsticks and thighs. Place the chicken breast side up in a slow cooker large enough to comfortably hold it. (If you are using chicken parts, arrange the thighs and drumsticks on the bottom of the slow cooker with the breasts in a layer on top.)

Juice one of the lemons (about 3 tablespoons juice). Whisk the juice together with the soy sauce and chicken stock and pour over the chicken.

Stuff the rinds of the juiced lemon into the cavity of the chicken along with a few unpeeled garlic cloves. Quarter the remaining lemon and arrange it along with the rest of the unpeeled garlic cloves and the sprigs of thyme around the chicken.

Place the lid on the slow cooker and cook on HIGH for 4 to 6 hours.

Remove the chicken from the slow cooker and allow it to rest on a baking sheet or carving board, tented with foil, for about 20 minutes. The wings and drumsticks may fall away as you lift the chicken.

TO MAKE THE GRAVY

While the chicken is resting, strain the cooking liquid from the bottom of the slow cooker into a measuring cup. Add more water if necessary to make 2 cups of liquid. In a small separate bowl, whisk together the flour with ½ cup of the cooking liquid until no lumps remain. Combine the cooking liquid, flour mixture, and the 2 cups of chicken stock in a saucepan over medium heat. Bring to a simmer and whisk gently until the gravy thickens, 3 to 5 minutes. Remove from the heat. Season the gravy with salt and pepper to taste.

To serve, remove the skin from the chicken and discard. Use your fingers to pull the meat away off the bones; it should come away easily with gentle pressure,

but use a knife as needed. Serve the breasts, thighs, and drumsticks right away with gravy, if desired, and tear the remaining meat into shreds for use as leftovers. Leftovers will keep for up to 3 to 4 days refrigerated or for 3 months frozen.

ROASTED CHICKEN THIGHS *and* SQUASH OVER POLENTA

SERVES 4 TO 6

We at The Kitchn recently declared chicken thighs to be the Next Big Thing. Boneless, skinless chicken thighs are an inexpensive cut of meat (even when organic and well-raised), and they're just impossible to mess up. We like to roast them or grill them, and even when cooked a few minutes too long, they're still tender and succulent. In this recipe we simply throw them on a sheet pan with cubed squash and some herbs and roast them together for one hearty, healthy dinner. Served over polenta, as here, or with pasta, this is a delicious weeknight meal ready in just about 30 minutes.

2 pounds boneless, skinless chicken thighs

3 pounds butternut squash, peeled and cut into ¾-inch cubes (about 4 cups)

3 teaspoons kosher salt
Freshly ground black pepper

¼ cup olive oil

8 garlic cloves, smashed

2 tablespoons cider vinegar

1 tablespoon finely chopped fresh rosemary

1 tablespoon honey

1 teaspoon red pepper flakes (optional)

FOR THE POLENTA

4 cups water or chicken broth

1 cup coarsely ground cornmeal

½ cup finely grated Parmesan cheese
Olive oil
Salt and freshly ground black pepper
Aged balsamic vinegar, for serving

Preheat the oven to 450°F. Mix the chicken thighs and squash in a large bowl. Toss with the salt and a generous quantity of black pepper.

In a food chopper, small food processor, or mortar and pestle, blend the olive oil, garlic, vinegar, rosemary, honey, and red pepper flakes to create a thick sauce. Toss with the chicken thighs and squash, and spread in one layer on a sheet pan. Roast for 25 minutes, or until the chicken is browned and the squash is tender. The chicken should reach an internal temperature of 165°F. Remove the chicken and squash from the pan and place them in a serving bowl, covered with foil to keep the food warm. Carefully drain any juices left in the baking pan into a small bowl and reserve.

TO MAKE THE POLENTA

While the chicken is roasting, heat 4 cups of water or broth to a boil in a 3-quart (or larger) saucepan. Add the cornmeal very slowly, whisking constantly. When the cornmeal is incorporated, turn the heat down to a bare simmer. The cornmeal should cook slowly, with a bubble plopping up to the surface every 30 seconds or so. Stir every 5 to 10 minutes. After about 20 to 25 minutes, the polenta should be quite thick and creamy. Remove the pan from the heat and stir in the cheese, a drizzle of olive oil, and salt and pepper to taste.

Serve the polenta in shallow pasta bowls, with a piece of chicken and a scoop of squash on top. Drizzle the plates with a few spoonfuls of pan juices from the chicken and a few drops of aged balsamic vinegar just before serving.

COLD PEANUT SESAME NOODLES
with PAN-SEARED CHICKEN

SERVES 4 AS A MAIN DISH OR 6 AS A SIDE DISH

Here's something you probably crave and might never make: cold sesame noodles with a rich yet light peanut sauce. Hold the chicken if you're a vegetarian, but otherwise, cook some chicken breasts on the stovetop in minutes, or experiment with other protein such as last night's leftover sliced steak. This is the stuff of takeout dreams, straight from your own home kitchen.

2 boneless, skinless chicken breasts (about 1 pound)
  Salt and freshly ground black pepper
4 teaspoons peanut oil
3 garlic cloves, minced
  1½-inch piece fresh ginger, peeled and minced
½ pound soba noodles
1 English (seedless) cucumber, about 12 inches long
2 medium carrots
5 scallions (white and light green parts), chopped
1 tablespoon black sesame seeds

FOR THE SAUCE
¼ cup natural peanut butter
3 tablespoons soy sauce
2 tablespoons rice vinegar
2 tablespoons sesame oil
2 tablespoons sugar
½ to 1 teaspoon red pepper flakes

Season the chicken breasts with salt and pepper. Heat 2 teaspoons of the peanut oil in a medium skillet over medium heat. Cook the garlic and ginger for about 2 minutes, then remove and set aside.

Add the remaining 2 teaspoons of oil, increase the heat slightly, and add the chicken breasts. Cook until golden on each side, 3 to 4 minutes per side. Turn the heat to low, cover the pan, and cook for about 10 minutes or until the chicken is no longer pink inside and an instant read thermometer inserted in the thickest part of the breasts reads 165°F. Remove the chicken from the pan and set aside to cool.

Bring a large stockpot of water to a boil and cook the noodles according to the package directions, then drain and run under cool water. Peel and julienne (see page 116) the cucumber and carrot. Set aside.

TO MAKE THE SAUCE

In a large bowl, whisk together the peanut butter, soy sauce, vinegar, oil, sugar, pepper flakes, and reserved garlic and ginger. Add to the bowl with the sauce and toss to coat. Add the cucumber, carrots, scallions, and sesame seeds.

To serve, mound noodles onto individual plates. Slice the chicken into thin, diagonal strips and place on top of the noodles. Serve immediately. Leftovers will keep in the refrigerator, tightly covered, for up to 2 days.

MIDDLE EASTERN TURKEY BURGER

MAKES 4 BURGERS

This spin on kofta, Middle Eastern meatballs, is perfect for the hot summer months when lamb or beef might feel too heavy. The herb yogurt sauce, our own take on the much-loved Greek tsatziki, packs a flavorful punch, and a few warmed pitas complete the meal. It's a refreshing new regular for your weeknight dinner repertoire.

FOR THE TURKEY PATTIES

- ¼ teaspoon coriander seeds
- ¼ teaspoon cumin seeds
- 1 pound ground turkey (dark meat preferable)
- ¼ cup finely diced red onion, from ¼ medium onion
- 1 tablespoon finely chopped mint
- 1 tablespoon finely chopped dill
- ½ teaspoon salt
- ¼ teaspoon freshly ground black pepper

FOR THE TSATZIKI

- ½ English cucumber
- ½ teaspoon salt
- 1 cup plain Greek yogurt
- 1 tablespoon finely chopped mint
- 1 tablespoon finely chopped dill
- 1 teaspoon freshly squeezed lemon juice
- ¼ teaspoon freshly ground black pepper

FOR ASSEMBLING THE BURGERS

- 4 pieces pita, flatbread, or naan
- 2 tablespoons olive oil
- 2 medium tomatoes, cut into ¼-inch slices
- 4 large leaves of butter lettuce
- 8 ounces crumbled feta

TO MAKE THE TURKEY PATTIES

In a small skillet over medium-high heat, toast the coriander and cumin seeds until fragrant, 1 to 2 minutes. Remove from the heat and grind, using a mortar and pestle or a spice grinder.

In a large bowl, combine the turkey, onion, mint, dill, spices, salt, and freshly ground black pepper. Mix the ingredients until just combined and form into 4 patties, handling the turkey as little as possible. Using your thumb, create a small indentation in the middle of each burger patty to ensure even thickness after cooking.

TO MAKE THE TSATZIKI

Peel the English cucumber and halve it lengthwise. Using a small spoon, gently scoop out and discard the soft core of each cucumber half. Using a box grater or a mandoline, grate the cucumber on the widest setting into long threads and mix with the salt. Allow the cucumber to sit briefly, about 5 minutes, then squeeze out the excess moisture using your hands. You should have about ½ cup of cucumber. Put the cucumber in a medium bowl and mix in the yogurt, mint, dill, lemon juice, and pepper. Cover the bowl and set it aside in the refrigerator.

TO COOK AND ASSEMBLE THE BURGERS

Preheat the oven to 250°F and wrap the pita in foil. Place the bread in the oven while you finish the burgers.

In a large skillet, heat 1 tablespoon of oil over medium-high heat until shimmering. Add two patties at a time and cook them for 5 to 6 minutes per side, disturbing the burgers as little as possible. Repeat this process with the remaining tablespoon of oil and turkey patties.

When the patties are done, transfer them to a plate. Spread a spoonful of tzatziki across each piece of bread. Layer on the tomato slices and lettuce, sprinkle 2 tablespoons of crumbled feta on top, and then place a patty on top of the cheese and fold the bread over the turkey burger. Serve immediately.

HERB-BRINED PORK CHOPS

MAKES 4 SERVINGS

There's something really satisfying about a nice thick pork chop. Here is a basic brined chop that is easy to make for a weeknight dinner. It goes well with any side: a tender green salad or a hearty grain dish. We serve it smeared with Dijon mustard or fruit chutneys, although the meat turns out so succulent (thanks to the brine) that it really can stand alone.

This recipe includes directions for making a basic brine, including rosemary, garlic, sugar, salt, and pepper, but branch out and try your own combo. Salt is essential, but everything else is optional. Consider ginger, fresh herbs, juniper berries, cloves, cinnamon sticks, vanilla bean, mustard seed, coriander seed, star anise, hot pepper flakes, or Sichuan peppercorns.

FOR THE BRINE
- 4 cups water
- ¼ cup kosher salt
- ¼ cup sugar
- 2 garlic cloves, minced
- 2 tablespoons chopped fresh rosemary
- 2 teaspoons black pepper

FOR THE PORK CHOPS
- 4 boneless pork chops, 1 inch thick (about 2 pounds)
  Salt and freshly ground black pepper
- 1 tablespoon olive oil

In a small saucepan, bring 1 cup of the water to a boil. Add the salt and sugar to the boiling water, stirring over high heat until they are dissolved. Chill the remaining 3 cups of water in the freezer or with ice cubes. Add the salt and sugar mixture to the cold water. Stir in the garlic, rosemary, and black pepper. Chill the brine in the refrigerator.

Place the pork in a stainless-steel bowl, a glazed ceramic dish, or a resealable plastic bag big enough to fully submerge the pork in the brine. Pour the brine over the pork, making sure the pork is completely covered in liquid. If you're using an open dish or bowl, cover it with plastic wrap and weigh it down with a plate if necessary to keep the meat submerged.

Chill for at least 1 hour, or for up to 2 days in the refrigerator.

Preheat the oven to 400°F. Place a cast-iron, stainless-steel, or other ovenproof skillet in the oven on a center rack. Take the pork out of the refrigerator and remove the meat from the brine solution. Pat the meat dry, season it with additional salt and pepper, and set it on the counter until the oven is ready. Discard the brine.

When the oven reaches 400°F, carefully remove the hot skillet and place it over medium-high heat on the stovetop, leaving the oven on. Add the olive oil to the pan and lay the pork chops in the center about an inch apart. Sear for about 3 minutes, or until the undersides of the pork chops have a golden crust.

Flip the pork chops and immediately place the pan in the oven. Cook for 5 to 7 minutes, or until the center of the chops is just barely pink and registers 140–145°F on an instant read thermometer.

Place the pork chops on a plate and tent with foil while you plate the rest of your meal. Spoon some of the pan juices over the pork chops just before serving.

Leftover pork will keep covered in the fridge for sandwiches the next day.

SOUTHWEST-SPICED
PORK TENDERLOIN

SERVES 6

No matter what dinner situation you find yourself in, you can count on this spicy pork tenderloin to come through for you. Serve thick-cut medallions fanned over creamy polenta for a dinner party or slice the meat thin for easy tacos on movie night. It makes a quick meal; you can pick up the tenderloin on your way home from work and sit down to eat half an hour later.

Don't limit yourself to the Southwestern-style spices we suggest here, either. The simplicity of this dish lends itself to variation, and flavoring mild-flavored pork tenderloin is a delicious way to experiment with a whole range of spices in your cupboard. Swap out the chili powder, cumin, paprika, and cinnamon for about 3 tablespoons of woodsy herbes de Provence or Chinese five-spice powder.

2 to 2½ pounds pork tenderloins
1 tablespoon chili powder
1 tablespoon ground cumin
1 tablespoon smoked paprika
2 teaspoons ground cinnamon
2 teaspoons coarse or kosher salt
½ tablespoon freshly ground black pepper
1 teaspoon vegetable oil

Place in the oven a cast-iron skillet, roasting pan, or other ovenproof cooking dish large enough to hold the pork tenderloins. Preheat the oven to 450°F.

Pat the pork dry and cut off any large pieces of surface fat. Mix together the chili powder, cumin, paprika, cinnamon, salt, and pepper in a small bowl. Rub the mixture into the surface of the pork on all sides.

Remove the hot pan from the oven and swirl 1 teaspoon of vegetable oil in the bottom. Set the pork in the pan. Roast for 10 minutes, then carefully flip the pork over with tongs or a spatula. Reduce the oven temperature to 400°F and cook the pork for an additional 10 to 15 minutes. The pork is done when its internal temperature registers 140–145°F in the thickest part of the meat and the pork still looks slightly pink on the inside.

Transfer the pork to a cutting board, tent with foil, and let it rest for 10 minutes before slicing. For extra-thin slices to use in sandwiches, cool the pork completely in the refrigerator before slicing. Leftovers will keep for 1 week refrigerated in an airtight container.

SLOW COOKER CARNITAS

MAKES 20 TO 30 TACO-SIZE SERVINGS

We originally published this pork taco filling recipe during a heat wave that hit New York one summer. Rather than turn on the oven, we touted the virtues of using a slow cooker on a hot day. Normally thought of during the colder months, the slow cooker is actually a great way to cook when it's too steamy to turn on the stove, and you'd rather be outside swimming or running through the sprinklers than tending a pot for dinner. What's more, this taco filling will serve the crowd of neighbors who come in dripping wet from the pool party.

1 boneless pork butt (6 to 8 pounds; also called pork shoulder)
2 tablespoons coarse kosher salt
1 tablespoon ground cumin
1 tablespoon freshly ground black pepper
1 tablespoon dried oregano
2 teaspoons ground cinnamon
1 teaspoon cayenne pepper, or to taste
8 garlic cloves, smashed
4 chipotle peppers (canned or dried)
1 cup tomato juice
1 cup orange juice

FOR SERVING
Corn tortillas (warmed)
Sour cream
Cilantro
Chopped red onion
Lime wedges

Trim excess fat from the meat and discard. In a small bowl, combine the salt, cumin, pepper, oregano, cinnamon, and cayenne. Rub the mixture all over the meat. Place the pork butt in a large slow cooker. In a medium bowl, mix together the garlic, chipotle peppers, tomato juice, and orange juice. Pour the liquid over the meat and cook on LOW for 8 hours. The meat is done when it is fall-apart tender.

When the meat is cool enough to handle, lift it from the juices and place it in a large bowl. Remove the bone, if there is one, then shred the meat. Skim the fat from the juices in the slow cooker, and add 1 cup of the liquid to the meat. Keep the remaining juices as a medium for reheating the pork.

For carnitas tacos, reheat the meat and serve it in warmed corn tortillas with sour cream, cilantro, red onion, and lime wedges.

LAMB LOIN CHOPS
with CHIMICHURRI

SERVES 4

When we talk about quick meals, we too often stick to chicken breasts and steak—familiar cuts of meat for many. But lamb chops are just as convenient, and they are hearty and delicious, especially when paired with this piquant sauce. Chimichurri is an Argentine specialty, usually served over steak, but also terrific with rice and eggs. There are many variations, but this sauce always includes lots of olive oil, garlic or shallots, fresh herbs, and an acid such as lemon juice or vinegar. The defining flavor is a fluffy heap of cilantro or flat-leaf parsley—or, as we do it here, both. As Sara Kate puts it, this is a dance party for your mouth.

2 pounds bone-in lamb loin chops, at least 1 inch thick (about 8 chops)
Kosher salt

FOR THE CHIMICHURRI

1 jalapeño pepper
3 teaspoons chopped fresh oregano
2 garlic cloves, finely minced

1 bay leaf, crumbled or finely chopped
Juice of 1 lemon (about 3 tablespoons)
½ teaspoon sweet paprika
¼ teaspoon red pepper flakes, or to taste
½ cup extra-virgin olive oil
½ cup (packed) finely chopped fresh flat-leaf parsley
½ cup (packed) finely chopped cilantro
Salt and freshly ground black pepper

FOR THE LAMB CHOPS

2 large garlic cloves, cut in half lengthwise
Freshly ground black pepper
Canola or grapeseed oil

Remove the lamb chops from their packaging and sprinkle very generously with salt. Use as much as a whole teaspoon on each side—the chops should be thickly covered with salt. Place the chops on a plate and let them rest at room temperature for 20 minutes.

Meanwhile, make the chimichurri. Using tongs, hold the jalapeño pepper over the flame of your stove (or put it in a pan and set it under the broiler) until the skin starts to blister and develop black spots, about 3 to 4 minutes. Set aside. When the pepper is cool enough to handle, remove the stem. Chop the pepper (skin and all) and place it in a medium bowl. Mix in the oregano, garlic, bay leaf, lemon juice, paprika, and red pepper flakes.

Heat the oil in a 2-quart saucepan over medium heat until it bubbles slightly but is not yet smoking. Remove the pan from the heat and stir in the jalapeño and spice mixture; it should sizzle. Stir in the parsley and cilantro, then taste and season with salt and pepper.

Allow the sauce to sit, covered, at room temperature for at least 30 minutes before using. (If you do not plan to use the sauce within a few hours, wait to add the fresh herbs until you are ready to use the sauce.)

TO PREPARE THE LAMB CHOPS

Preheat the oven to 400°F. Rinse the lamb chops thoroughly under running water. Pat them very dry with paper towels. Rub the chops lightly with the garlic, then season them generously with freshly ground black pepper.

Choose an ovenproof skillet large enough to easily hold all the chops. Grease the pan lightly with canola oil or another oil with a high smoke point and heat over medium-high heat until very hot but not smoking. Use tongs to place the chops in the pan. Cook for 3 minutes on each side, until the chops develop a golden brown crust. After 6 minutes total of searing, place the pan in the oven and cook for 6 to 10 minutes more, or until a thermometer inserted into a chop reads 140°F. Remove the pan from the oven and place the chops on a cutting board. Cover with foil and let them rest for 5 minutes.

Serve the lamb chops hot, generously drizzled with chimichurri.

Tip from The Kitchn

We use lamb loin chops here (instead of shoulder chops) because they tend to be thicker, a little more satisfying, and juicy like a good steak. Lamb's flavor is best when the meat is cooked medium-rare to medium, with a juicy pink interior. The thicker cut also makes for a more relaxed cooking time, with some room for error.

We learned the trick of rubbing the lamb with salt before cooking from Terry at blue-kitchen.com, who recommends this technique as a way to quickly tenderize cuts of meat that might otherwise be a little tough. We use this trick regularly when preparing our weeknight meals.

PAN-FRIED STRIPED BASS FILLETS *with* BROWN BUTTER *and* CAPERS

SERVES 4

Drag a simple fillet through a dusty flour bath, pop it into a hot buttery pan, and you will be 3 minutes away from dinner. A satisfying pan sauce comes together once you remove the fish. Throw some capers into the pan and pour off an inch or two from the top of your glass of white wine. This is one of those magical dishes that seems so sophisticated yet is prepared casually. See photograph on page 280.

- ¼ cup all-purpose flour
- 2 teaspoons salt
- 1 teaspoon finely ground black pepper
- 4 6-ounce striped bass fillets, skin on
- 6 tablespoons unsalted butter
- ¼ cup coarsely chopped capers
- ¼ cup white wine
- 2 tablespoons freshly squeezed lemon juice
- 1 tablespoon chopped fresh flat-leaf parsley
- 4 lemon wedges

Mix the flour, salt, and pepper in a shallow bowl. Dredge the fish fillets in the flour mixture and shake off any excess flour.

In a large skillet over medium heat, melt 3 tablespoons of the butter until gently bubbling. Set the fish in the pan, skin side down, and cook until browned and crisp, 2 to 3 minutes. Turn the fillets over and cook them until they are opaque in the center and the butter has begun to brown, about 3 minutes. Transfer the fillets skin side up to plates and cover.

Turn the heat down to low. Add the capers, wine, and lemon juice to the pan. Cook for about 2 minutes before stirring in the remaining 3 tablespoons of butter.

Serve the fish on individual plates or on a serving platter, then drizzle the sauce over the fillets, sprinkle with parsley, and garnish with lemon wedges.

FOOLPROOF SALMON BAKED
with OLIVE OIL *and* HERBS

SERVES 4

Many home cooks are afraid of overcooking, undercooking, or otherwise ruining an expensive piece of fish. This recipe is the place to start for a cook intimidated by fish—it's foolproof. The keys are the low baking temperature and the olive oil. The fish basically poaches in a very shallow pool of olive oil, protected from overbaking by the oil below and a paste of herbs on top. Even if it cooks for 5 minutes too long, it will still be moist, tender, and falling apart on the fork.

¼ cup plus 2 tablespoons olive oil
1¼-pound salmon fillet
Flaked sea salt and freshly ground black pepper
1 large shallot, roughly chopped (about ¼ cup)
¼ cup (loosely packed) fresh dill fronds
¼ cup (loosely packed) fresh flat-leaf parsley or tarragon leaves
Zest of 1 lemon

Heat the oven to 250°F. Pour ¼ cup olive oil into a small baking pan just large enough to hold the salmon in one piece. Lay the salmon, skin side down, in the olive oil. Sprinkle generously with salt and pepper.

Blend the shallot, dill, parsley, and lemon zest in a food chopper or small food processor. (Alternately, chop the shallot and herbs very fine and mix thoroughly with the other ingredients.) Blend in the remaining 2 tablespoons of olive oil. Pat this herb paste over the salmon.

Bake the salmon for 22 to 28 minutes, depending on the thickness of the salmon fillet. To check for doneness, insert the tines of a fork into the thickest part of the fillet and gently pull. If the fish flakes easily, then it is done. If it is still gooey, and if the fork is difficult to pull out, bake the salmon for 5 more minutes and check again.

To serve the salmon, gently slide a spatula under the fish and remove it to a cutting board. Use a sharp knife to cut the fillet into four equal pieces. If desired, lift the fish away from the skin to serve.

Serve with rice or fresh bread and a generous green salad.

BAKED BROWN RICE, LENTILS,
and CAULIFLOWER
with CUCUMBER YOGURT SAUCE

SERVES 4 TO 6

This generous vegetarian dish is inspired by the rice and lentils staple of Middle Eastern home cooking known as mujaddara. *While we often rhapsodize over the simplicity of* mujaddara, *we also wanted to amp up the vegetables and color in this otherwise simple, starchy dish. So we pile on cauliflower and red peppers and serve a cool cucumber yogurt sauce as an accompaniment. (See photograph on page 128.)*

2 tablespoons unsalted butter
1 large onion (about 1 pound), sliced into thin half-moons
1½ teaspoons salt, plus more to taste
¾ cup dried brown or green lentils
½ cup medium-grain brown rice
3½ cups low-sodium chicken or vegetable broth
1 small head cauliflower (about 2½ pounds), cut into bite-sized florets (about 4 cups)
1 12-ounce jar roasted red peppers, drained and chopped (about 1 cup)
4 garlic cloves, minced
½ cup chopped fresh flat-leaf parsley leaves
2 tablespoons olive oil
2 tablespoons rice vinegar
1 teaspoon smoked paprika
½ teaspoon freshly ground black pepper, plus more for the cauliflower
½ teaspoon ground cumin
¼ teaspoon ground cinnamon

FOR THE YOGURT SAUCE
1 cup plain Greek yogurt
½ large cucumber, peeled, seeded, and finely chopped
1 teaspoon freshly squeezed lemon juice
1 teaspoon lemon zest
¼ teaspoon ground sumac
¼ teaspoon ground cumin
Salt and freshly ground black pepper

Preheat the oven to 325°F. Heat a wide Dutch oven or heavy, ovenproof pot, 5 quarts or larger, over medium-high heat. Melt the butter, and when it foams up, add the onion and sprinkle with 1 teaspoon of salt. Cook, stirring occasionally, over medium-high heat for about 15 to 20 minutes, or until the onions are soft and pale brown with crispy dark edges.

When the onions have finished cooking, stir in the lentils and rice and add the broth. Bring the pot to a boil on the stovetop, cover the dish with a lid, and bake the lentils and rice in the oven for 60 minutes, or until the rice and lentils are tender and have absorbed the liquid.

While the brown rice and lentils are cooking, toss the cauliflower, red peppers, garlic, and parsley in a large bowl. Stir in the oil, vinegar, paprika, the remaining ½ teaspoon of salt, and a generous quantity of black pepper.

Remove the lentils and rice from the oven and turn the oven up to 450°F. Remove the lid and stir in the cumin, cinnamon, and the ½ teaspoon of black pepper. Taste and season with more salt if desired. Spread the cauliflower and red pepper mixture over the rice and lentils, and return the pot to the oven for 25 minutes or until the cauliflower is browned and crisp-tender.

TO MAKE THE YOGURT SAUCE

In a medium bowl, mix together the yogurt, cucumber, lemon juice and zest, ground sumac, cumin, and salt and pepper to taste. Set the sauce aside to let the flavors meld while the lentils, rice, and vegetables finish baking.

When the cauliflower has cooked, serve the rice and lentils immediately, scooped up with the vegetables, and topped with the cucumber yogurt.

SPICED LENTIL SOUP
with LEMON YOGURT

SERVES 6 TO 8

This is the soup you forget about and then return to and fall in love with all over again. You can make a big pot of lentil soup in about 30 minutes, and it will last all week. A bowl for lunch is hearty and filling enough to last you until dinner, but it's also one of the healthiest dishes you can put on the table. If you think of lentil soup as bland and boring, it's time to open up the spice cupboard and give this recipe a try.

- 4 slices thick-cut bacon, chopped (or 1 tablespoon olive oil for vegetarians)
- 1 medium yellow onion, diced small
- 1 large or 2 small carrots, peeled and diced small
- 3 celery stalks, diced small
- 2 garlic cloves, minced
- 2 tablespoons tomato paste
- 1 tablespoon smoked paprika
- 1 teaspoon ground cumin
- 1 teaspoon salt
- ½ teaspoon ground cinnamon
- 6 cups low-sodium chicken or vegetable broth
- 1½ cups dried green or brown lentils
- 1 bay leaf
  Freshly ground black pepper, to taste
- ½ cup plain whole-milk or nonfat yogurt
  Zest and juice of 1 lemon
- ½ cup chopped celery leaves

Set a 6-quart or larger pot over medium heat. Add the bacon and cook slowly until the fat has rendered and the bacon is crispy. Remove the bacon with a slotted spoon and transfer to a paper towel. Crumble the cooled bacon and set aside. Pour off all but 1 tablespoon of the bacon fat. If using olive oil, simply heat the oil and continue to the next step.

Turn the heat to medium-high and cook the onion until it softens and is almost translucent, about 5 minutes. Add the carrots and celery and cook for another minute or two. Stir in the garlic, tomato paste, paprika, cumin, salt, and cinnamon. Cook until fragrant, about 30 seconds.

Add ¼ cup of the broth and use the back of your spoon to scrape up any brown bits on the bottom of the pan. Cook for 30 seconds.

Add the remaining broth, lentils, and bay leaf to the pan and stir. Bring the pot to a boil, then reduce the heat to low. Simmer, uncovered, for 20 to 30 minutes, until the lentils are soft. Taste and add salt and pepper as needed.

Meanwhile, whisk together the yogurt, lemon zest, and lemon juice.

To serve, ladle a cup of soup into each bowl. Top with a dollop of the yogurt mixture and a pinch of the cooked bacon and celery leaves.

The soup will keep refrigerated in an airtight container for up to a week or frozen in individual portions for up to 2 months.

ONE-POT COCONUT CHICKPEA CURRY

SERVES 6

It's important to have at least one dish in your weeknight dinner repertoire that can be assembled mostly out of pantry staples. This curry relies on canned goodies and pantry essentials—chickpeas, coconut milk, tomatoes, onions, garlic—that are always on hand in Faith's pantry, and maybe in yours as well. Together they make a mild, toothsome chickpea curry, stewed in a creamy sauce of coconut milk, scented with cardamom and cumin, and perked up with a final squeeze of lemon. Baby spinach adds a swirl of green, if you're lucky enough to have some in the refrigerator (or the freezer).

- 2 teaspoons garam masala
- 1 teaspoon cumin seeds
- 1 teaspoon ground ginger
- 4 green cardamom pods
- 1 tablespoon unsalted butter or ghee
- 1 small yellow onion, diced
- 4 large garlic cloves, minced
- 1 tablespoon grated ginger, from a 3-inch peeled piece of ginger
- 1 14.5-ounce can diced tomatoes
- 2 15-ounce cans chickpeas, drained
- 1 14-ounce can coconut milk, well shaken
- 5 ounces baby spinach (about 5 cups, loosely packed); if using frozen, 1 cup thawed and drained spinach
  Juice of 1 lemon (about 3 tablespoons)
- 1 teaspoon salt, or to taste
  Cooked white or brown rice, for serving

Mix the garam masala, cumin, and ground ginger in a small cup or ramekin. Use the flat of a chef's knife to gently crack the cardamom pods, and add the cracked pods to the cup as well.

Heat the butter in a heavy pot or Dutch oven over medium heat. Add the onion and cook for about 10 minutes, browning the onion and letting it develop dark color, although without burning it entirely. Stir in the garlic and ginger and cook for 2 minutes.

Add the spices from the cup and stir them into the onion mixture. Add the tomatoes and chickpeas and sauté for about 2 minutes. Take the pan off the heat and stir in the shaken coconut milk. Return the pan to the heat and bring to a gentle boil. Turn down the heat and simmer for about 30 minutes, or until the chickpeas are tender and the sauce has reduced slightly.

Add the baby spinach in handfuls, stirring in each handful to help it wilt before adding the next. Stir in the lemon juice. Taste and season with salt.

Serve immediately over rice, or let cool and refrigerate. The curry will hold up well in the refrigerator in an airtight container for up to 5 days.

Tip from The Kitchn

This is not a spicy curry at all; it's mild enough for young children. If you'd like more heat, add 1 to 2 chopped jalapeño peppers with the garlic and ginger.

Want a little something extra in this curry? Add chopped cauliflower or 1-inch chunks of potatoes with the coconut milk and simmer until tender.

BLACK BEAN EDAMAME BURGERS

MAKES 12 BURGERS

Creating a really good veggie burger has been something of an ongoing labor of love at The Kitchn. Our quest ended when Megan Gordon brought us this recipe: a perfect blend of mushrooms, grains, vegetables, and bright green edamame. This burger has all the best flavors, textures, and spices and is tender yet satisfying.

You should know up front that these veggie burgers are not a quick prospect. The chopping alone will take you through an episode or three of your favorite podcast. It's worth it. This recipe makes a big batch, so you can freeze unbaked patties for quick meals down the road.

- 3 tablespoons olive oil, plus extra for the baking pan
- ½ cup farro (or 1 cup cooked brown rice, page 199)
  Kosher salt
- 1 medium yellow onion, diced small
- 3 medium carrots, peeled and shredded
- 2 garlic cloves, minced
- 16 ounces cremini mushrooms, stems removed, caps diced small
- 2 15.5-ounce cans black beans, rinsed and drained
- 1½ cups panko bread crumbs
- 1 cup frozen edamame, thawed
- ¼ cup chopped fresh cilantro
- ¼ cup chopped fresh flat-leaf parsley
- 1 tablespoon Dijon mustard
- 1 tablespoon soy sauce
- 1½ teaspoons chili powder
- 1 teaspoon ground cumin
- 1¼ teaspoon salt
  Pinch of freshly ground black pepper
- 2 large eggs
  Thin slices of cheese, for serving (optional)
- 12 hamburger buns

Heat ½ tablespoon of the olive oil in a medium saucepan. Add the farro and cook over medium heat, stirring, until fragrant, 2 minutes. Add 1½ cups of water and a pinch of salt, and bring to a boil. Cover and simmer for 20 minutes. Check the farro and continue to simmer

for another few minutes until the farro is chewy but not mushy. Remove the pan from the heat and drain off any remaining water.

In a large, deep skillet, heat the remaining 2½ tablespoons of olive oil over medium heat. Add the onion and cook until translucent, 5 to 8 minutes. Add the carrots and garlic and cook until fragrant, 2 minutes. Add the mushrooms and cook until softened and cooked through, another 3 to 4 minutes. Set the mushroom and vegetable mixture aside to cool.

In a food processor or blender, pulse 1 cup of the black beans to a chunky puree. Transfer to a large mixing bowl. Mix in the remaining black beans, cooked farro, cooled mushroom and vegetable mixture, panko bread crumbs, edamame, cilantro, parsley, mustard, soy sauce, chili powder, cumin, salt, and pepper. Allow to cool until the mixture is no longer steaming.

Taste and adjust the seasonings to your liking. Whisk the eggs in a small bowl and stir them into the vegetable mixture. Cover and refrigerate the burger mixture for at least 30 minutes or for up to a day.

When ready to cook the veggie burgers, heat the oven to 400°F. Line a baking sheet with parchment or some other nonstick liner.

Form handfuls of the mixture into patties roughly 4 inches in diameter and ¾ inch thick. Lay them on the baking sheet spaced an inch or two apart. Bake the burgers in batches if all the patties don't fit; alternately, form some patties and freeze them for later (see below).

Bake the burgers for 20 to 25 minutes, until the tops are dry and the patties feel firm around the edges. If desired, top the burgers with cheese and run them under the broiler for 30 to 60 seconds until the cheese has melted. Serve the patties warm on rolls with ketchup, mustard, mayo, and any other favorite toppings.

Baked patties will keep in the refrigerator for up to 1 week in an airtight container. Unbaked patties can be frozen for up to 3 months: freeze the shaped patties on a parchment-lined baking sheet until solid, then stack the burgers between layers of wax paper and seal inside a freezerproof container. Increase the baking time by 5 to 10 minutes for frozen patties.

SPINACH, MUSHROOM, *and* FONTINA QUESADILLAS

MAKES 4 QUESADILLAS

The name of the game is "get dinner on the table." When you want something fast and easy, a quesadilla will never let you down. As you can see by this recipe, quesadillas certainly don't need to use Mexican ingredients—in fact, as long as you have tortillas, you have the perfect vehicle for whatever odds and ends you have in the fridge. A handful of spinach, a container of mushrooms, a pile of cheese, and dinner is minutes away.

- 1 teaspoon olive oil
- 8 ounces cremini mushrooms, stems removed and caps sliced ⅛ inch thick or thinner (about 3 cups)
- ½ teaspoon salt
- ¼ teaspoon dried thyme or 1 teaspoon fresh thyme
  Freshly ground black pepper
- 6 ounces baby spinach (5 to 6 cups, loosely packed)
- 4 teaspoons unsalted butter
- 4 9- to 10-inch flour tortillas
- 2 cups shredded fontina cheese

Warm the olive oil in a deep skillet over medium heat. Add the mushrooms and ¼ teaspoon of the salt. Cook, stirring frequently, until all the liquid released from the mushrooms has evaporated and the mushrooms are soft and golden, about 10 minutes total. If the mushrooms start to scorch before cooking through, reduce the heat slightly. Stir in the thyme and black pepper to taste.

Add the baby spinach, the remaining ¼ teaspoon salt, and 1 tablespoon water to the pan. Stir until the spinach has completely wilted and tastes tender, 2 to 4 minutes. Taste and add salt and pepper as needed. Transfer the mushroom and spinach mixture to a clean bowl.

Wipe the skillet clean. Over medium heat, swirl 1 teaspoon of butter to coat the bottom of the pan. Lay one tortilla in the pan. Sprinkle ½ cup of cheese over the entire tortilla, and then spread a quarter of the mushroom-spinach mixture over just half of the tortilla (to make it easier to fold the quesadilla without the filling falling out).

When the cheese has melted and the underside of the tortilla is speckled with golden spots, fold the tortilla in half and slide it onto a plate. Repeat with the remaining tortillas. Slice the quesadillas into wedges to serve.

GREEN PAPAYA PAD THAI

SERVES 4 TO 6

This twist on the Thai food favorite is a game changer; instead of using traditional rice noodles you shred green papaya on a box grater or mandoline. The result is a lighter, fresher, and more toothsome dish, with all the deep flavors you find in good old-fashioned Pad Thai.

A note on some of the ingredients: a green papaya is simply an unripe papaya. Most Asian markets carry it. The other ingredients that may seem hard to come by, such as palm sugar and tamarind paste, can also be found at an Asian grocery store or online.

1 whole green papaya

FOR THE PAD THAI SAUCE

¼ cup fish sauce

2 tablespoons palm sugar (or granulated sugar)

1 tablespoon tamarind paste

4 to 6 tablespoons vegetable oil

2 cups thinly sliced chicken, beef, or pork (optional)

8 ounces firm tofu, cubed

6 small garlic cloves, minced

2 small shallots, minced

3 large eggs

1 cup bean sprouts, washed and dried

½ cup chopped flat Chinese chives (¼-inch pieces)

½ cup julienned radishes

½ cup minced roasted peanuts

Chili powder

Freshly ground black pepper

Lime wedges, for serving

Wash the papaya. Remove the skin and wash the fruit again. Slice the papaya in half lengthwise and scoop out the white seeds. (You'll only be using one half of the papaya.) Cut one half into strips, or use a box grater to make long shreds, like noodles.

Prepare the Pad Thai sauce. In a small saucepan, combine the fish sauce, palm sugar, and tamarind paste. Cook the sauce over medium heat, stirring to break up the lumps, until the mixture bubbles and thickens slightly, about 2 minutes. Remove the pan from the heat and set aside.

If you're adding chicken, beef, or pork, heat 2 table-spoons of the oil in a wok or large frying pan on high heat and cook the poultry or meat for 3 to 4 minutes. Remove the meat to a small bowl and set aside.

Heat another 2 tablespoons of oil over medium-high heat in the same pan. Thoroughly dry the tofu cubes with a towel and add them to the pan when the oil is just barely smoking. Fry the tofu, agitating the pan in order to cook all sides, until a crisp of brown skin forms, about 2 to 3 minutes. Lift the tofu croutons from the pan with a slotted spoon and drain them on a paper bag or stack of several paper towels.

In the same pan, heat the remaining 2 tablespoons of oil on high heat and add the garlic and shallots. Cook for 1 minute, stirring constantly with a wok spatula or a large wooden spoon. Add the cooked meat, if using.

Crack the eggs into the pan and stir aggressively for a few seconds until they begin to set. Add the papaya noodles and stir for 1 minute until they are well coated with cooked egg. Add about ½ cup of the Pad Thai sauce, stirring constantly until the contents of the pan are well coated with the sauce. Add the tofu croutons, all but a pinch of the bean sprouts, and the chives. Stir well then immediately remove the pan from the heat and divide the Pad Thai between four to six plates or present it in one large serving bowl.

Top the Pad Thai with the remaining sprouts, rad-ishes, peanuts, a pinch or two of chili powder (depending on your taste for heat), a few cracks of ground black pepper, and wedges of lime.

This dish will keep in a sealed container in the refrig-erator overnight, but it is best served immediately.

WHITE BEAN *and* ROASTED TOMATO CHILI

SERVES 6

Want to see home cooks get really worked up? Ask them about the perfect pot of chili. Everyone has their own idea of how chili should be made. Whether you think meat is essential, coffee and cocoa allowable, or—the paramount divider—beans or no beans, the best pot of chili is your own, because you get to call all these decisions yourself, which is part of the fun. Here's our idea of a darn good chili with lots of creamy white beans, tomatoes blitzed and roasted in the oven, and a classic mix of spices.

- 2 28-ounce cans peeled and diced tomatoes, well drained
  Olive oil
- 1 pound ground beef chuck
- 1 large onion (about 1 pound), diced
- 1 red bell pepper, diced
- 1 green bell pepper, diced
- 2 stalks celery, diced (about 1 cup)
- 6 garlic cloves, minced
- 1 tablespoon chili powder
- 2 teaspoons ground cumin
- 1 teaspoon paprika
- 1 teaspoon chipotle powder
- ½ teaspoon freshly ground black pepper
- 3 15-ounce cans cooked white beans, such as Great Northern, drained
- 4 cups low-sodium chicken broth
- 2 teaspoons salt, plus more to taste

FOR SERVING

  Sliced avocado
  Shredded Cheddar cheese
  Corn chips

Heat the oven to 450°F. Spread the tomatoes in a 9 x 13-inch or similar roasting dish and drizzle liberally with olive oil. Roast the tomatoes for 20 to 30 minutes, stirring occasionally, until the tips of the tomatoes are blackened and any juices have reduced considerably. Remove the dish from the oven and set aside.

Meanwhile, heat a heavy 4-quart pot or Dutch oven over medium-high heat and add the ground beef. Cook, stirring frequently and breaking up the crumbles, until the meat is browned and begins to crisp up. A dark crust may form on the bottom of the pan; this is expected and desired.

Turn the heat down to medium and push the meat to the sides of the pan. Drizzle olive oil on the bottom of the pan, unless there is substantial fat already remaining from the meat. Add the onion, bell peppers, celery, and garlic, and cook for 5 to 8 minutes, stirring the vegetables together with the meat, until the vegetables are golden and soft.

In a separate small bowl, whisk together the chili powder, cumin, paprika, chipotle powder, and the black pepper. Add the spices to the vegetables and meat and stir thoroughly. Fold in the white beans and the roasted tomatoes. Pour in the chicken broth and bring the pot to a simmer. Lower the heat and simmer for at least 30 minutes, or up to 3 hours if you can spare the time. Stir in the salt. Taste and add more seasoning or salt if desired.

Serve the chili hot with avocado, shredded Cheddar cheese, or corn chips, if desired. Leftovers will keep for up to 5 days in the refrigerator in an airtight container and can be frozen for up to 6 months.

MARGHERITA PIZZA *(and Beyond)*

MAKES TWO 10-INCH PIZZAS

Finding a truly great slice of pizza is a quest for many food lovers, and leads pizza-pie hounds to fill web message boards with critical dissections of restaurants' crusts, wood oven technique, and topping philosophy. But the hunt does not have to take you beyond your own kitchen, since you are more than capable of making radically good pizza at home. No wood oven required, and no special sauce—just a bright and piquant uncooked tomato sauce and some great homemade dough.

1 recipe Pizza Dough (recipe follows), separated into 2 balls

½ cup Fresh Tomato Pizza Sauce (recipe follows)

1 cup grated Parmesan cheese

1 8-ounce ball whole-milk mozzarella cheese, chopped or torn into small pieces

Kosher salt and freshly ground black pepper

Extra virgin olive oil

½ cup (loosely packed) finely sliced fresh basil leaves

Position an oven rack to the upper third of the oven and place a pizza stone or upside-down large, heavy baking pan on the rack. Heat the oven as hot as it will go—at least 500°F.

Using the heel of your hand, gently press and stretch the first ball of dough on a well-floured surface into an 11- to 12-inch circle, about ¼ inch thick, and lay it on a sheet of parchment. Repeat the process with the second ball of dough.

Spread about ¼ cup of pizza sauce over each disk of dough and sprinkle each with about ¼ cup Parmesan cheese. Spread half of the mozzarella cheese over each disk, then sprinkle another ¼ cup Parmesan cheese over each pizza. Sprinkle lightly with salt and pepper and drizzle with olive oil.

Open the oven and slightly pull out the oven rack with the baking stone or sheet on it. Carefully lift one pizza by grasping the parchment sheet by the corners, and place the pizza on the stone. Bake the pizza for 5 to 10 minutes (baking time will vary greatly depending on how hot the oven is and how thin you were able to stretch the dough). The pizza is done when the edges have browned deeply and the cheese is melted and bubbling.

Carefully remove the pizza from the oven by picking up the edges of the parchment and sliding the pizza onto a platter or wood cutting board. Sprinkle with half of the basil. Let cool for 3 to 5 minutes to let the cheese set. Repeat with the second pizza.

To serve the pizzas, cut with a pizza cutter or kitchen shears and eat immediately.

Pizza Dough

MAKES TWO 10-INCH PIZZAS

¾ cup (6 ounces) lukewarm water

1 teaspoon active dry yeast or instant yeast

2 cups unbleached all-purpose flour, plus more as needed

1½ teaspoons salt

In a large bowl or in the bowl of a stand mixer, combine the water and yeast and stir with a fork to dissolve the yeast. The mixture should look cloudy and begin to foam. Place the paddle attachment on the mixer, add the flour and salt to the bowl, and mix until a shaggy dough is formed. If the dough is too wet, add more flour as needed.

Turn the dough out onto a clean work surface, along with any loose flour still in the bowl. Or, if using a stand mixer, switch to the dough hook. Knead the dough until all the flour is incorporated, and the dough is smooth and elastic, about 5 minutes. The dough should still feel moist and slightly tacky. If it's sticking to your hands and the countertop or the sides of the stand mixer bowl like bubble gum, work in more flour 1 tablespoon at a time until it is smooth.

If you have time at this point, you can let the dough rise, covered in an oiled bowl in a warm place until doubled in size (about 1 hour and 30 minutes). After the dough has risen, you can use the dough or wrap it in plastic wrap and refrigerate it for up to 3 days. (Bring the dough to room temperature before proceeding.)

Cover the dough with the upside-down mixing bowl or a clean kitchen towel while you prepare the pizza toppings, or let the dough rest overnight.

Fresh Tomato Pizza Sauce

MAKES ABOUT 2 CUPS, ENOUGH FOR 6 TO 8 PIZZAS

- 1 15-ounce can whole or diced tomatoes
- 4 garlic cloves, roughly chopped
- 1 teaspoon balsamic vinegar, or to taste
   Olive oil
   Salt and freshly ground black pepper

In a blender or food processor, blend the tomatoes with the garlic, balsamic vinegar, and a drizzle of olive oil. Season to taste with salt and pepper.

The sauce will keep for up to a week in the fridge and much longer frozen. Freeze in ½- to 1-cup portions in individual freezer bags, then defrost overnight, snip off a corner, and squeeze out the sauce. Or freeze in muffin cups, then slip the frozen disks into a large bag. (Each muffin cup will hold enough sauce for 1 to 2 pizzas.)

PIZZA TOPPING IDEAS

▼

Every topping is fair game, including some you may not have considered. We love unorthodox flavors such as potato and sauerkraut. Here are other favorites.

> Very thin sweet potato slices, caramelized onions, finely chopped fresh rosemary, Gruyère cheese

> Very thin white potato slices, caramelized onions, sliced prosciutto, Gorgonzola cheese

> Diced fresh tomatoes, crispy cooked sausage, chopped fresh kale, mozzarella cheese

> Roasted diced butternut squash, cooked bacon, chopped spinach, smoked mozzarella cheese

> Sliced black olives, sliced artichoke hearts, soft goat cheese

> Thinly sliced smoked German sausage, sauerkraut, fresh mozzarella cheese

> Ricotta instead of red tomato sauce, thinly sliced garlic, fresh dill, fresh basil, red pepper flakes, Parmesan cheese

FREEZING TIP

To freeze a ball of pizza dough, coat it lightly with olive oil, then slip it into a freezer bag. Pizza dough can be frozen for up to 3 months. When you're ready to use the dough, put it in the fridge for at least 12 hours. Let it warm up at room temperature for about 30 minutes before stretching it out.

THREE BEST PASTA SAUCES

Aside from the fact that homemade pasta sauce always tastes better than the stuff out of the jar, another reason to make your own is because of the way it makes the house smell, especially the long and slow cooking Bolognese Sauce. These are three very straightforward pasta sauces we feel any cook would want to know how to prepare. Why not make a double batch and freeze some?

Bolognese Sauce
SERVES 4 TO 6

  2 tablespoons extra-virgin olive oil
  4 garlic cloves, minced
  2 medium carrots, peeled and minced
  1 yellow onion, diced (about 1 cup)
  1 celery stalk, diced
  ¼ teaspoon salt
  2 pounds ground meat or poultry, such as pork, beef, veal, turkey, or a combination
  ¼ cup tomato paste
  1 cup dry red wine
  2 cups canned crushed tomatoes (San Marzano variety, if possible)
  Salt and freshly ground black pepper, to taste
  Parmesan cheese

In a large nonreactive saucepan, heat the olive oil over medium heat. Add the garlic, carrots, onion, celery, and salt. Cook, stirring, until the onions are soft but not brown.

Add the meat and turn the heat to high, stirring the meat into the onion mixture and breaking up any lumps. Cook until the meat is browned, 8 to 10 minutes, stirring occasionally.

Push the meat to the sides of the pan and add the tomato paste, mashing it into the pan for a minute or so, allowing it to caramelize. Combine the paste with the meat mixture and pour in the wine, scraping the bottom of the pan to incorporate any toasted bits. Cook until the liquid has evaporated, about 5 minutes.

Add the tomatoes and their juices, bring the pot to a boil, then lower to a simmer and cook uncovered, stirring occasionally, until the sauce is thick but not dry, about 2½ hours. If at any point the vegetables appear to dry out, add enough water to just barely cover them.

Before serving, check for final seasoning and add salt and pepper if needed.

Cook a heftier noodle, such as fettuccine, tagliatelle, or rigatoni, to al dente. Add the pasta directly to your sauce along with a splash of the salty pasta water. Grate in a generous amount of Parmesan cheese, toss, and serve with a drizzle of olive oil.

The sauce will keep in a sealed container in the refrigerator for a week, or in the freezer for up to 2 months.

Wild Mushroom Ragu
SERVES 4 TO 6

  ½ ounce dried porcini mushrooms (about ½ cup)
  3 tablespoons olive oil
  ½ large onion, chopped (about ½ cup)
  ½ cup chopped shallots (from about 4 shallots)
  ¼ teaspoon salt, plus more to taste
  1 pound small, fresh wild mushrooms, sliced ¼ inch thick
  3 garlic cloves, smashed to a paste with a pinch of salt
  1 teaspoon fresh thyme leaves
  2 tablespoons tomato paste
  ½ cup dry red wine
  2 cups low-sodium vegetable, chicken, or beef stock, heated
  Freshly ground black pepper
  ½ cup freshly grated Parmesan cheese
  3 tablespoons chopped fresh flat-leaf parsley

In a small saucepan, bring 1 cup water and the dried porcini mushrooms to a boil. Remove the pan from the heat and let the mushrooms stand for 15 minutes. Strain the soaking liquid into a bowl through a sieve lined with a paper towel or a coffee filter. Roughly chop the porcini. Set the liquid and mushrooms aside.

In a heavy saucepan, heat the olive oil over medium heat. Add the onion, shallots, and salt and stir well. Cook until the onion and shallots are soft, about 5 minutes. Stir in the garlic paste, the rehydrated porcini mushrooms, and

the fresh mushrooms. Add another pinch of salt and the thyme, toss briefly, and cover the pan. Cook for another 3 minutes, shaking the pan a few times.

Uncover the pan, turn the heat up slightly, and continue to cook, stirring frequently, until all the liquid has evaporated, about 5 minutes. When the pan is dry and the mushrooms begin to brown, move them to the sides of the pan and add the tomato paste, mashing it into the pan for a minute or so, allowing it to caramelize. Combine the paste with the mushrooms.

Pour in the wine and stir constantly. When the wine has evaporated, pour in ½ cup of the strained mushroom stock and ½ cup of the warmed meat or vegetable stock. Bring the pot to a boil and scrape up any brown bits on the bottom of the pan. Lower the heat to a gentle simmer and cover. Cook for about 15 minutes, shaking the pan slightly every few minutes.

When the liquids have almost evaporated, pour in the remaining mushroom broth and another ½ cup of the warmed meat or vegetable stock. Cook for another 20 to 30 minutes, occasionally stirring the sauce and adding stock a tablespoon at a time to keep the mushrooms moist. The sauce is ready when the mushrooms are tender and the liquid has thickened. Season with freshly ground black pepper, to taste.

Toss with freshly cooked rigatoni or other sturdy pasta shape. Top the dish with grated fresh Parmesan cheese and chopped fresh flat-leaf parsley.

The sauce will keep in a sealed container in the refrigerator for a week or in the freezer for up to 2 months.

Five-Ingredient Marinara Sauce
SERVES 4 TO 6

      3 tablespoons olive oil
6 to 8 garlic cloves, crushed and chopped
      1 28-ounce can plum tomatoes (San Marzano variety, if possible)
     ¼ teaspoon salt
         Dried red pepper flakes (optional)
    10 fresh basil leaves, cut in chiffonade (page 117)

In a large nonreactive saucepan, heat the olive oil over medium heat. Add the crushed garlic and sauté for a minute, stirring with a wooden spoon. Add the tomatoes and their juices and bring the mixture to a boil. Lower the heat to a simmer and season the sauce with the salt and the red pepper flakes, if using. Break up the tomatoes with the back of a spoon and cook, stirring frequently, until thickened, about 15 minutes. Stir in the basil and cook another few minutes until the basil is wilted. Taste for seasoning and add more salt and pepper flakes as desired.

Serve over a freshly cooked tender pasta shape like garganelli. Top the dish with freshly grated Parmesan cheese and chopped fresh flat-leaf parsley.

The sauce will keep in a sealed container in the refrigerator for a week, or in the freezer for up to 2 months.

SEARED SCALLOPS
with LEMONY FETTUCCINE
ALFREDO *and* ARUGULA

SERVES 4 TO 6

Pull this recipe out when you really want to wow your guests. From the plump, perfectly seared scallops to the creamy lemon-scented pasta on which they rest, this is the kind of dish that elicits gasps when you bring it from the kitchen. Yet it also comes together in about 20 minutes with a bare handful of ingredients—minimal fuss, 100 percent impressive.

This dish won't hold for very long once it has been prepared, so have all your ingredients, pans, dinner plates, and side dishes ready to go before you hit the stove. You need to serve this as soon as it's ready.

     2 pounds large sea scallops (or 5 per person)
        Salt and freshly ground black pepper
     1 pound dried fettuccine pasta
     9 tablespoons unsalted butter
     1 cup heavy cream
     2 cups shredded Parmesan cheese
        Zest and juice of 1 lemon
     4 cups (loosely packed) arugula
        Lemon wedges, for serving

Check the scallops and remove any side muscles that are still attached. (The side muscle is a tough, rectangular tag of tissue on the side of the scallop. To remove it, pinch it with your fingers and tear it away.) Pat the scallops dry, sprinkle them with salt and pepper, and set them aside.

Bring a large pot of water to a rolling boil and add 1 tablespoon of salt. Add the fettuccine to the pot and swirl until all the pasta is submerged. Cook the pasta until al dente, 6 to 8 minutes.

Meanwhile, in a 4-quart or larger pot, melt 8 tablespoons of the butter and the cream over medium heat until the mixture begins to steam. Add half of the Parmesan cheese, the lemon zest, and the arugula. Stir until the arugula is wilted. Remove the pot from the heat.

Once the pasta has finished cooking, drain it and use tongs to immediately place it into the pan with the warm sauce, tossing it gently until it is well coated. Add the remaining Parmesan cheese and the lemon juice and toss. Taste and add more salt if needed.

Warm the remaining 1 tablespoon of butter in a stainless-steel or cast-iron skillet over medium-high heat. Arrange the scallops in the pan 1 inch apart. (To avoid crowding the pan, cook the scallops in batches if necessary.) Sear the scallops for 2 minutes on one side and then flip them. Sear the other side for another 2 to 3 minutes. The tops and bottoms should be golden brown, and the sides should be opaque all the way to the center.

Divide the pasta among serving bowls and top with five scallops per person. Garnish each plate with a lemon wedge or two. Serve immediately.

WHITE SPINACH LASAGNA
with SAUSAGE

MAKES ONE 9 × 13-INCH LASAGNA

Lasagna is the ultimate comfort food: filling, gooey, flavorful, freezable for rainy days, and portable for friends in need. Here's a white version with a splash of greens and meat so you feel like you're eating a balanced meal and not just the world's most comforting food.

5 tablespoons unsalted butter
⅔ cup all-purpose flour
5 cups whole milk
1½ cups finely grated Parmesan cheese
1 teaspoon salt
½ teaspoon freshly ground black pepper
About 10 ounces spinach, coarsely chopped (7 cups)
Olive oil
1½ pounds sweet Italian sausage, casings removed
1-pound box no-cook lasagna noodles
1 15-ounce container whole-milk ricotta cheese (about 1½ cups)

Melt the butter in a saucepan over medium-high heat. Stir in the flour, whisking vigorously for 2 minutes. Gradually whisk in the milk. Bring the pot to a boil, stirring. Reduce the heat to low. Simmer for 5 minutes, or until thickened. Remove the sauce from the heat. Whisk in 1 cup of the Parmesan cheese, and the salt and pepper. Stir in the spinach and set the sauce aside.

Preheat the oven to 350°F. Grease a 9 × 13-inch baking dish with olive oil.

Cook the sausage in a skillet over high heat, breaking up the clumps, until the sausage is no longer pink, about 4 to 5 minutes.

Spread 1½ cups of the sauce in the baking dish. Layer with 4 to 5 noodles, nestling them in however possible, breaking them to make them fit if necessary. Top with 2 cups of the sauce. Sprinkle on half the sausage and dot with ½ cup of the ricotta. Layer 4 to 5 more noodles on top, spread on another 2 cups of sauce, sprinkle the remaining sausage on top, and dot with another ½ cup ricotta. For the final layer, top with 4 to 5 noodles, spread the remaining 1½ cups of sauce, and dot with the remaining ½ cup ricotta. Bake the lasagna, covered with foil, for 50 minutes.

Remove the baking dish from the oven. Preheat the broiler. Uncover the lasagna; top with the remaining Parmesan cheese. Broil until bubbling, 1 to 2 minutes.

The lasagna can be covered and refrigerated, unbaked, for up to two days before baking, or it can be frozen, brought back to room temperature, and baked according to the directions above.

RISOTTO with CHANTERELLE MUSHROOMS, CARAMELIZED ONIONS, and PARMESAN CHEESE

SERVES 4 TO 6

Despite its reputation as fancy restaurant food, risotto is actually just Italian home cooking, Nonna-style. We think every cook should know the formula for a simple risotto. Good risotto depends on fat, short-grained rice, like Arborio, that can absorb a lot of liquid and give off a creamy, starchy sauce. While this is a terrific date-night dish, this risotto of buttery chanterelles and soft caramelized onions also offers a template for your own creations.

Heads-up: The longer risotto sits, the more it will lose the special creaminess that makes it so unique and irresistible. Therefore, have the rest of your meal ready and plan to make the risotto and bring the finished dish directly from the stove to the dinner table. (You can keep risotto warm for a scant hour in a slow cooker set on LOW, but it's still best right out of the pan.) That said, leftover risotto is fantastic for shaping into patties and frying quickly on the stovetop.

- ½ pound chanterelle mushrooms, or another flavorful mushroom
- 6 tablespoons unsalted butter, plus more as needed
- 2 onions, thinly sliced
-   Salt and freshly ground black pepper
- 6 to 8 cups low-sodium vegetable or chicken stock
- 1 shallot, minced (about 2 tablepsoons)
- 2 to 3 garlic cloves, minced
- 2 cups Arborio, carnaroli, or vialone nano rice
- ½ cup white wine
- 1 cup freshly grated Parmesan cheese
- ¼ cup chopped fresh flat-leaf parsley, for garnish

Brush any dirt from the mushrooms and trim the ends of the stems. Slice the caps and stems thin. Set aside.

Melt 1 tablespoon of the butter in a large sauté pan over medium heat. Add the onions and a generous pinch of salt, as well as a generous amount of black pepper. Cook, stirring occasionally, until the onions are caramelized deep brown and smell sweet, about 30 minutes. Transfer the onions to a clean dish and cover with foil to keep warm.

Warm the stock in a medium saucepan over low heat. It should be just barely steaming by the time you start the risotto. Once it is warm, remove the pan from the heat.

While the stock is warming, melt 1 tablespoon of the butter in a 4-quart (or larger) pot and add the mushrooms. Cook without stirring for a few minutes. Once the mushrooms start to release their liquid, stir them occasionally until all the liquid is evaporated and the mushrooms are golden brown, another 10 to 12 minutes. Add more butter to the pan as necessary if the pan looks dry. Transfer the cooked mushrooms to the dish with the onions and cover. (If the brown glaze coating the bottom of the pan starts to look or smell burnt while cooking the onions and mushrooms, deglaze it with a few tablespoons of water and continue cooking.)

In the same pan used to cook the onions and mushrooms, melt 2 tablespoons of the butter over medium heat. Add the shallot and garlic and cook until the shallot is translucent and the garlic is fragrant, about 1 minute. Add the rice to the pan and stir to coat every grain with fat. Cook, stirring, for 3 to 5 minutes or until the rice is aromatic and the edges of the grains have turned translucent but the centers are still opaque.

Add the wine to the pan and scrape up any browned bits from the bottom of the pan as the wine bubbles. Let it reduce until the pan is nearly dry again.

Begin adding the warm stock one ladle at a time. Before adding more stock, wait until the rice almost absorbs each portion of stock. This gradual addition of liquid is key to releasing the rice's starches to create a delicious sauce, so don't rush this step. You may not need to use all of the stock. Lower the heat as needed to keep the risotto at a gentle simmer.

Begin tasting the rice after about 12 minutes to gauge doneness. Add salt, as needed, to taste. The risotto is ready when the rice is al dente (when it still has a bit of chew) and the dish has the consistency of thick porridge. If you run a spatula through the risotto, the risotto should flow slowly to fill in the space.

Add a final ladleful of broth along with the remaining 2 tablespoons of butter and the Parmesan cheese to enrich the risotto and make it extra-creamy. Fold in the onions and mushrooms, and then immediately divide the risotto between individual bowls or serve family style from a large platter. Top each serving with a sprinkle of parsley.

PASTA CASSEROLE
with BROCCOLI *and* GOUDA CHEESE

SERVES 6

Pasta casseroles are usually a guilty pleasure, packed with cream and three kinds of cheese. But we prefer a lighter pasta bake, one that puts fresh ingredients forward yet lends itself to weeknight convenience. This is one of the quickest casseroles we know. This dish bakes up bubbly and comforting, but at the same time it gives you your daily serving of vegetables, too.

　　Olive oil
　　Kosher salt
1　pound dried orecchiette or medium shell pasta
1　small head fresh broccoli (about 1½ pounds), stalk removed, florets reserved
½　cup chopped fresh flat-leaf parsley leaves
2　large shallots, finely chopped (about ¼ cup)
15　ounces small-curd cottage cheese
1　cup plain whole-milk or low-fat yogurt
1　large egg, beaten
1½　teaspoons salt
　　Freshly ground black pepper
4　ounces aged Gouda cheese, grated (about 3 cups)

Heat the oven to 350°F and lightly grease a 9 × 13-inch baking dish with olive oil. Fill a large pot three-quarters full with water, salt it generously, and bring to a boil. Add the pasta and cook until al dente, or according to package directions. Drain, return to the cooking pot, and set aside.

　　Fold the broccoli florets into the pasta, along with the parsley and shallots.

　　In a separate bowl whisk together the cottage cheese, yogurt, egg, and salt. Fold this mixture into the pasta and season generously with black pepper. Fold in three-quarters of the Gouda cheese.

　　Spread the casserole ingredients into the prepared baking dish. Sprinkle the top with the remaining cheese. Drizzle lightly with olive oil. (At this point the casserole may be covered and refrigerated for up to 24 hours. Let it come to room temperature before baking it.) Bake for 30 to 35 minutes, or until the cheese on top has melted and the pasta is lightly golden. Serve immediately.

PESTO FOR ALL
SEASONS *with* SPAGHETTI

SERVES 6 TO 8

Very few things evoke summer more than pesto. In late September, Sara Kate strips her basil of its last leaves and makes pesto to freeze for the months ahead. Later in the season, she uses other leafy greens that survive the first frost—such as chard, kale, and collards. In the spring, try spinach.

½　cup chopped walnuts
8　ounces kale, spinach, collards, chard, or other greens, trimmed and rinsed
1　cup shredded Parmesan cheese
½　cup extra-virgin olive oil
4　garlic cloves, chopped
2　teaspoons lemon juice
1　teaspoon salt
½　teaspoon freshly ground black pepper
1　pound spaghetti, cooked

Preheat the oven to 350°F. Spread the nuts in a single layer on a rimmed baking sheet and roast them until they are golden and fragrant, about 10 minutes.

　　Meanwhile, bring a large pot of salted water to a boil. Have a colander ready in the sink. Have a large bowl of cold water ready. Drop the greens into the boiling water. When the water returns to a boil, swirl the greens around a few times until they become limp.

　　Drain the greens and plunge them into the cold water. Drain them again, then place them on a clean dishtowel and blot away the moisture. Chop finely.

　　Place the nuts, greens, Parmesan cheese, oil, garlic, lemon juice, salt, and pepper in a blender and puree until uniformly smooth. You may need to add more olive oil to reach your desired consistency.

　　Serve the pesto tossed with the cooked spaghetti.

　　To store, place the pesto in a storage container with plastic wrap pressed directly on the surface of the pesto and refrigerate. The pesto will stay fresh for up to 3 days in the refrigerator. To freeze, place desired portions in small containers with plastic wrap pressed directly on the surface of the pesto, or place in plastic freezer bags, and freeze for up to 2 months.

CLASSIC MEATBALLS
with **PASTA SHEETS**

SERVES 4 TO 6

We talk a lot about food and love on The Kitchn. Even on the most harried evening, the act of cooking expresses love and care for your family or friends and yourself, as you take the time to nourish everyone with handcrafted food. And if a quick weeknight meal is like an affectionate kiss on the cheek, these meatballs are a lavish embrace of pure, unadulterated passion, with their slow-cooked sauce and velvety classic Italian taste, piled high on sheets of pasta and falling apart at the touch of a fork. Don't blame us if they prompt marriage proposals; we're all for love.

FOR THE MEATBALLS

- ½ cup fine dried bread crumbs
- ½ cup whole milk
- ½ pound ground pork
- ½ pound ground beef, such as ground chuck
- ½ pound ground veal
- 1 teaspoon coarse kosher salt
  Freshly ground black pepper
- ¼ cup finely chopped fresh flat-leaf parsley
- 1 tablespoon finely chopped fresh sage
- ½ teaspoon cayenne pepper, or to taste
- 1 small yellow onion, finely grated
- 2 large garlic cloves, finely grated
- ⅓ cup freshly grated Parmesan cheese
- 2 large eggs, beaten
  Double batch of Five-Ingredient Marinara Sauce (page 211)

FOR SERVING

- 1 pound dried lasagna noodles
  Freshly grated Parmesan cheese

TO MAKE THE MEATBALLS

Put the bread crumbs in a small bowl and pour the milk over them. Stir them together and set them aside for at least 10 minutes so that the crumbs can soften and absorb the milk.

Mix the pork, beef, and veal together thoroughly in a large mixing bowl. Stir in the salt and a generous amount of black pepper, then add the parsley, sage, and cayenne. Stir in the onion, garlic, and Parmesan cheese. Mix the ground meat with your hands until all the seasonings are very thoroughly distributed through the meat. Stir in the bread crumb mixture and the eggs, and mix thoroughly.

Cover the bowl and put the meatball mixture in the refrigerator for at least 30 minutes, and for up to 24 hours. At this point you can also freeze the meat in a sealed container for up to 3 months for later use.

TO COOK THE MEATBALLS

Shape the seasoned ground meat into 1½-inch meatballs. Place the raw meatballs into the pan of cooked marinara and bring it to a gentle simmer over medium heat. Cover and cook the meatballs over low heat for at least 30 minutes, turning once and uncovering the pan halfway through. Cook the meatballs until they are fully done and no longer bright pink inside. The internal temperature should reach 165°F.

This cooking method produces a very smooth and tender meatball. If you want a little bit of crispness to the meatballs, you can sear them or broil them briefly first to develop a crust and then finish cooking them in the sauce.

TO SERVE

Cook the lasagna noodles according to the package directions. Drain the noodles and snip them into squares using kitchen shears. Place several squares on each pasta plate and cover generously with sauce and a few meatballs. Serve with plenty of fresh Parmesan cheese.

Tip from The Kitchn

We realize that not all meat-loving cooks are enamored of veal. We prefer pasture-raised veal that has been butchered in a humane way, and we appreciate the way it adds a delicate texture to meatballs like these. Nevertheless, we respect that many people choose not to eat veal (or lamb, for that matter), and if you fall into that group we recommend substituting ground chicken thighs for the veal. The chicken will lighten the meatballs in a similar way, although it won't impart quite the same velvety texture.

EASIEST BEEF STEW

SERVES 6 TO 8

Among food writers, Laurie Colwin is one of our heroines. Though most of her work was fiction, and she died far too young at the age of forty-eight, she left behind two gorgeous books about food. This recipe is adapted from the first book, Home Cooking, *where she preaches the value of cooking casually, with spirit and joy. This is not the average American beef stew that may come to mind. The rich and creamy stew we offer here is more of a traditional Beef Bourguignon, delicious on its own or served over a bed of egg noodles or creamy polenta (page 190).*

- 2 cups unbleached all-purpose flour
- 2 tablespoons paprika
- 3 teaspoons freshly ground black pepper
- 3 pounds stewing beef, beef chuck, or shoulder roast, cut into 1-inch cubes
- ½ cup olive oil, or as needed
- 2 cups red wine
- 1 14.5-ounce can tomato puree
- ¼ cup tomato paste
- 2 teaspoons kosher salt
- 8 garlic cloves, peeled and chopped
- 4 large carrots, peeled and cut into chunks
- 4 large yellow onions, peeled, cut into eighths, roots left intact
- 2 medium russet potatoes (about 6 ounces each) peeled and cut into 1-inch chunks
- 1 sprig fresh rosemary
- 2 sprigs fresh thyme
- 1 bay leaf
- 1 10-ounce package broad egg noodles
- 2 tablespoons unsalted butter
- ½ cup chopped fresh flat-leaf parsley
   Flaked sea salt

Preheat the oven to 300° F.

In a large mixing bowl, combine the flour, paprika, and 2 teaspoons of the black pepper. Toss in the beef cubes and carefully turn the mixture over several times until the meat is well coated. You may have to do this in several batches, setting each batch of floured meat aside on a plate before adding the next batch.

Heat 1 to 2 tablespoons of the olive oil in a large, deep, heavy-bottomed casserole or a 6- to 8-quart Dutch oven over medium heat, making sure the bottom of the pan is evenly coated. Being careful not to overcrowd the pan, brown the meat over medium heat in batches, adding more olive oil as needed, using metal tongs to turn the cubes of meat so that each side is browned. Remove the pan from the heat. When the pan is cool enough to handle, wipe out any burnt flour.

Over high heat, return the pot to the burner and pour in the red wine, tomato puree, tomato paste, salt, and the remaining teaspoon of pepper, scraping up the bits from the bottom of the pan while stirring. Cook the mixture, stirring constantly, until the liquid begins to thicken (about 5 minutes). Remove the pan from the heat.

Place half of the meat into the pot and sprinkle with half of the garlic. Add half of the carrots, half of the onions, and half of the potatoes. Add the remaining browned meat, and the remaining garlic, carrots, onions, and potatoes. Top with the rosemary, thyme, and bay leaf.

Cover the pot and place it in the oven for at least 3 hours, removing the cover for the final 20 minutes of cooking.

Meanwhile, cook the noodles according to the package instructions. Drain and toss with the butter.

Discard the rosemary, thyme sprigs, and the bay leaf from the pot. To serve, place a handful of noodles in each serving bowl and ladle the stew over the noodles. Top with the parsley and sea salt.

This dish can be stored in a sealed container in the refrigerator for up to 5 days.

PAN-SEARED RIB-EYE STEAK
with PAN SAUCES

SERVES 2

The first, and most important, step in cooking a great steak is to buy a great steak. The beef should come from cows that have been at least partially grass-fed and humanely butchered—the meat tastes better. Look for steaks that have been dry-aged, because this process intensifies the flavor. Remember, no matter how expensive the meat is, it will still be cheaper than eating out on Valentine's Day! Expect to pay at least $10 to $15, if not more, for a pound of steak. If the meat costs less than that, pass it up. A good rib eye will have some fat marbling around the edges. A one-pound steak will easily feed two, and can be stretched to three or even four people with a side salad and a grain dish.

1 tablespoon kosher salt

2 teaspoons freshly ground black pepper

1 tablespoon peanut, safflower, vegetable, or canola oil

1-pound rib-eye steak, 1 to 1½ inches thick

½ cup low-sodium beef or chicken stock

½ cup dry red wine

1 tablespoon unsalted butter

Blot the steak dry with paper towels or a clean rag. If the steak has been refrigerated, let it come to room temperature.

Put a cast-iron skillet in the oven, and preheat the oven to 475°F.

Mix the salt and pepper in a small bowl. Pour the oil into a second small bowl. Brush the oil all over the steak, coating it generously on both sides and the ends. Sprinkle the salt and pepper mix generously on both sides of the meat, patting it into the steak so it sticks.

Once the oven reaches 475°F, carefully remove the hot cast-iron skillet from the oven. Place it over high heat and use long, sturdy kitchen tongs to place the steak on the hot pan. It should sizzle immediately.

Cook the steak over high heat for 30 to 60 seconds, until the steak develops a nice crust. Flip it over and cook it for an additional 30 to 60 seconds. Then, again carefully, put the skillet in the oven. Cook for 3 to 4 minutes.

Open the oven and carefully flip the steak, using the long tongs. Close the oven and cook for an additional 2 minutes. Remove the skillet from the oven. Use an instant read thermometer to test the steak for doneness: it should be 125–130°F for medium-rare. If you prefer your steak closer to medium, add 1 to 2 minutes to the oven time and check for a temperature of 140°F. Take the steak out of the oven and turn off the heat.

Remove the steak from the pan (do not clean out the pan!) and place the steak on a large cutting board. Cover the steak with aluminum foil and let it rest for about 5 minutes.

Meanwhile, make the sauce. Place the skillet with the steak drippings over medium heat. Add the stock and red wine. Bring to a boil, lower the heat, and simmer until the liquid reduces by at least half. Scrape up any small bits of meat still clinging to the skillet and whisk in the butter.

Slice the steak against the grain and fan slices out on each plate. Pour the sauce over the sliced steak and serve immediately.

VIETNAMESE BEEF PHO
(Vietnamese Noodle Soup)

SERVES 4 TO 6

With the rich broth, noodles, and assorted garnishes such as onions, herbs, chilies, and lime, pho (pronounced "fuh" not "foe") is a wonderful interplay of textures and flavors. Traditionally the soup is made with beef or chicken bones; this version uses store-bought beef broth, so that the meal can come together in no time. It's simple to make this dish vegetarian: Just use more vegetables instead of steak and a vegetable broth instead of beef broth.

FOR THE BROTH

- 2 large onions, quartered
- 4-inch piece ginger, peeled and quartered lengthwise
- Two 3-inch cinnamon sticks
- 2 pieces whole star anise
- 3 whole cloves
- 2 teaspoons coriander seeds
- 6 cups low-sodium beef (or vegetable) broth
- 1 tablespoon soy sauce
- 1 tablespoon fish sauce
- 3 carrots, coarsely chopped

FOR TOPPING THE BROTH

- ½ pound London broil, sirloin steak, or round eye, placed in the freezer for 15 minutes
- 3 scallions, green and white parts, thinly sliced
- 1 chili pepper (Thai bird, serrano, or jalapeño), sliced crosswise and paper-thin
- 1 lime, cut into wedges
- 1 cup bean sprouts
- Large handful of chopped fresh herbs: cilantro, mint, basil, Thai basil

FOR SERVING

- 1 pound dried flat rice noodles (known as bánh pho; use ⅟₁₆-, ⅛-, or ¼-inch width depending on availability and preference), cooked according to package instructions
- Hoisin sauce, Sriracha, or Thai chili sauce

TO PREPARE THE BROTH

Using tongs, char the onions and the ginger over an open flame or directly under a broiler until slightly blackened, about 5 minutes on each side. Rinse with water.

In a large pot, dry-roast the cinnamon, star anise, cloves, and coriander over medium-low heat for about 1 minute, stirring to prevent burning. When the spices are aromatic, add the stock, soy sauce, fish sauce, carrots, and charred onions and ginger. Bring the mixture to a boil, reduce the heat, and simmer, covered, for 30 minutes. Set a fine-mesh strainer over a second pot, and strain the broth into it, discarding the solids. Keep the broth hot over low heat until ready to serve.

TO PREPARE THE TOPPINGS

Remove the steak from the freezer and cut it across the grain into ¼-inch-thick slices. Arrange it along with the other toppings on a platter.

TO SERVE

Divide the cooked noodles among deep serving bowls. Divide the beef slices evenly among the bowls and arrange them over the noodles. Ladle about 1½ cups of hot broth over the meat into each bowl. (The broth will instantly cook the thin-sliced beef.) Serve with toppings as desired.

The broth can be prepared ahead of time and stored in a sealed container in the refrigerator for up to 3 days, or in the freezer for up to 2 months.

TRICOLOR SLAW *with* LIME DRESSING

SERVES 6

We love this crunchy, colorful slaw. It's fresh and zingy, without the creamy heaviness of mayo-based coleslaws. This is our know-it-by-heart summer salad for picnics and barbecues.

- ½ head green cabbage (about 1 pound), cored and finely shredded with a mandoline or chef's knife
- ½ head red cabbage (about 1 pound), cored and finely shredded with a mandoline or chef's knife
- 1 pound carrots, peeled and grated with a box grater
- 1 large bunch cilantro, leaves roughly chopped
- ½ cup neutral oil, such as peanut or safflower
- ⅓ cup lime juice (from 3 to 4 limes)
- 2 teaspoons sugar
  2-inch knob ginger, peeled and finely grated (about 2 teaspoons)
  Kosher salt and freshly ground pepper

Toss the cabbages and carrots together in a large bowl with the cilantro. Stir together the oil and lime juice in a small bowl or measuring cup, and whisk in the sugar. Add the ginger to the dressing. Toss the dressing with the slaw, and season generously with salt and pepper. Don't skimp on the salt, as it makes this salad come alive.

The slaw is best served within a day or two, cold from the fridge, but you can refrigerate it for up to 3 days, or until it loses its crispness.

Tip: The recipe calls for half a head each of red and green cabbage, so ask at the produce section of your grocery store whether they'll sell you half heads of cabbage. Most will happily split up cabbages for you, so you're not left with double what you need.

Tip from The Kitchn

You can shred the cabbage with a chef's knife or mandoline, but this is a great recipe for using your food processor. Faith speeds through a batch of shredded cabbage thanks to the shredding blade.

SPRING BABY GREENS *with* HERBS *and* MEYER LEMON VINAIGRETTE

SERVES 4

Come spring, when the greens are just sprouting and the chives are blooming, take advantage of all of these petite and pungent ingredients and make a simple side salad to complement just about any meal. Serve as a lighter complement to a heavy meat-based meal, or even with a hearty egg dish for a weekend brunch. Farmer's markets are the place to find super-fresh tender spring greens and blossoms.

- 6 cups washed baby greens (arugula and baby spinach), torn into bite-sized pieces
- ½ cup chopped fresh herbs (lemon thyme, lemon verbena, Thai basil, and flat-leaf parsley)
  Zest of 1 Meyer lemon
- ¼ cup chopped fresh chives (and blossoms) or spring garlic

FOR THE VINAIGRETTE
  Juice of 1 Meyer lemon (about 2 tablespoons)
- ⅓ cup extra-virgin olive oil
- 1 tablespoon honey, or to taste
  Salt and freshly ground black pepper, or to taste

2 to 3 chive blossoms, for garnish

In a large mixing bowl, combine the greens, herbs, lemon zest, and chives.

In a small bowl or jar, whisk or shake the lemon juice, oil, honey, and salt and pepper until completely emulsified. Taste and adjust the seasonings.

Divide the salad greens among four salad plates and drizzle with the vinaigrette. Pull the chive blossoms apart and scatter the petals evenly over each salad. Serve immediately.

WILTED RAW KALE SALAD

SERVES 4 TO 6

Want to take raw kale from good to great? Use your fingers. Kale makes a delicious and healthful salad green, but it can also be tough and somewhat bitter. By massaging the fibrous leaves, you bring out their sweetness and transform them into something tender and more easily digestible. Eat this as a salad with Parmesan cheese (or other toppings), or keep the massaged kale on hand to add to sandwiches, frittatas, and homemade pizza.

- 1 bunch kale, preferably dinosaur (lacinato) variety (about 6 ounces), ribs removed and discarded, leaves chopped into ¼-inch ribbons
- 1 tablespoon extra-virgin olive oil
- ½ teaspoon salt
- 1 tablespoon freshly squeezed lemon juice (from about ½ lemon)
- ½ cup grated Parmesan cheese

In a large bowl, combine the kale, oil, and salt. Toss the kale, vigorously massaging the oil and salt into the leaves with your fingers for about 3 minutes, until the kale has softened.

Toss with the lemon juice and top with the Parmesan cheese. Serve immediately. The kale salad will keep refrigerated in an airtight container for 3 days.

WATERMELON SALAD
with FETA *and* MINT RIBBONS

SERVES 4 TO 6

We've been known to eat a bowl of watermelon and nothing else on a hot summer night. What elevates this dish more than anything is using very fresh, in-season watermelon. So while you might be tempted to give it a shot when those melons from mystery climates show up in the colder months, promise us you'll wait for watermelon's prime time: in May, June, and July. It'll be worth the wait.

- 6 cups bite-size watermelon cubes (from a watermelon weighing about 2 pounds)
- 1 cup thinly sliced radishes (about 5 radishes)
- 2 tablespoons extra-virgin olive oil
- 2 tablespoons lime juice (from 1 lime)
- 3 ounces very cold feta cheese, drained and crumbled
- ¼ large red onion, sliced very thin (about ¼ cup)
- ½ cup (loosely packed) fresh mint leaves, cut in chiffonade

  Flaked sea salt and freshly ground black pepper, to taste

Pour off any juice that has gathered around the watermelon. In a large mixing bowl, toss the watermelon gently with the radishes, oil, and lime juice. Add the feta cheese crumbles, and toss just until the watermelon begins to look lightly coated. Transfer to a serving dish and top with red onion slices and mint. Garnish generously with black pepper. Taste. If desired, add a sprinkle of salt. Serve immediately.

THREE JAM JAR DRESSINGS

Salad dressing seems as if it should be easy to make, yet when it comes to dinnertime, no one wants the job. The key to a good dressing is simple: taste it as you go. You can follow a recipe like the ones here, which involve adding everything to a jar and shaking like crazy, but when it comes down to it, pay attention to your taste buds. You want to ensure that the balance of fat (milk, cheese, and/or oil), acid (lemon juice or vinegar), and flavorings is right for you. Heavier dressings like the Buttermilk Chive and the Miso Tahini stand out with hearty greens such as romaine lettuce and kale, and raw vegetables such as radishes, carrots, beets, and celery. The lemon vinaigrette complements any salad, especially ones with tender greens.

Buttermilk Chive Dressing
MAKES 8 OUNCES (1 CUP)

- ⅔ cup well-shaken buttermilk
- ⅓ cup plain yogurt
- 2 teaspoons freshly squeezed lemon juice
- 1 teaspoon Dijon mustard
- 2 tablespoons finely chopped chives
- ½ teaspoon salt
- Freshly ground black pepper, to taste

In a 12-ounce or larger lidded jar, combine all of the ingredients with a generous amount of black pepper. Shake aggressively until the dressing is well combined. Taste for seasoning. Store in a tightly sealed jar in the refrigerator for up to 3 days. Shake well before using.

Miso Tahini
MAKES 6 OUNCES (¾ CUP)

- ¼ cup tahini
- 1 tablespoon white miso paste
- 1 tablespoon plus 1 teaspoon freshly squeezed lemon juice (from about ½ lemon)
- ¼ cup or more hot water
- Freshly ground black pepper, to taste

In an 8-ounce or larger lidded jar, combine all of the ingredients. Shake aggressively until the dressing is well combined. Add more warm water as necessary to reach your desired consistency. Taste for seasoning.

Store in a tightly sealed jar in the refrigerator for up to 3 days. Dressing thickens up as it sits, so you will need to add more water to thin it. Shake well before using.

Lemon Vinaigrette
MAKES 6 OUNCES (¾ CUP)

- ½ cup olive oil
- ½ teaspoon grated lemon peel
- ¼ cup freshly squeezed lemon juice (from 2 lemons)
- 1 tablespoon very finely minced shallot
- ¼ teaspoon coarse salt
- Freshly ground black pepper, to taste

In an 8-ounce or larger lidded jar, combine all of the ingredients. Shake aggressively until the dressing is well combined. Taste for seasoning. Store in a tightly sealed jar in the refrigerator for up to 3 days. Shake well before using.

WEDGE SALAD *with* BACON, MAPLE-FRIED RED ONIONS, *and* BUTTERMILK CHIVE DRESSING

SERVES 4

The wedge salad is one of life's great pleasures. If you've ever been to an old-time diner or a classic steak house, you know what we mean. But in our ever-lasting efforts to make dishes more creative and healthy, we offer this twist on the original. Instead of only iceberg lettuce, try wedging other nutritious salad greens, such as romaine and radicchio.

- 2 tablespoons olive oil
- ½ medium red onion, thinly sliced (about 1 cup)
  Kosher salt, to taste
- 1 tablespoon maple syrup
- ½ teaspoon vinegar, such as cider or sherry vinegar
- 4 to 6 strips thick-cut bacon
- 4 to 6 long baguette slices (sliced diagonally)
- 1 large garlic clove
- ½ romaine heart
- ½ head radicchio
- ⅓ small head iceberg lettuce
- 1 recipe Buttermilk Chive Dressing (page 225)
- 3 ounces crumbled blue cheese

Heat a wide frying pan over medium-high heat. Pour 1 tablespoon of the oil into the pan and heat until shimmering. Add the onion slices and a pinch of salt and stir. Arrange the onion evenly over the pan and reduce the heat to low. Cook, stirring occasionally, for about 10 minutes. When the slices of onion begin to show color, drizzle the maple syrup and vinegar over them and stir to coat. Continue cooking, stirring every minute, for about 10 minutes, raising the heat slightly in the last minute to help crisp the onions.

Remove the onion from the pan and spread it out evenly on a plate to cool, using two forks to separate the strands as much as possible.

Cook the bacon over low heat until crisp. Set aside on paper towels. When it is completely cooled, crumble the bacon.

Brush the baguette slices with the remaining 1 tablespoon of olive oil and rub them with the garlic. Toast under the broiler, in a toaster oven, or on a grill until golden brown.

Remove the root end from the lettuces, and cut each piece into 4 wedges. Place one wedge of each on four individual salad plates. Dress each plate with ¼ cup of the dressing. Top with the fried onions, bacon pieces, and crumbled blue cheese. Garnish with a piece of toasted bread.

TOMATO SALAD *with* BASIL *and* BURRATA

SERVES 4 TO 6

When the tomatoes are the stars of the garden, this is the salad to make. Decadent, creamy burrata, which is an extra-rich fresh mozzarella with a topknot and center that oozes out, mixes with the tomato juices and fragrant basil to bring the most flavorful, summery ambrosia to your table. Try to find heirloom tomatoes in a range of colors; they are widely available at markets in the height of summer.

- 2 small shallots, minced (about ¼ cup)
- 3 teaspoons balsamic vinegar
- 2 tablespoons extra-virgin olive oil
- 2 pounds tomatoes (about 3 medium tomatoes)
- 1 8-ounce piece burrata cheese, pulled into bite-size pieces
- ¼ cup fresh basil leaves, cut in chiffonade (page 117)
  Flaked sea salt and freshly ground black pepper

In a medium mixing bowl, toss the shallots with the vinegar and oil. Set aside for at least 30 minutes, or up to 3 hours.

Toss the tomatoes with the dressing. Arrange the tomatoes on a platter, drizzling with more vinaigrette as needed. Scatter the burrata on top of the tomatoes. Top with the sliced basil and a pinch of salt and black pepper.

GREENEST GREEN GODDESS SALAD

SERVES 6 TO 8

Here is the greenest salad. A throwback to Sara Kate's home state of California, this hippie salad was popular in the 1970s, when it was prepared frequently in her family home. Traditionally, the Goddess concept applies to the dressing, whose bright hue comes from loads of herbs. Here's a meal in a bowl that simply challenges the cook to push the earth's emerald gifts to the limit. Focus on what is in season and the flavors you love. Aside from the ingredients in the recipe below, you could add cilantro, blanched green beans, blanched green cauliflower, sliced cucumber, shredded green apples, or chopped green onions; the possibilities are fun to consider.

- 2 cups broccoli florets
- ½ pound salad greens, such as spinach or baby mixed greens
- 1 avocado, sliced
- 1 green bell pepper, sliced
- 2 celery stalks, sliced thin
- ¼ cup chopped bright green celery leaves
- 1 cup Green Goddess Dressing (recipe follows)
- ½ cup chopped dry-roasted pistachios or pepitas

Bring a medium pot of salted water to a boil and prepare a large bowl with ice water. Add the broccoli florets to the boiling water and cook until bright and tender, about 2 minutes. Drain the broccoli and immediately plunge it into the ice bath to stop the cooking process. Let it sit for a few minutes and then drain it.

In a large salad bowl, combine the salad greens, broccoli, avocado, bell pepper, celery, and celery leaves. Toss with ½ cup of dressing. Add more if needed. Top with pistachios and serve immediately.

Green Goddess Dressing
MAKES ABOUT 1 CUP

- ½ cup whole-milk yogurt
- ⅓ cup mayonnaise
- ¼ cup roughly chopped fresh flat-leaf parsley
- 3 tablespoons roughly chopped fresh chives
- 1 tablespoon roughly chopped fresh tarragon
- 3 tablespoons freshly squeezed lemon juice (from about 1 lemon)
- ¼ teaspoon lemon zest
- 1 tablespoon white wine vinegar
- 2 anchovy fillets, roughly chopped
- 1 small garlic clove, finely chopped
  Kosher salt, to taste

Place all of the ingredients in a blender or food processor and process until smooth and pale green. Taste and adjust seasoning as desired. The dressing will keep in a tightly sealed container for up to 5 days in the refrigerator.

GRILLED CAESAR SALAD

SERVES 4

You can throw pretty much any vegetable or fruit on the grill. Romaine, held together neatly with its strong root end and tall, alert leaves, is the perfect lettuce for the grill (or grill pan). Even better if you've just cooked a piece of meat on the same grill. It's the ultimate way to elevate a salad without making it fussy.

FOR THE DRESSING

  2 small garlic cloves, minced
  3 anchovy fillets, rinsed and minced
  1 large egg yolk
  1 teaspoon Dijon mustard
  ½ cup extra-virgin olive oil
  3 tablespoons freshly squeezed lemon juice
     (from about 1 lemon)
  1 teaspoon cider vinegar
  ½ teaspoon salt, plus more to taste
     Freshly ground black pepper, to taste
  ¼ cup finely grated Parmesan cheese

FOR THE SALAD

  2 large heads romaine, sliced in half lengthwise,
     roots trimmed clean but left intact
  3 tablespoons extra-virgin olive oil
  8 baguette slices (cut on the bias, ½ inch thick and
     about 6 inches long)
     Freshly ground black pepper, to taste

TO PREPARE THE DRESSING

Using a mortar and pestle or the back of a spoon in a medium bowl, mash the garlic and anchovies to form a paste. If you're using a mortar and pestle, transfer the mixture to a medium bowl. Add the egg yolk and the mustard, and whisk to combine. Add a very slow stream of olive oil while continuing to whisk. As the dressing begins to emulsify, gradually add more olive oil, whisking constantly. The finished dressing should have a mayonnaise-like consistency. Whisk in the lemon juice and vinegar, then season to taste. Stir in the Parmesan cheese and set aside. You should have about ¾ cup of dressing.

TO MAKE THE SALAD

Preheat the grill or grill pan to medium-high. Brush the cut side of the half heads of romaine with 1 tablespoon of the olive oil and grill cut side down for a minute or two, until the lettuce is seared with grill marks. Place half a head of romaine on each plate.

Brush the baguette slices on both sides with 2 tablespoons of the olive oil. Grill on both sides until browned.

Drizzle each half head of romaine with a quarter of the dressing. Garnish with two pieces of grilled baguette. Sprinkle with a few cracks of freshly ground black pepper. Serve immediately.

FENNEL *and* RADICCHIO SALAD *with* FARRO *and* PECANS

SERVES 4 TO 6

Some salads are delicate starters for dinner; others can fill a lunchbox. This is one of the latter. It starts with a robust, colorful blend of cold-weather greens—fennel, romaine, radicchio—and is plumped out by chewy, filling farro. A tangy, garlicky, citrusy dressing makes it even more delicious.

  ⅔ cup farro
  1 cup pecans
  ½ cup extra-virgin olive oil
     Juice of 1 medium orange (about 1/3 cup)
  2 tablespoons rice vinegar
  2 large garlic cloves, grated
  1 small head fennel, top removed, quartered, and
     shaved into paper-thin slices with a mandoline
     or food processor
  1 head radicchio, cored, quartered, and sliced into
     ribbons (page 117)
  1 romaine heart, cored, quartered, and sliced into
     ribbons (page 117)
     Flaked sea salt and freshly ground black pepper
  2 ounces aged Gruyère cheese, shaved into ribbons
     with a vegetable peeler

Heat 1⅔ cups salted water in a saucepan. When it comes to a boil, add the farro and stir. Cover and turn the heat to low. Simmer, covered, for about 30 minutes, or until the farro has absorbed the liquid. It should still be chewy. Spread the cooked farro into a single layer on a large plate or baking sheet to cool completely.

Heat a shallow skillet over medium-high heat. Toast the pecans, turning frequently, over medium heat for 5 minutes or until their edges turn dark and they smell toasted. Remove the pecans to a plate to cool.

To make the dressing, whisk together the oil, orange juice, rice vinegar, and grated garlic. Set aside.

Toss the fennel, radicchio, and romaine in a large bowl, and mix with the cooked farro. Toss with the dressing, and season to taste with generous amounts of salt and pepper. Toss with the pecans and the Gruyère just before serving.

BEET SALAD *with* HORSERADISH CRÈME FRAICHE *and* PISTACHIOS

MAKES 4 TO 6 SERVINGS

If you can read a recipe, you can make this salad, but your guests will think you are a restaurant-trained chef. Tender beets, dressed and rolled in pistachio crumbs, give the impression of a Turkish dessert. Spooning the horseradish cream onto the plate first gives you the opportunity to pull the beet morsels across the plate so that it looks like a painter's canvas, with streaks of purple and splatters of green.

- 4 medium beets
- 1 tablespoon olive oil, plus more for drizzling
- 1½ teaspoons lemon juice
  - Coarse salt, to taste
- 8 ounces arugula (about 4 to 6 cups)
- ¼ cup crème fraîche
- 2 teaspoons prepared horseradish
  - Zest of ½ lemon (about 1 teaspoon)
- ½ cup lightly toasted, finely chopped pistachios
  - Freshly ground black pepper, to taste

Preheat the oven to 400°F.

Wash and trim the beets. Place them in a foil packet, drizzle with olive oil, and roast for 45 minutes to an hour, or until knife tender. Let the beets cool and then peel them. Slice each beet into bite-size pieces. You can wrap them in plastic wrap and store them in the refrigerator for up to 2 days.

In a mixing bowl, whisk together the olive oil and lemon juice. Add salt to taste. Toss the dressing with the beets to coat, then remove the beets with a slotted spoon and set aside.

Place the arugula in the bowl and toss to coat with the dressing that remains in the bottom of the bowl.

In a small bowl, combine the crème fraiche, horseradish, and lemon zest.

Sprinkle the pistachios over the beets so that each side is coated with nuts, pressing the nuts into the beets if necessary to help them stick.

Divide the horseradish crème fraiche equally among serving plates, top each plate with a scoop of arugula, then place a few chunks of beets on top. Season to taste with salt and pepper. Serve immediately.

QUICK SAUTÉED GREENS *with* GINGER

SERVES 4 TO 6

Here's the simple way to work greens into your diet. Try mixing some of the tender greens, like spinach, with some of the heartier ones, like kale. The result will have a variety of textures and flavors. Serve it on top of a bed of rice, or it's not completely unheard of to eat this meal straight from the pan. Just saying . . .

- 1 large bunch greens such as chard, collards, kale, or mustard greens (about 8 ounces)
- 1 tablespoon extra-virgin olive oil
- 4 garlic cloves, thinly sliced
  - 1½-inch piece ginger, peeled and minced
- ¼ teaspoon red pepper flakes (optional)
- 1 tablespoon freshly squeezed lemon juice
- ½ teaspoon salt, plus more to taste

LEMONY ASPARAGUS RIBBONS

SERVES 4

If you've never had asparagus raw, try this version. When shaved into long, thin ribbons, this spring vegetable makes a beautifully crisp and flavorful salad or side dish. This is one occasion when you should be looking for fatter asparagus stalks. We like to use a vegetable peeler to cut the ribbons (it feels safer), but a mandoline also works. Sliced into thin strips, the raw asparagus is crunchy yet pliable enough to wrap around a fork.

1 pound trimmed asparagus (about 20 spears)
3 tablespoons extra-virgin olive oil
1 tablespoon plus 1 teaspoon freshly squeezed lemon juice (from about ½ lemon)
  Flaked sea salt and freshly ground black pepper
⅓ cup finely chopped almonds, toasted
⅓ cup shredded Parmesan cheese (about 1 ounce)

Rinse the greens well and dry them on a clean kitchen towel. Tear or cut the leaves away from the stems and discard the stems, or reserve them for another use. Coarsely chop the leaves. Set a small cup of water by the stove.

In a large skillet over medium-high heat, heat the oil and cook the garlic, ginger, and pepper flakes (if you're using them) very briefly, about 15 seconds. Gradually add the greens, stirring between each addition. Add a splash of water with each mounding handful of greens.

Stir in the lemon juice and salt. Turn the heat down to medium-low and cook the greens until they are tender, 5 to 10 minutes depending on the type of greens; for example, chard might take only 5 minutes, while kale might need 10 minutes. Serve immediately.

Using a vegetable peeler and working one stalk at a time, lay the asparagus flat on a cutting board and run the vegetable peeler along its length from the bottom to the tip, creating very thin, long strips.

In a large bowl, whisk together the oil and lemon juice and season to taste with salt and pepper.

Add the asparagus ribbons and gently toss with your hands until evenly coated. Transfer the asparagus to a serving dish or to individual plates. Scatter the almonds and Parmesan cheese across the top of the asparagus. Serve immediately.

CRISPY PAN-FRIED BEANS
and WILTED GREENS

SERVES 4 AS A MAIN DISH; 6 TO 8 AS A SIDE DISH

We have to give a shout-out to Heidi Swanson of 101 Cookbooks and Yotam Ottolenghi of Ottolenghi Restaurant for opening our eyes to the incredible possibilities of pan-fried beans. This dish is such a surprising combination of flavors and textures, from the blistered, yet creamy, white beans to the silky ribbons of lemon-kissed chard. They create a tasty symmetry that we never tire of eating, whether as a simple lunch at home or tossed with pasta for dinner. Although this dish calls for canned beans, it works best with homemade beans (page 241), as they will hold their shape a little better.

It's important to use a cast-iron skillet for this recipe, to help the beans crisp up. This is nearly impossible to do in a nonstick pan.

- 1 tablespoon plus 1 teaspoon vegetable or grapeseed oil
- 1 large yellow onion, thinly sliced
- 1 to 2 teaspoons salt
- 1 12-ounce bunch Swiss chard, rinsed and patted dry, center stems removed from the leaves and chopped into bite-size pieces, leaves cut crosswise into ribbons, reserved separately
- 2 garlic cloves, minced
- 1½ teaspoons za'atar spice blend (see Tip)

- 1 15.5-ounce can (2 cups) Great Northern, cannelloni, or other white beans, drained and rinsed
- Zest and juice of 1 lemon
- Extra-virgin olive oil for serving

Heat 1 teaspoon of the oil in a large, deep cast-iron skillet over medium-high heat. Cook the onion with ½ teaspoon of salt until it is just starting to turn translucent, about 5 minutes. Add the chard stems and cook until they are tender and the onion is very soft, another 6 to 8 minutes. Stir in the garlic and cook until fragrant, about 30 seconds.

Add the chard leaves in handfuls to the pan, stirring to coat them with the onion and garlic. Sprinkle the za'atar, 1 teaspoon salt, and 2 tablespoons water over the greens and cook, stirring, until the chard is completely wilted and tender, 3 to 5 minutes. Remove the chard and onion to a large bowl and wipe out the skillet.

Place the skillet over high heat. When the pan is very hot, warm the remaining 1 tablespoon of oil, enough to coat the bottom of the pan. Add the beans with a sprinkle of salt and spread them into a single layer. Cook the beans for 2 minutes without stirring. The beans will sizzle and pop as they fry. Stir and shake the pan to distribute them into a single layer again. Continue stirring and shaking the pan every 2 minutes, until all the beans are blistered.

Fold the beans into the bowl with the chard and onion, and toss with the lemon juice and zest. Taste and season with more salt if needed. Serve immediately, drizzling a little extra-virgin olive oil over each dish. Add a poached egg, a scoop of pasta, or a piece of toast to make a more complete meal. The beans will lose their crispiness as they cool, but leftovers still make a tasty meal. This dish will keep refrigerated in an airtight container for up to a week.

Tip from The Kitchn

If you don't have za'atar in your cupboard, you can make your own by combining equal parts fresh or dried thyme, ground sumac, and sesame seeds. Or skip the sumac and just use equal parts of thyme and sesame.

ROASTED EGGPLANT *with* SMOKED ALMONDS *and* GOAT CHEESE

SERVES 6

We have made salads from all sorts of vegetables: fennel, cabbage, potato, sweet potato. But an eggplant salad is more rare, even though the eggplant's tender, unctuous innards seemed like they would go so well with other salad staples. So we stepped up to the challenge and created this dish. We love the natural smokiness of roasted eggplant, so here is a lesson in how to play up that flavor with smoked paprika and smoked almonds, as well as to play off the rich ingredients with sharp acids from lemons and creamy goat cheese. All together these flavors create a "salad" that is one of our all-time favorite vegetable side dishes.

2	large eggplants (about 2½ pounds)
	Kosher salt
½	cup olive oil
2	tablespoons cider vinegar
1	tablespoon honey
1	teaspoon smoked paprika
1	teaspoon ground cumin
4	large garlic cloves, minced
3	tablespoons freshly squeezed lemon juice (from about 1 lemon)
1	tablespoon soy sauce
1	cup fresh flat-leaf parsley leaves, roughly chopped
½	cup smoked or roasted almonds, roughly chopped
2	ounces goat cheese, crumbled and divided
¼	cup finely chopped scallions

Place a rack in the middle of the oven. Preheat the oven to 400°F. Line a large baking sheet with parchment. Cut the eggplant into 1-inch cubes and place them in a large bowl. Sprinkle the eggplant lightly with kosher salt and set aside in a large bowl while making the marinade.

In a small bowl, whisk together the oil, vinegar, honey, smoked paprika, and cumin. Dab away any extra water that has beaded on the eggplant and toss with the marinade. Stir in the garlic. Spread the eggplant on the prepared baking sheet and slide the sheet into the middle of the oven. Reserve the bowl.

Roast the eggplant for 40 minutes, or until very tender and slightly browned. Stir every 15 minutes and check after 30 minutes to make sure it isn't burning. Remove the eggplant from the oven and let it cool a little while making the dressing.

In the large bowl used for marinating the eggplant, whisk together the lemon juice and soy sauce. Return the roasted eggplant to the bowl and toss with the lemon juice mixture. Fold in the parsley leaves, smoked almonds, and most of the goat cheese, reserving a little.

Spread the finished salad in a serving bowl and sprinkle the reserved goat cheese and scallions on top. Serve immediately, while warm. Leftovers keep well in a covered container in the refrigerator for up to 3 days.

Tip from The Kitchn

Look for smoked almonds in the snack aisle of your grocery store, not with the baking ingredients. If you can't find them, roasted almonds make a fine substitute.

ROASTED BRUSSELS SPROUTS, CAULIFLOWER, *and* RADISHES *with* GARLIC AÏOLI

SERVES 4

Roasted vegetables are our most relied-upon side dish for any meal. Weeknight dinner? Fancy dinner party? Leisurely Sunday lunch? Yes, yes, yes. Vegetables pick up depth and spark when they are roasted in the oven, and they can be simple and hands-off, or dressed up with a sauce, like the luxurious garlicky aïoli we offer here.

Nearly any vegetable can be roasted in the oven, even ones you might not have considered, such as cabbage, broccoli, and radishes. We included radishes in this mix for their color and for the extra-juicy flavor they release in the heat of the oven.

8 ounces radishes, trimmed and quartered
8 ounces Brussels sprouts, trimmed and halved
12 ounces cauliflower (about ½ large head), trimmed, halved, and cut into 1-inch pieces
1 tablespoon vegetable or grapeseed oil, or any other oil with a high smoke point
1 teaspoon kosher salt
Freshly ground black pepper
Garlic Aïoli for dipping (recipe follows)

Place an oven rack in the center of the oven and preheat the oven to 425°F.

Mix the radishes, Brussels sprouts, and cauliflower in a large bowl and toss with the oil, salt, and a generous amount of black pepper. Spread the vegetables on a large baking sheet in a single layer. Roast for 18 to 25 minutes, or until tender with blackened, crisped edges, stirring every 8 to 10 minutes. Remove the vegetables from the oven. Taste and season with additional salt and pepper, if desired.

Serve immediately with a spoonful of Garlic Aïoli for dipping.

Garlic Aïoli

MAKES ABOUT 1 CUP

This is homemade mayonnaise—with a kick of garlic. The most reliable way to make a creamy aïoli is in a small food processor, but if you don't have one, you can use a whisk and a bowl.

5 garlic cloves, peeled and smashed
2 teaspoons Dijon mustard
½ teaspoon salt
1 large egg yolk
⅔ cup extra-virgin olive oil
1 to 2 tablespoons freshly squeezed lemon juice (from about ½ lemon)
1 tablespoon warm water

Combine the garlic, mustard, and salt together in the bowl of a food processor and blend until smooth, or pound to a smooth paste in a mortar and pestle. With the food processor running (or while whisking briskly by hand) beat in the egg yolk. Then slowly add ¼ cup of the oil. Add the lemon juice and the water. Add the remaining oil very slowly while whisking or processing. The mixture should emulsify and become a creamy sauce.

Taste for seasoning, and add more salt if desired. Cover and refrigerate until ready to serve. The aïoli is best served within 24 hours, although it can be refrigerated in an airtight container for up to 5 days.

TIPS FOR ROASTING VEGETABLES

While this recipe explains how to prepare one particular mix of vegetables in the oven, the process can be extended to nearly any vegetable. The main key to roasting any vegetable is to cut the vegetable pieces the same size so they all cook at the same rate.

Don't be afraid to roast at high heat—up to 425°F—and to let the vegetables get a little blackened around the edges to develop flavor.

SMASHED POTATO SALAD

SERVES 4 TO 6

If you don't have a great potato salad recipe up your sleeve, now is a good time to get one. Some of us eschew mayonnaise-laden potato salads, so here we offer the option of rich whole-milk yogurt. If you're as opinionated as we are about what makes a great potato salad, start with this recipe, but then tinker with the balance of flavors. Want it more pungent? Increase the shallots. Want it sweeter? Stir a little honey into the sauce. Is the mustard too strong? Turn it down a notch. Now you're ready at a moment's notice to make your favorite potato salad.

- 2 pounds petite red potatoes, scrubbed and quartered
- ¾ cup mayonnaise or whole-milk yogurt
- 1¼ teaspoons dry mustard powder
- 1 heaping teaspoon prepared Dijon mustard
- ½ cup finely chopped celery
- 2 shallots, finely chopped (about ¼ cup)
- ¾ teaspoon kosher salt
  Freshly ground black pepper, to taste
- ½ cup thinly sliced scallions, green tops only, for garnish

In a large pot of salted water, bring the potatoes to a boil. Cook the potatoes until they are tender and easily pierced with a knife, about 20 to 25 minutes total. Drain the potatoes and return them to the pot.

In a small bowl, mix the mayonnaise, dry mustard, Dijon mustard, celery, shallots, salt, and a generous amount of pepper. Scoop this mixture onto the potatoes and smash using a potato masher or the back of a large serving fork until your desired texture is reached. Taste for seasoning and refrigerate until chilled. When ready to serve, transfer to a salad bowl and top with the scallions.

The potato salad will keep, covered, in the refrigerator for up to 2 days.

BACON-CHEDDAR TWICE-BAKED POTATOES

SERVES 4 TO 6

Twice-baked potatoes are an ingenious invention that turns the inside of a baked potato back into the shell, improved by cheesy and bacony leaps and bounds on its second round of baking. If you can find smoked Cheddar cheese, your potatoes will have even more of a campfire appeal.

- 4 medium russet potatoes
- 1 tablespoon olive oil
- 1 teaspoon salt, plus more to taste
- 6 strips thick-cut smoked bacon (or 8 strips thin-cut bacon), diced
- 1 large yellow onion, diced small
- 2 garlic cloves, minced
- ½ cup sour cream or whole-milk yogurt
- 1 cup sharp Cheddar cheese, shredded
  Freshly ground black pepper, to taste
- ¼ cup minced fresh chives

Preheat the oven to 425°F.

Scrub the potatoes clean and pat them dry. Rub them with olive oil, and sprinkle them with salt. Prick the potatoes a few times with the tines of a fork. Place them a few inches apart on a baking sheet. Bake for 50 to 60 minutes, until they are completely soft when pierced with a fork and the skins are dry.

While the potatoes are baking, warm a skillet over medium-low heat and cook the diced bacon until the bacon has crisped to your liking. Remove the bacon with a slotted spoon and drain on paper towels.

Pour off all but 1 teaspoon of the bacon fat. Add the onion and ½ teaspoon of the salt to the pan and cook over medium-low heat until the onion is deep golden and caramelized, 8 to 10 minutes. Stir in the garlic and cook for another 30 seconds. Remove the pan from the heat.

When the potatoes are cool enough to handle, slice them in half and scoop the insides into a medium-sized bowl, leaving a ¼ inch or so of potato next to the skin. Mash the potato flesh with the onion, garlic, bacon, sour cream, and about ¾ cup of the cheese. Season to taste with salt and pepper.

Arrange the potato skins on the baking sheet. Divide the filling among the potato skins and sprinkle the tops with the remaining ¼ cup of cheese. At this point, the potatoes can be baked right away or refrigerated and baked later.

Bake for another 15 to 20 minutes, until the cheese has melted and the peaks of the mashed potatoes are crispy. Potatoes that have been refrigerated may take a little longer to finish in the oven. Serve immediately with a sprinkling of chives on top.

POTATO, SQUASH, *and* GOAT CHEESE GRATIN

SERVES 6

Elizabeth Passarella contributed to The Kitchn for many years, and some of our best and most popular recipes came out of her oven. For us, this gratin expresses Elizabeth's tastes and sensibility very well. It is casual yet elegant, a joyful jumble of squash and potatoes with a grace note of aromatic basil. Its fresh flavors and almost unbelievable simplicity stand fussier, richer gratins on their heads. Our readers return to this dish again and again, and so do we.

- 1 pound yellow summer squash (about 4 medium squashes), cut into ⅛-inch slices with a mandoline or food processor
- 2 pounds small red potatoes, cut into ⅛-inch slices with a mandoline or food processor
- ⅓ cup extra-virgin olive oil
  Salt and freshly ground black pepper
- 6 ounces soft goat cheese, crumbled
- ½ cup whole milk
- ⅔ cup freshly grated Parmesan cheese
- ¼ cup finely chopped fresh basil leaves

Preheat the oven to 400°F. Lightly grease a 9 × 13-inch baking dish with olive oil or cooking spray.

In a large bowl, toss the sliced squash and potatoes with the olive oil and a generous amount of salt and pepper.

Spread a third of the squash and potato slices in the bottom of the prepared baking dish. There is no need to layer them or evenly divide the squash and potato slices. Just tumble them in and spread in an even layer. Scatter half of the goat cheese evenly over the squash and potato slices. Repeat with another third of the squash and potatoes and the remaining goat cheese. Top with the remaining squash and potatoes.

Pour the milk over the entire dish. Top with the Parmesan cheese. Cover tightly with foil or an ovenproof lid. Bake, covered, for 30 minutes, then uncover and bake for an additional 15 to 20 minutes, or until the top browns and the potatoes are tender. Remove the baking dish from the oven and sprinkle with the fresh basil. Let stand for 10 minutes then slice and serve.

Serve the gratin alone for dinner with a green salad, or as a side to roast chicken or a bowl of soup.

CITRUSY QUINOA SALAD
with AVOCADO, CUCUMBER, *and* ALMONDS

SERVES 4 TO 6

Once we nailed down how to cook quinoa perfectly every time (our post on making quinoa still brings thousands of readers to our site every day), a whole new world of seed salads opened up. Tossed with grapefruit segments, cucumber, and toasted almonds, and topped with creamy avocado, this quinoa salad makes a great lunch dish, or a side for dinner.

- 1 cup quinoa
- 3 tablespoons extra-virgin olive oil
- 2 cups low-sodium vegetable or chicken broth
  Zest and juice of ½ lemon (about 1 teaspoon zest and 1½ tablespoons juice)
- 1 large shallot, minced
- ½ tablespoon sherry vinegar
- 1 Ruby Red grapefruit
- ⅓ seedless English cucumber (about ¼ pound), unpeeled and diced small
- 2 celery stalks, diced small
- ½ cup sliced toasted almonds
  Kosher salt, to taste
  Freshly ground black pepper, to taste
- 1 ripe avocado, thinly sliced, for serving
  Flaked sea salt

Rinse the quinoa for 2 to 3 minutes in a fine-mesh strainer, rubbing vigorously. Drain. Heat a 2-quart saucepan over medium-high heat and add a teaspoon of oil. When the oil is hot, add the quinoa and cook, stirring to coat the quinoa with olive oil, for 1 minute. (The quinoa may pop, so be prepared to stir right away.) Pour in the broth, bring to a boil, cover, and turn the heat down to low. Cook for 15 minutes or until most of the liquid is absorbed. Turn off the heat and let the quinoa sit, with a folded dishtowel over the pot lid, for 5 minutes.

Line a large baking sheet with parchment and spread out the cooked quinoa in an even layer. Let it cool while you prepare the remaining ingredients.

Whisk together the lemon juice, shallot, and sherry vinegar. Slowly stream in the remaining oil while whisking, until the vinaigrette is emulsified. Set aside.

To prep the grapefruit, peel away the top and bottom of the grapefruit rind until you can see the flesh. With a sharp knife, peel away all rind and pith along the curve of the grapefruit. Then cut between the white segments and cut out the flesh. Roughly chop the grapefruit segments and set aside.

Transfer the quinoa to a large bowl and add the cucumber, celery, grapefruit, and lemon zest. Add the vinaigrette and toss gently.

Fold in the almonds. Taste and adjust the salad to taste with salt and pepper. At serving time, top the salad with the avocado, a sprinkle of flaked sea salt, and freshly cracked black pepper. This dish will keep in the refrigerator for 1 day in a sealed container.

WHEAT BERRY SALAD *with* BLOOD ORANGES, FETA, *and* RED ONION VINAIGRETTE

SERVES 4 TO 6

This salad, like many recipes, was born from a surplus of one ingredient discovered in the back of a cupboard. Wheat berries are the entire wheat kernel, minus the hull, so hardly any nutrition has been stripped away. They are loaded with fiber, protein, and iron, but can act just like rice, with the added bonus that they have a chewier bite that will hold up alongside bold salad ingredients such as the blood oranges, feta, and red onion vinaigrette we offer here.

- 1½ cups soft wheat berries
- ½ cup Red Onion Vinaigrette (recipe follows)
- 2 blood oranges
- 3 ounces feta cheese, crumbled (about ½ cup)
- ⅓ cup chopped fresh flat-leaf parsley

Bring 1½ quarts of salted water to a boil in a medium saucepan. Add the wheat berries and reduce the heat to a simmer. Cook the wheat berries until they are tender

with a slight crunch, about 1 hour. Drain and spread out onto a baking sheet to cool completely.

In a medium bowl, combine the wheat berries with the Red Onion Vinaigrette. Stir to combine. Peel and cut the blood oranges into segments (supremes) and chop them into small dice, reserving the juices. Add the orange pieces with their juices, the feta, and parsley to the wheat berries. Toss and serve. Leftovers will keep, covered and refrigerated, for 3 days.

Red Onion Vinaigrette
MAKES ABOUT ½ CUP

- 1 teaspoon olive oil
- ½ medium red onion, sliced thin (about 1 cup)
- ½ teaspoon salt
- 1 garlic clove, minced
- ½ teaspoon fresh thyme leaves (from about 3 sprigs)
- ¼ cup extra-virgin olive oil
- 2 tablespoons cider vinegar
- 2 teaspoons sugar
-   Freshly ground black pepper, to taste

Heat the olive oil in a skillet over medium-low heat. Add the onion, season with the salt, and cook, stirring occasionally, until soft, about 10 minutes. Add the garlic and thyme and cook for another 1 to 2 minutes.

Transfer the onion mixture to a blender and add the extra-virgin olive oil, vinegar, sugar, and a few cracks of black pepper. Blend until smooth. Taste for seasoning.

CRISPY BROWN RICE SALAD
with PEANUTS *and* CILANTRO

SERVES 4 TO 6

Here's a fresh rice salad to bring on a picnic or have ready for dinner on a hot summer night. Apples lend an unexpected sweetness, while crispy onions (found packaged in the Italian section of most grocery stores), peanuts, and toasted sesame seeds make this salad delightfully crunchy. Make the rice the night before and the whole dish will come together in a flash.

- 1 cup brown rice
- 1 Granny Smith apple, cored and cut into ½-inch dice
- ½ cup finely chopped cilantro leaves
- ¼ cup roughly chopped dry-roasted peanuts

FOR THE DRESSING

- 2 garlic cloves, minced
- 1 tablespoon honey
- 1 teaspoon white miso
- 2 tablespoons olive oil
- 2 tablespoons white wine vinegar

FOR SERVING

-   Coarse kosher salt, to taste
-   Handful of cilantro leaves and stems, chopped
- ¼ cup crispy onions
- 4 tablespoons toasted sesame seeds

Cook the brown rice according to package directions or the directions on page 199. Fluff and cool to room temperature.

Combine the apple, cilantro, peanuts, and cooled rice in a large bowl.

TO MAKE THE DRESSING
In a small bowl, whisk together the garlic, honey, miso, oil, and vinegar.

TO ASSEMBLE THE SALAD
Stir the dressing into the rice mixture until all the ingredients are coated. Season to taste with kosher salt. Serve garnished with extra cilantro, crispy onions, and sesame seeds.

POT BEANS *with* BASIL, PARMESAN CHEESE, *and* TOMATOES

SERVES 4 TO 6

Dried beans are a humble kitchen staple that can become glamorous in the right setting. They are inexpensive, rich in protein, and, when cooked from scratch, make their own deep and delicious sauce that puts canned beans to shame. We like to cook a pot of beans on Sunday, either simmering them slowly over low heat or baking them, hands off, in the oven—so we give you both methods here. The stovetop method is perhaps most common, but we are huge fans of the oven method for cooking beans. Cooking beans in the oven is a little quicker and more hands off, and we feel that the final result is a creamier texture.

Sometimes we want to dress our beans up just a little, and this simple recipe shows off their flavor with Parmesan cheese, basil, garlic, and tomato. These beans are swimming in a savory, cheesy liquor—delicious enough, and satisfying too, to eat as a main course for dinner. This delicious recipe can provide the base for meals throughout the week—think inside tacos, alongside grilled chicken, or under braised vegetables.

- 1 pound dried beans, such as pinto beans or Good Mother Stallard beans
- 1 tablespoon olive oil
- 1 small yellow onion, diced
- 2 garlic cloves, minced
  Pinch of red pepper flakes (optional)
- 1½ teaspoons salt, plus more if necessary
  Freshly ground black pepper, to taste
- 2 large tomatoes, seeded and roughly chopped
- 1 cup freshly grated Parmesan cheese
- 1 cup (loosely packed) finely shredded fresh basil

Rinse and drain the beans. Place them in a bowl and cover with water by 1 to 2 inches. Soak the beans overnight before cooking. (If you're short on time, put the beans in a pot, cover with water by 2 to 3 inches, and bring to a boil. Remove the pot from the heat and let the beans stand for 1 hour.)

STOVETOP METHOD

Heat the olive oil over medium-low heat in a 3-quart or larger saucepan or Dutch oven. Sauté the onion and garlic until translucent, about 5 minutes. Stir in the red pepper flakes, if you're using them. Drain the presoaked beans and stir them into the onion and garlic.

Pour in enough water to cover the beans by 1 inch, and raise the heat. Bring the pot to a boil, then lower the heat to a bare simmer, cover, and cook the beans until they are tender. The total cooking time will vary greatly depending on the size of the beans (larger beans will usually take a little longer to cook), their freshness, and how long they soaked. Expect to cook the beans for at least 90 minutes and for up to 3 hours. Keep an eye on the water and add more if the beans begin to dry out.

After 1 hour, begin checking the beans for tenderness. When the beans are barely tender, stir in 1½ teaspoons of salt and give them a taste. Add more salt and pepper as desired.

When the beans are tender to your liking, turn off the heat and stir in the tomatoes, Parmesan cheese, and basil. Serve immediately.

OVEN METHOD

Follow the directions given above for soaking the beans. Preheat the oven to 325°F. Drain the presoaked beans. In an ovenproof pot or Dutch oven, bring the beans to a boil on the stove. Turn off the heat and cover the pot with a tight-fitting lid. Cook the beans in the oven for 75 minutes, then check for tenderness. Continue checking the beans every 15 minutes until they are tender to your liking. Add the salt near the end of the cooking process. When the beans are done, remove them from the oven and stir in the tomatoes, Parmesan cheese, and basil. Serve immediately.

Tip from The Kitchn

You can also skip the onion, garlic, tomato, Parmesan cheese, and basil entirely and just cook a plain pot of beans for use in meals. One pound of dried beans will yield about 5 cups cooked beans, equal to about three 15-ounce cans of beans.

BRAISED GREEK
GREEN BEANS *with* TOMATO

SERVES 4 TO 6

While green beans are wonderful when barely cooked or raw, they need to be fresh off the vine to be enjoyed that way. More mature green beans are tough and fibrous, but after a long, slow simmer with tomatoes and a touch of cinnamon, they become velvety soft.

1	pound fresh or frozen green beans
2	tablespoons olive oil
1	large onion, finely chopped
4	garlic cloves, thinly sliced
¼ to ½	teaspoon red pepper flakes, or to taste
1	28-ounce can whole tomatoes, drained
½	cup dry white wine
½	teaspoon ground cinnamon
	Freshly ground black pepper
¾	teaspoon salt
1	lemon, cut into wedges, for serving

If the green beans are frozen, thaw them at room temperature for about 30 minutes while preparing the rest of the ingredients. If they're fresh, wash them and snap off the ends.

Heat the olive oil in a Dutch oven or heavy lidded pot over medium heat. Sauté the onion and garlic gently over medium heat for 8 to 10 minutes, or until they are soft and golden. Stir in the red pepper flakes. (Using the full ½ teaspoon will give the beans an energetic kick of heat, while the ¼ teaspoon will add only a mild piquancy.) Add the tomatoes and stir to break them up. Sauté for another 5 minutes, until the tomato begins to break down.

Stir in the green beans and toss them to coat with the onion, tomatoes, and oil. Stir in the wine, cinnamon, and a generous quantity of black pepper and bring to a simmer over medium-high heat. Cover and turn the heat down to a bare simmer. Cook for 30 minutes, and then remove the lid and cook uncovered for an additional 15 to 30 minutes or until the beans are tender to your liking.

Stir in the salt and taste. Add more if desired. Serve with lemon wedges on the side.

CORN *and* BLACK BEAN SKILLET *with*
CARAMELIZED CHEDDAR CHEESE

SERVES 4 TO 6

Your best bet for a potluck offering is a side dish with savory flavors and bright colors, such as this skillet dish; just as good at room temperature as it is warm. Emma says the secret to this Tex-Mex dish lies in slowly caramelizing the Cheddar cheese, which builds up layers of smoky flavor.

2	cups fresh or frozen corn kernels, thawed
½	green bell pepper, diced
½	red bell pepper, diced
2	large garlic cloves, minced
1	15-ounce can roasted diced tomatoes, well drained
1	15-ounce can black beans, well drained
1	teaspoon salt, or to taste
1	teaspoon ground cumin
½	teaspoon chipotle powder, or to taste
¼	teaspoon ground cinnamon
	Freshly ground black pepper
2	cups shredded Cheddar cheese (8 ounces)
½	cup finely chopped fresh cilantro (optional)

In a large bowl, stir together the corn kernels, bell peppers, garlic, tomatoes, and black beans. Stir in the salt, cumin, chipotle powder, cinnamon, and a generous amount of black pepper. Taste and add more salt or more chipotle for spiciness, if desired. Fold in the cheese.

Set a cast-iron or heavy skillet over medium heat. Spread the corn mixture in the pan. Cook for 30 minutes, stirring every 5 minutes. The cheese will melt and start to form a crust on the bottom of the pan. With each stir, scrape up the crust and fold it back into the vegetables. (If the mixture smokes, turn down the heat a little or scrape the skillet a little more frequently.) After about 30 minutes, when the sauce has become thick and creamy, turn off the heat and stir in the cilantro, if using.

Let the vegetables cool slightly before serving. Serve with rice and chicken, or wrapped up in tortillas with grilled peppers and onions. This dish will keep in the refrigerator in an airtight container for up to 1 week.

DESSERTS

RUSTIC APRICOT GALETTE

MAKES ONE 12-INCH GALETTE

A galette is one of those dishes that is more of a formula than a recipe. Once you learn the basics, you can make a galette with other stone fruits such as peaches, nectarines, plums, or even apples or pears, flavored with a dash of cinnamon. With apricots you have the best of summer—a ripe, sweet fruit that speaks for itself, needing very little added sugar. In the desperate months of winter, we've even made this galette with frozen fruit and eaten it as a picnic on the living room floor. It's great for breakfast the next morning.

FOR THE CRUST

- 1½ cups unbleached all-purpose flour
- 1 tablespoon sugar
- ½ teaspoon salt
- 10 tablespoons cold unsalted butter, cut into ¼-inch cubes
- ¼ to ½ cup ice water

FOR FILLING AND BAKING THE GALETTE

- 3 tablespoons granulated sugar
- 1 tablespoon (packed) brown sugar
- 2 tablespoons unbleached all-purpose flour
- ⅛ teaspoon salt
- Pinch of freshly grated nutmeg
- 1½ pounds ripe apricots, pitted and cut into eighths
- 1 tablespoon unsalted butter, cut into ¼-inch cubes
- 1 tablespoon heavy cream

  Whipped cream or crème fraîche, for serving

TO PREPARE THE CRUST

Combine the flour, sugar, and salt in a food processor. Pulse a few times to combine. Scatter the butter pieces over the mixture and pulse until the pieces are about the size of peas. (Or whisk the flour and sugar together in a large bowl and work the butter in with a pastry blender or two knives.)

Sprinkle the ice water, 1 tablespoon at a time, over the mixture and pulse once or mix after each addition. Continue adding water and pulsing until the dough forms small crumbly lumps, like cottage cheese. The dough should clump when pinched together. Be careful not to overprocess the dough; it should not form into a ball while still in the food processor.

Dump the dough out onto a lightly floured work surface and pat it into a 1-inch-thick disk without handling it too much. Do not knead the dough. Wrap it in plastic wrap and refrigerate for at least 30 minutes. (Or wrap it well in plastic wrap and freeze it for up to 3 months. To use, defrost in the refrigerator overnight.)

TO PREPARE THE FILLING

In a large bowl, combine all but 1 teaspoon of the granulated sugar, the brown sugar, flour, salt, and nutmeg. Add the apricots and toss until they are evenly coated.

TO ASSEMBLE AND BAKE THE GALETTE

Position a rack in the lower third of the oven and preheat the oven to 400°F. Line a baking sheet with parchment paper and set aside.

On a lightly floured work surface, roll out the pastry to a 14-inch-diameter circle. Transfer the dough to the prepared baking sheet.

Arrange the fruit mixture in the center of the crust, leaving a 2-inch border of dough around the edges. Fold the edges over the filling, pinching pleats in the crust as you proceed. Dot the exposed fruit with the cubed butter. Brush the edges of the crust with the cream, and then sprinkle with the remaining 1 teaspoon of sugar.

Bake the galette for 40 minutes, and then lower the oven temperature to 350°F and bake for another 10 to 20 minutes, or until the crust is golden brown and the edges are slightly caramelized. Remove the pan from the oven and set it on a wire rack for a few minutes to cool slightly. Slip the parchment paper with the galette off the baking sheet and onto the wire rack, and allow the galette to cool completely, or serve it warm. Top with a dollop of whipped cream or crème fraîche.

The galette can be stored covered in plastic wrap in the refrigerator for up to 2 days.

CHUNKY CHOCOLATE CHERRY OATMEAL COOKIES

MAKES ABOUT 42 COOKIES

How many favorite ingredients can you cram into a single cookie? Quite a few, it turns out! Dried cherries, walnuts, oats, chocolate, and a dash of cinnamon all find a home here, and the nubby cookies that result definitely walk the line between snack and dessert. Mixing by hand encourages the chewy, dense texture that makes these cookies so great, so leave your mixer in the cupboard.

- 1 cup walnuts
- 1 cup dried cherries
- 7 ounces dark chocolate (typically 2 bars)
- ¾ cup (packed) brown sugar
- ¾ cup granulated sugar
- ½ cup (1 stick) unsalted butter, softened
- 2 large eggs
- 1 teaspoon vanilla extract
- 1 teaspoon salt
- 1 teaspoon baking soda
- ½ teaspoon ground cinnamon
- 2 cups all-purpose flour, sifted
- 1 cup old-fashioned rolled oats

Heat the oven to 375°F. Line a baking sheet with parchment or a nonstick baking liner.

Pour the walnuts onto the baking sheet and toast until browned and fragrant, about 10 minutes. Cool slightly and then chop roughly. Allow the walnuts to cool completely before using them. Line the baking sheet with a new sheet of parchment paper.

Cover the cherries with 1 cup boiling water and let them stand for 10 minutes to plump up. Drain and pat them dry. Chop the chocolate bars into small pieces.

In a large mixing bowl, mix together the sugars with a wooden spoon or stiff spatula, removing any lumps. Mix in the butter, working the sugar into the butter until completely combined. Add the eggs one at a time, stirring to form a completely smooth batter. Stir in the vanilla, salt, baking soda, and cinnamon.

Add the flour all at once and stir the batter gently until the ingredients are well combined. Fold in the rolled oats, walnuts, cherries, and chocolate until all the ingredients are combined.

Drop mounded golf-ball-sized tablespoons of dough onto the prepared baking sheet, spaced 1 to 2 inches apart. Bake the cookies until the craggy tips and edges just start to darken, 9 to 11 minutes. Let the cookies cool on the baking sheet for 5 minutes, then transfer to a cooling rack to cool completely. Repeat with the remaining cookie dough.

These cookies will keep in an airtight container at room temperature for 1 week.

PERFECTED CHOCOLATE CHIP COOKIES

MAKES 2 DOZEN 3½-INCH COOKIES

It's hard to improve on the basic chocolate chip cookie. We decided to work with the best of the best recipes and combine them into one that incorporates all our favorite things about the most memorable chocolate chip cookies—from Jacques Torres's big gooey cookie, to the classic recipe by Ruth Graves Wakefield, owner of the original Toll House Inn where this cookie madness started. If you plan far enough ahead to give the dough a one-day rest in the refrigerator, you will notice a huge difference in flavor and texture.

- 2 cups unbleached all-purpose flour
- 1 teaspoon baking soda
- ½ teaspoon fine salt
- 14 tablespoons (1¾ sticks) unsalted butter, at room temperature
- 1 cup (packed) dark brown sugar
- ½ cup granulated sugar
- 1 large egg
- 2 teaspoons pure vanilla extract
- 12 ounces bittersweet chocolate chips or chunks
  Flaked sea salt

Sift the flour, baking soda, and salt into a bowl. Set aside.

In the bowl of a stand mixer, or in a large bowl using a hand mixer, cream the butter and sugars together on

medium speed until the butter is pale yellow. (Or beat vigorously by hand with a wooden spoon.) Add the egg and vanilla. Reduce the speed to low, slowly add the dry ingredients, and mix until just combined, 5 to 10 seconds. Fold in the chocolate chips.

Press plastic wrap against the surface of the dough or turn it out onto the plastic wrap and wrap tightly. Refrigerate it for at least 24 and for up to 72 hours.

When you're ready to bake the cookies, preheat the oven to 350°F. Drop mounded Ping-Pong ball–sized tablespoons of dough onto a baking sheet, spaced 2½ inches apart. Sprinkle lightly with flaked sea salt. Bake the cookies until they are light brown, but still soft in the middle, about 15 minutes. Cool slightly then remove from the cookie sheet onto a wire rack. Serve warm for best texture. The cookies will keep in a sealed container at room temperature for up to 5 days.

CUT-OUT SUGAR COOKIES with TANGY BUTTERCREAM ICING

MAKES 2½ TO 4 DOZEN COOKIES, DEPENDING ON SIZE

We'll let a rave reader review on this classic cookie recipe speak for itself. From thethinchef: "Hands-down the BEST cut-out sugar cookie I have ever made. Not only are they a dream to work with, but they are DELICIOUS!" That's just a taste of the enthusiasm for this recipe, which provides an alternative to the often boring yet obligatory holiday sugar cookie. Our sugar cookies have a tender, flaky texture and notes of vanilla, almond, and lemon. We're so glad readers love these cookies as much as we do.

- 1 cup (2 sticks) unsalted butter, softened at room temperature for 1 hour
- 2 ounces cream cheese (¼ of an 8-ounce package), softened at room temperature for 1 hour
- 1 cup sugar
- 1 large egg
- ½ teaspoon vanilla extract
- ½ teaspoon almond extract
  Zest of 1 lemon

- 3 cups all-purpose flour
- 1½ teaspoons baking powder
- ½ teaspoon salt
- 1 recipe Tangy Buttercream Icing (recipe follows)

In the bowl of a stand mixer, or in a large bowl using a hand mixer, cream the butter and cream cheese with the sugar until light and very smooth. Add the egg and beat until golden. Mix in the vanilla extract, almond extract, and lemon zest.

Whisk together the flour, baking powder, and salt in a separate bowl, then add the dry mixture, bit by bit, to the butter mixture until fully incorporated. Mix just until a soft dough forms.

Prepare two large, identically sized rectangles of parchment or wax paper. Pat the dough out into a rectangle on one piece of paper, then cover with the second piece of paper. Using a rolling pin, roll out the dough to about ¼ inch thick. Place the dough on a large baking sheet and cover with plastic wrap, then refrigerate for at least 1 hour, or overnight. The dough can be refrigerated for up to 5 days, or frozen for up to 3 months, well wrapped. Let the dough thaw overnight in the refrigerator before baking the cookies.

Preheat the oven to 350°F. Remove the chilled dough from the fridge and cut it into shapes with cookie cutters or biscuit cutters. Place the cut-out cookies on baking sheets lined with parchment paper or a silicone liner such as a Silpat.

Bake the cookies for 8 to 15 minutes, depending on their shape and size. Small cookies may begin browning after 7 minutes (ideally, these cookies will not brown at all). The finished cookies will have slightly golden-brown bottoms, but they will feel very soft and underbaked until they cool. Let the cookies cool on the baking sheets for 10 minutes, then remove them carefully to a cooling rack to let them cool completely before icing or decorating them. The finished cookies will keep for up to 5 days in a tightly covered container at room temperature. Finished cookies can also be frozen for up to 3 months. To freeze finished cookies, cool completely then stack between layers of wax paper or plastic wrap in an airtight container. Cover the top layer of cookies with several layers of wax paper and foil or plastic.

Decorating Sugar Cookies

> Decorating Cookies Before Baking. To add color
and sparkle to cookies before baking, whisk 1 large egg
yolk with 1 tablespoon water in a small bowl. Brush a
light coating of egg wash on the unbaked cookies, then
sprinkle with colored sugar. (The best sugar for this is the
chunky decorating sugar, since it won't melt or burn as
quickly as finer sugars.)

> Decorating Baked Cookies. Once baked cookies
have cooled, they can be frosted with any frosting or
glaze and then sprinkled with decorating sugar or candy
sprinkles.

Tangy Buttercream Icing

**MAKES ENOUGH TO GENEROUSLY FROST 2 TO 3 DOZEN
COOKIES, DEPENDING ON SIZE**

*This tangy frosting is an upgrade from the simplest
buttercream, rich with cream cheese and just sweet enough.*

- ½ cup (1 stick) unsalted butter, softened at room
temperature for 1 hour
- 4 ounces cream cheese, softened at room temperature
for 1 hour
- 3 cups confectioners' sugar
- 1 teaspoon pure vanilla extract
- ¼ teaspoon salt

In the bowl of a stand mixer, or in a large bowl using a
hand mixer, whip the butter and cream cheese together
until very smooth and creamy. Add the confectioners'
sugar, vanilla, and salt. Whip until very smooth. The frosting can be stored in an airtight container in the refrigerator for up to a week, or frozen for up to 3 months.

POACHED PEARS *with* RED WINE
and CARDAMOM SYRUP

SERVES 6

*Poached pears are Faith's idea of a party trick—the dinner
host's dream dessert. They look fancy, but they cook ahead
of time and hold perfectly in the fridge until you're ready for
them. And while they are cooking, they perfume the house
so sweetly. These pears can be served on their own, or laid
on top of a square of baked puff pastry, or drizzled with
Bourbon Crème Anglaise (page 150). The leftover red wine
poaching syrup is wonderful over vanilla ice cream.*

- 6 ripe yet firm pears (about 2 pounds), peeled, stems
intact
- 1 750-milliliter bottle dry yet mellow red wine, such
as Merlot
- 1½ cups sugar
- 6 whole green cardamom pods
- 1 cinnamon stick

Cut the pears in half lengthwise and use a melon baller
or teaspoon to scoop out the seeds and central core.

In a 4-quart (or larger) pot, stir together the red wine
and sugar. Lightly smash the cardamom pods with the
flat of a chef's knife. Add the pods and the cinnamon to
the pot and bring to a boil. Stir for 1 minute or until the
sugar dissolves, then lower the heat to a simmer and slip
the pears into the liquid.

Simmer the pears for about 30 minutes or until they
are tender, stirring occasionally to make sure the pears
are submerged. Remove the pot from the heat and let
the pears cool in the poaching liquid for about 30 minutes, then remove the pears from the pot. Slice the pear
halves into thinner slices to serve immediately, or refrigerate the halves in an airtight container for up to 3 days.

To make the syrup, simmer the poaching liquid over
medium-low heat until it is reduced to about 2 cups.
Don't let it burn, and cover the pot slightly to keep the
red wine from spattering your stove. Strain out the spices
and refrigerate the syrup. It will keep for at least 1 week in
the refrigerator, or up to 1 year in the freezer, well sealed.

To serve the pears, drizzle them with warmed syrup.

ONE-BOWL BIRTHDAY BUTTER CAKE (OR CUPCAKES) *with* DOUBLE CHOCOLATE FROSTING

**MAKES ONE 9 × 13-INCH CAKE,
A 9-INCH TWO-LAYER CAKE, OR 18 CUPCAKES**

In Faith's house, birthday cake means just one thing: yellow cake with chocolate frosting. A plain butter cake is such a good dessert to know, perhaps even by heart. And this simple one is not only reliably moist and fluffy, but it's nearly as fast to make as a box mix. Don't just take our word on that—one of our contributors, Nina Callaway, did a side-by-side test of this cake recipe with a box mix, and found our from-scratch version took a mere 13 seconds longer. Surely anyone has 13 seconds to spare for a cake this tasty?

½ cup (1 stick) unsalted butter, softened at room temperature for 1 hour
1½ cups sugar
2 large eggs
2 large egg yolks
2¼ cups all-purpose flour
3½ teaspoons baking powder
1 teaspoon salt
1¼ cups whole milk
1 teaspoon vanilla extract

Position an oven rack in the center of the oven and heat the oven to 350°F. Prepare a 9 × 13-inch pan or two 9-inch round cake pans by greasing them thoroughly with butter or baking spray. Sprinkle a little flour into the pans, tilt and shake to distribute evenly, then tap out the excess flour over the sink. If you are making cupcakes, grease or line 18 muffin cups.

Use a hand mixer or stand mixer to cream the butter and sugar until fluffy and light. With the mixer running, add the eggs and egg yolks one by one and beat until they are fully incorporated and the batter is creamy. Beat in the flour, baking powder, and salt, and finally the milk and vanilla. When the milk is added the batter will look lumpy at first. Beat the batter on low for 30 seconds, then on high for 3 minutes.

Immediately pour the batter into the prepared pans and smooth the top of the batter. Place the pans on the center oven rack. For a 9 × 13-inch pan, bake for 25 to 30 minutes, or until the top springs back slightly when pressed and a skewer or knife inserted in the center comes out clean. For round 9-inch cake pans, bake for 20 to 25 minutes. For cupcakes, bake for 18 to 20 minutes.

Let the cakes cool in their pans on wire racks for 20 minutes, then flip each pan over onto the rack and tap gently all over. Lift the pan slightly. If the cake doesn't feel like it's releasing, lay a slightly damp kitchen towel over the pan and tap again. If necessary, let the cakes cool more. If the cakes have been baked thoroughly, they should fall right out of the pans once they've cooled a little and the sides of the cake have shrunk back from the pan. For cupcakes, cool for 20 minutes on cooling racks. Remove the cupcakes by gently tipping the pan on its side, or by pulling them out by their liners.

Cool the cakes completely before frosting.

Double Chocolate Frosting

MAKES ENOUGH TO FROST A TWO-LAYER 9-INCH CAKE OR 18 CUPCAKES

Deep, dark chocolate frosting is a foil for sweet butter cake, and here that darkness comes from bittersweet chocolate and a dose of cocoa powder. This stuff is also really good on graham crackers. (Don't ask how we know.)

4	ounces bittersweet (70% cacao) chocolate
1	cup heavy cream
¼	cup unsweetened cocoa powder
1	teaspoon pure vanilla extract
¼	teaspoon salt
3 to 3½	cups confectioners' sugar

Finely chop the chocolate and place it in the bowl of a stand mixer or in a metal mixing bowl. Warm the cream over medium heat until bubbles form around the edges and the surface vibrates. Pour the cream over the chocolate and let the mixture stand for 5 minutes.

Beat the chocolate cream with the paddle attachment or with a hand mixer for 3 minutes or until smooth and glossy brown and somewhat cooled. Beat in the cocoa powder, vanilla, and salt. Beat in enough confectioners' sugar to form a thick, glossy icing.

Leftover icing can be refrigerated for up to 5 days, well covered.

HOW TO DIVIDE CAKE BATTER EVENLY

For perfectly even cake layers, place an empty cake pan on a kitchen scale and zero it out. Pour in 19 to 20 ounces of batter. Pour the rest of the batter into the other pan and weigh it. It should also read 19 to 20 ounces.

HOW TO SUCCESSFULLY FROST A CAKE
▼

Here are a few tips for creating a glamorous birthday centerpiece. If you want a higher ratio of icing to cake, split each layer of a two-layer cake in half by carefully slicing it as evenly as possible with a long serrated knife to create four thin layers.

To frost the layer cake, smear a spoonful of frosting on the cake plate or rotating cake stand to hold the cake in place. Place four strips of parchment paper or wax paper around the edge of the plate. Set the bottom cake layer on the plate so that the strips are tucked just under the edges of the cake layer.

Cover the bottom layer with frosting. Stack the layers one on top of the other, with a thin layer of frosting between each. Then use an offset spatula to frost the entire cake with a thin layer of icing. Let this thin crumb layer dry for 15 minutes (this helps you keep the final layer crumb-free).

Fill a tall glass with very hot water. Use an offset spatula to roughly ice the cake with thick dabs of frosting. Wipe the spatula clean. Dipping the spatula in hot water frequently, run it over the cake sides and top until the frosting is smooth. Finish with sprinkles or decorating sugar.

NO-BAKE BANANA *and* PEANUT BUTTER CARAMEL ICEBOX CAKE

SERVES 6 TO 8

We're always happy to read comments from readers who try our recipes. One of the most wildly popular recipes we ever published is for No-Bake Strawberry Icebox Cake, a cake that doesn't need the oven. Instead, it's a magic trick of graham crackers, whipped cream, and fruit that melds into a tender, cakey dessert. Readers love its cool simplicity, its generous proportions, and how it transcends the sum of its parts.

This icebox cake is constructed on the same principle, with vanilla whipped cream, bananas, and a homemade peanut butter caramel sauce that really sets it off. Summer picnic? Office potluck? We have you covered.

FOR THE PEANUT BUTTER CARAMEL SAUCE

- ½ cup sugar
- ½ cup heavy cream
- ¼ cup creamy peanut butter
- Generous pinch of kosher salt

FOR THE CAKE

- 4 ounces cream cheese, very soft
- 1 14-ounce can sweetened condensed milk
- 2¾ cups heavy cream
- 2 teaspoons pure vanilla extract
- ½ teaspoon salt
- ½ cup finely chopped peanuts
- ½ cup finely chopped pecans
- 4 sleeves graham crackers (about 19 ounces, or 28 to 30 whole crackers)
- 3 small to medium bananas

TO MAKE THE PEANUT BUTTER CARAMEL SAUCE

Mix the sugar with 2 tablespoons of water in a 2-quart saucepan. Heat over medium to high heat, stirring occasionally, until the mixture comes to a rolling boil. Stop stirring and cook over high heat for 5 to 10 minutes, until the sugar develops brown streaks.

Swirl the pan by the handle and watch for the first sign of smoke. As soon as the caramel turns dark brown and smokes, take the pan off the heat and whisk in the heavy cream. Be careful—the mixture will steam and bubble up violently. Return the pan to the heat and bring the caramel sauce to a simmer over low heat. Add the peanut butter and salt and whisk until the sauce is very smooth, then remove the pan from the heat.

TO ASSEMBLE THE CAKE

In the bowl of a stand mixer fitted with the paddle attachment, or in a large bowl using a hand mixer, whip the cream cheese until it is very smooth and creamy. Add the sweetened condensed milk very gradually, whipping continually and stopping to scrape down the bowl as necessary. When the milk is smoothly incorporated, and with the mixer still going, slowly pour in the cream. Add the vanilla and salt and whip on medium or high speed for 5 to 10 minutes, or until the cream holds soft peaks.

Mix the peanuts and pecans together in a bowl and set aside. If the peanut butter caramel has cooled too much to pour easily, warm it gently over low heat, then transfer it to a glass measuring cup.

Spread a spoonful of the whipped cream over the bottom of a 9 × 13-inch baking pan, or a similarly sized platter. (This keeps the graham crackers from sliding around.) Lay down six or more graham crackers, enough to completely fill the bottom of the pan. Lightly cover the top of the graham crackers with a quarter of the remaining whipped cream.

Peel and quarter the bananas lengthwise, then chop them fine. Arrange a third of the bananas over the whipped cream. Sprinkle with ¼ cup of the mixed nuts, and drizzle about a quarter of the peanut butter caramel sauce over the top. Make another layer with graham crackers, whipped cream, bananas, nuts, and caramel, then repeat again. (You will have three layers of crackers, whipped cream, bananas, nuts, and caramel.)

Top with a final layer of crackers. Swirl the remaining whipped cream on top, sprinkle with the remaining nuts, and drizzle on the remaining peanut butter caramel sauce.

Refrigerate the cake uncovered for 4 hours, or until the crackers have softened completely. This cake is best when made no more than 12 hours ahead of time. It will last 3 days, covered, in the refrigerator.

THREE ESSENTIAL ICE CREAMS: VANILLA, CHOCOLATE, and GREEN TEA

Once you get rolling with homemade ice cream, it's hard to stop. Here are three classic flavors to get you started. For the chocolate and green tea we borrow a method from Jeni Britton Bauer of Jeni's Splendid Ice Creams. She uses cream cheese and cornstarch instead of eggs to thicken the mixture. While we love the rich flavor that eggs impart in a vanilla ice cream, without eggs, the flavored ice creams have a more pure flavor.

Basic Vanilla Ice Cream
MAKES 1 QUART

- 4 large egg yolks
- ⅔ cup sugar
- 1½ cups whole milk
- 1 vanilla bean, split and scraped, or 1 teaspoon pure vanilla extract
- 1½ cups heavy cream

In a large metal mixing bowl, prepare an ice bath and set aside.

In a medium mixing bowl, use a whisk to beat the egg yolks and sugar until the eggs are pale yellow.

Place a large saucepan with the milk over medium heat and bring to a simmer. Add the vanilla bean or vanilla extract, and cook over medium-low heat. Remove the pan from the heat and pour about 1 cup of the hot milk into the egg mixture, whisking constantly. Return the pan of milk to the stove over low heat and slowly pour the egg mixture into the hot milk. Stir constantly with a wooden spoon until the custard has thickened slightly and registers 170°F degrees on an instant read thermometer.

Remove the mixture from the heat and allow it to cool. Remove the hull of the vanilla bean, if using, and stir in the heavy cream. Pour the mixture into a bowl through a fine-mesh strainer to remove any lumps.

Set the bowl in the ice water bath and let stand, stirring occasionally, until the custard is cooled, about 20 minutes. At this point you can churn the ice cream

or cover the surface of the custard directly with plastic wrap to prevent a skin from forming and refrigerate it for at least 3 hours or for up to 12 hours until you are ready to churn it.

Churn the mixture in an ice cream maker according to the manufacturer's instructions. The mixture will not be completely hard. To finish freezing, scoop the mixture into a lidded storage container, cover, and allow the ice cream to harden in the freezer for at least 1 hour before serving. The ice cream will keep in the freezer for about a week if sealed properly.

[Some of the] Best Chocolate Ice Cream
MAKES 1 QUART

- 2 cups whole milk
- 1 tablespoon plus 1 teaspoon cornstarch
- 8 ounces semisweet chocolate, chopped
- 2 ounces cream cheese, softened
- 1½ cups heavy cream
- ⅓ cup sugar
- Pinch of salt

In a large metal mixing bowl, prepare an ice bath and set aside.

In a small bowl, mix 2 tablespoons of the milk with the cornstarch. In a large bowl, combine the chocolate and cream cheese. Set aside.

In a large saucepan, combine the cream and the remaining milk with the sugar. Bring the milk and cream to a boil and cook over medium heat until the sugar dissolves, about 4 minutes. Take the pan off the heat, and then gradually whisk in the cornstarch mixture. Return the pot to a boil and cook over moderately high heat, stirring with a wooden spoon until the mixture is slightly thickened, about 1 minute.

Pour just enough of the hot milk over the chocolate and cream cheese to cover them. Stir until the chocolate is melted and the mixture is thick and silky. Add the salt. Gradually add the remaining hot milk mixture.

Set the bowl in the ice water bath and let stand, stirring occasionally, until the mixture has cooled off, about 20 minutes. At this point you can churn the ice cream or cover the surface directly with plastic wrap to prevent a skin from forming and refrigerate for at least 3 hours or up to 12 hours.

Churn the mixture in an ice cream maker according to the manufacturer's instructions. The mixture will not be completely hard. To finish freezing, scoop the ice cream into a lidded container, cover, and allow the ice cream to harden in the freezer for at least 1 hour before serving. The ice cream will keep in the freezer for about a week if sealed properly.

Green Tea Ice Cream
MAKES 1 QUART

2 cups whole milk

1 tablespoon plus 1 teaspoon cornstarch

2 ounces cream cheese, softened

¼ cup matcha tea powder (2 to 3 tablespoons for a less intense flavor)

Pinch of salt

1½ cups heavy cream

⅓ cup sugar

In a large metal mixing bowl, prepare an ice bath and set aside.

In a small bowl, mix 2 tablespoons of the milk with the cornstarch. In a large bowl, stir together the cream cheese, matcha tea powder, and salt. Set aside.

In a large saucepan, combine the cream and the remaining milk with the sugar. Bring the mixture to a boil and cook over medium heat until the sugar dissolves, about 4 minutes. Take the pan off the heat, and then gradually whisk in the cornstarch mixture. Return the pot to a boil and cook the mixture over medium-high heat until slightly thickened, about 1 minute.

Pour just enough of the hot cream and milk over the cream cheese mixture to cover it. Stir until the mixture is thick, silky, and uniformly green. Gradually add the remaining hot milk and cream.

Set the bowl in the ice water bath and let stand, stirring occasionally, until the mixture has cooled off, about 20 minutes. At this point you can churn the ice cream or cover the surface directly with plastic wrap to prevent a skin from forming and refrigerate it for at least 3 hours or for up to 12 hours.

Churn the mixture in an ice cream maker according to the manufacturer's instructions. The ice cream will not be completely hard. To finish freezing, scoop the ice cream into a lidded container, cover, and allow it to harden in the freezer at least 1 hour before serving.

The ice cream will keep in the freezer for about a week if sealed properly.

STRAWBERRY *and* HONEY SORBET

SERVES 2 TO 4

With just four ingredients, you can have homemade sorbet. Here is a recipe that uses strawberries and honey, but once you master the technique (in other words, in about five minutes) you can start fooling around with other flavor combinations. One of our favorites is peach and maple. Just aim for about a pound of fruit, start slow with the sweetener, and taste the puree. And if you're wondering about the vodka, it's not an effort to slip in a shot of booze; it actually helps lower the freezing point of the sorbet, giving it a softer texture and preventing it from getting too hard.

1 pint (1 pound) strawberries, hulled and quartered

¼ cup honey

1 tablespoon vodka, or flavored liqueur of choice, (optional)

¼ cup freshly squeezed lemon juice (from 1½ lemons)

Place the strawberries in a blender and puree until very smooth. Push the puree through a fine-mesh sieve to remove some of the seeds. Whisk in the honey, vodka (if you're using it), and lemon juice. (You'll want the puree to be on the sweet side, since freezing will dull the flavor.) Cover and chill the mixture.

Once the strawberry puree is completely chilled, pour it into an ice cream maker and freeze according to the manufacturer's instructions. Return the sorbet to the freezer for a couple more hours so it can continue to firm up. The sorbet can be stored in a lidded container in the freezer for up to 2 weeks, with a piece of plastic wrap pressed directly against the surface of the sorbet to prevent freezer burn.

MAGIC ONE-INGREDIENT ICE CREAM *(7 Ways)*

SERVES 4

We have some theories about why a recipe will go viral on the Internet. There is a certain combination of easy, cheap, and weird that causes a recipe to get passed from hand to hand, screen to screen, in an explosive train of links, growing more popular than it would with any promotion we could throw at it. So it was with this one-ingredient ice cream, which calls for nothing but bananas and your food processor. Blend the bananas long enough, and the fruit morphs into creamy ice cream, with the texture of soft serve and the natural sweetness of fruit. This is one of the biggest hits we've ever had, and it's time you tried it.

2 pounds very ripe bananas

Peel the bananas and cut them into small pieces (the smaller the better). Place them in a freezer-safe container. (Line the container with parchment paper or wipe a little oil inside to help the pieces release more easily, if desired.) Freeze the bananas overnight or until they are completely solid.

Place the frozen bananas in a food processor. Blend for 2 to 5 minutes, stopping frequently to scrape down the sides of the bowl. At first the bananas will simply turn into smaller chunks, and then into a fine grit. Keep blending, and add a spoonful of water if the banana pieces get stuck on the blade. They will suddenly turn into soft, creamy ice cream.

Eat the ice cream immediately, or return it to the freezer to harden a little more, if desired. Banana ice cream can be stored in an airtight container in the freezer for up to 2 weeks.

VARIATIONS

For flavor variations, blend bananas in a food processor until they are the consistency of soft serve ice cream, and then add the additional ingredients.

Nut and Honey Banana Ice Cream

Blend in ¼ cup almond or peanut butter and 2 tablespoons honey.

Nutella Banana Ice Cream

Blend in ⅓ cup Nutella spread.

Dark Chocolate Banana Ice Cream

Blend in 6 tablespoons cocoa powder, ¼ cup heavy cream, and 1 teaspoon vanilla.

Cinnamon Dulce Banana Ice Cream

Blend in ⅓ cup sweetened condensed milk and 1 teaspoon ground cinnamon.

Orange Dreamsicle Banana Ice Cream

Blend in ½ cup orange juice, ¼ cup heavy cream, and 1 teaspoon vanilla.

Strawberries and Cream Banana Ice Cream

Blend in ⅔ cup chopped frozen strawberries and ¼ cup heavy cream until smooth.

CINNAMON TOAST BREAD PUDDING CUPCAKES

MAKES 12 CUPCAKES

Our favorite parts of bread pudding are the crispy top and edges, so we devised these cupcake-sized puddings to give us more tasty bits. The crunchy, fragrant tops taste just like cinnamon toast. Any kind of bread can be used in bread pudding, but here we prefer richer challah or another egg-enriched bread. If you have a loaf of bread that is going stale but you're not quite in a bread pudding mood, toss the bread in the freezer—it will hold there until the craving strikes you for these cinnamon-laced treats.

FOR THE CINNAMON TOAST

- 12 ounces day-old challah bread
- ½ cup (1 stick) unsalted butter, melted
- ½ cup sugar
- 1 tablespoon ground cinnamon

FOR THE CUSTARD

- 1 cup cream
- 1 cup whole milk
- 2 large eggs
- 2 large egg yolks
- ¼ cup (packed) dark brown sugar
- 1 teaspoon pure vanilla extract
- ½ teaspoon ground cinnamon
- ½ teaspoon ground ginger
- ¼ teaspoon ground cloves
- ¼ teaspoon freshly grated nutmeg
- ½ teaspoon salt

FOR THE GLAZE

- 1 cup confectioners' sugar
- 1 to 2 tablespoons whole milk
- ⅛ teaspoon freshly grated nutmeg

TO PREPARE THE CINNAMON TOAST

Place a rack in the center of the oven and another rack near the top of the oven. Preheat the oven to 325°F. Prepare a twelve-cup muffin tin by lightly greasing the muffin wells or line the wells with aluminum liners. Prepare a large baking sheet by lining it with parchment paper.

Cut the bread into slices about ½ inch thick, and then cut the slices into squares about 1 inch to a side. In a large bowl, whisk together the melted butter, sugar, and cinnamon. Toss the bread in the melted butter until roughly coated.

Spread the bread on the prepared baking sheet and toast on the top oven rack for 25 minutes, stirring once, until the bread is crisp and beginning to brown around the edges. Reserve the large bowl and don't wipe it clean.

TO MAKE THE CUSTARD

While the bread is toasting, whisk together the cream, milk, eggs, egg yolks, and brown sugar in the large bowl used to coat the bread. Whisk in the vanilla, cinnamon, ginger, cloves, nutmeg, and salt.

Remove the bread from the oven and use the parchment paper to funnel the toasted bread pieces into the large bowl containing the custard. Stir the hot bread until it is thoroughly coated with the custard. Divide the bread and custard mixture evenly among the prepared muffin cups (they will be quite full). At this point the bread pudding can be covered and refrigerated overnight, if desired.

Bake the cupcakes on the middle rack in the oven for 30 to 35 minutes or until the tops are crisp and a toothpick inserted into the middle comes out clean. Let the cupcakes cool for at least 10 minutes before removing them from the pan.

TO MAKE THE GLAZE

In a medium bowl, stir together the confectioners' sugar, milk, and nutmeg until smooth. Add a little extra milk if the glaze seems too thick. Drizzle the glaze over the finished cupcakes before serving. Serve warm, or refrigerate in a covered container for up to 5 days. Warm the cupcakes briefly in the microwave or in the oven before serving.

NUTELLA CHEESECAKE BARS

MAKES ABOUT 20 BARS

On the Internet, Nutella is a phenomenon. We've watched our readers go wild for it in no-bake cookies, ice cream, or wedged between warm slices of bread. Any cookbook from The Kitchn should pay homage to our readers' love of this chocolate-hazelnut spread, so we offer this recipe. It's a double Nutella treat, with one layer smeared over a chocolate crust, and more Nutella swirled into the creamy cheesecake.

FOR THE CRUST

- 1½ cups finely ground chocolate graham cracker crumbs, from 10 to 12 crackers
- 1 tablespoon sugar
- 6 tablespoons unsalted butter, melted
- ¼ cup water

FOR THE CHEESECAKE FILLING

- 1 pound cream cheese, softened at room temperature for 1 hour
- 1 cup sour cream
- ⅔ cup sugar
- 2 large eggs
- 2 large egg yolks
- 2 tablespoons all-purpose flour
- 1 teaspoon pure vanilla extract
- ½ teaspoon salt
- 1¼ cup Nutella
- ¼ cup confectioners' sugar
- 1 to 3 tablespoons milk

Roasted, crushed hazelnuts, for serving

TO MAKE THE CRUST

Position one rack in the center and one rack in the bottom of the oven. Preheat the oven to 350°F. Lightly grease a 9-inch square baking pan with butter or baking spray.

Stir together the graham cracker crumbs, sugar, melted butter, and water until a soft dough forms. Press the dough into the bottom of the prepared pan. Bake the crust on the bottom oven rack for 20 minutes. Remove the crust from the oven and let it cool.

TO MAKE THE CHEESECAKE FILLING

Beat the softened cream cheese in the bowl of a stand mixer or in a large bowl with a hand mixer on medium speed until very smooth, about 2 minutes. Beat in the sour cream and sugar. Beat in the eggs and yolks one by one, then the flour, vanilla, and salt. Beat until smooth, stopping to scrape down the sides of the bowl periodically.

Gently spread ½ cup of the Nutella over the chocolate graham cracker crust. Pour the cream cheese mixture over the Nutella on the crust. Drop dollops of another ½ cup of Nutella into the cheesecake filling. Lightly run a knife through the mixture, swirling the Nutella throughout the cheesecake.

Bake the cheesecake in the center of the oven until it is set with a golden puffy top, 40 to 45 minutes. Transfer the cheesecake to a wire rack and let it cool for about 30 minutes. In a small saucepan over medium-low heat, warm the remaining ¼ cup Nutella until almost liquid. Whisk in the confectioners' sugar and milk to form a thick glaze. Drizzle the glaze over the cheesecake and smear it lightly.

Refrigerate the cheesecake for at least 3 hours or overnight. Cut into 2-inch-square bars and sprinkle with crushed hazelnuts to serve.

A NEAPOLITAN
TRIO OF PUDDINGS:
Vanilla, Chocolate, and Strawberry

Our most popular and appealing desserts are the homiest. We've noticed that when people are craving sweets, they return to the desserts of childhood, including creamy puddings like the ones Grandma used to make. Since launching The Kitchn, we've also seen a strong rise in readers interested in gluten-free desserts. Pudding offers a homey, easy dessert that just happens to be gluten-free. And the strawberry pudding is dairy-free.

Vanilla Pudding
SERVES 6

- 3 tablespoons cornstarch
- ¼ teaspoon salt
- 1 cup heavy cream
- 2 large egg yolks
- 2 cups 2% milk
- ⅓ cup sugar
- 1 vanilla bean, split and scraped, or 2 teaspoons pure vanilla extract

Whisk the cornstarch and salt together in a 1-quart mixing bowl, until no lumps remain. Slowly whisk in the cream. Whisk in the egg yolks. It is important that this mix be very smooth.

Warm the milk and the sugar over medium heat in a 3-quart saucepan. If you're using the vanilla seeds, they should be incorporated into the liquid. Drop the entire bean pod into the milk and warm the milk over medium heat until bubbles form around the inside edge of the pan and the entire surface of the milk begins to slowly simmer. Remove the vanilla bean pod and discard. Turn off the heat.

Pour 1 cup of the hot milk mixture into the bowl with the cornstarch and egg yolks. Whisk vigorously to combine. The mixture should come together smoothly, with no lumps. If you see any lumps, add a little more hot milk and whisk until smooth. Pour the combined mixture back into the pot slowly, whisking constantly. Turn the

heat back on to medium and bring the pot to a simmer while continuing to whisk. The custard will come to a boil with large bubbles that slowly pop up to the surface. Boil, whisking constantly, for 2 minutes. Turn off the heat. If you didn't use the vanilla bean, stir in the vanilla extract.

Spread the pudding into a container or individual dessert glasses or bowls. To avoid the "skin" that develops on top of cooling puddings, cover the surface with plastic wrap or buttered wax paper. Refrigerate the pudding for at least 1 hour, or until firm enough to be spooned out of the bowl.

The pudding can be stored for up to 3 days in the refrigerator. If you will be serving the pudding a day or more after cooking, whip the chilled pudding with a large whisk or in the bowl of a stand mixer for about 60 seconds to make it creamy and light again before serving.

Chocolate Pots de Crème
SERVES 6

½ cup heavy cream
6 ounces semisweet dark chocolate, finely chopped
2 large eggs, lightly beaten
½ cup whole milk
1 tablespoon brandy (optional)
1 teaspoon vanilla extract
Pinch of salt
Whipped cream, for serving

Warm the cream in a small saucepan over medium heat, stirring frequently. When the cream is bubbling around the edges of the pan, remove the pan from the heat and stir in the chocolate. Set it aside for 3 to 5 minutes, or until the chocolate has melted completely.

In a blender or food processor, combine the eggs, milk, brandy (if you're using it), vanilla, and salt. While the blender is running, pour in the chocolate cream and run on high speed for 1 minute or until the ingredients are very well combined. Divide the chocolate cream among six 4-ounce ramekins. Cover the tops of the custards loosely with plastic wrap and chill for at least 2 hours. Serve the pots de crème with small spoonfuls of unsweetened whipped cream.

The pots de crème will keep in the refrigerator for up to 3 days.

On Raw Eggs

If you are uncomfortable using raw eggs, you may very carefully heat them over a double boiler with the milk and cream until they reach 160°F; this process will basically pasteurize them. The eggs must be very well beaten before you add them to the milk and cream, and you must stir the mixture gently as you raise the temperature of the pan very gradually over a low flame; otherwise you will have scrambled eggs. Use a thermometer and remove the pan from the heat as soon as the mixture nears 160°F, making sure the mixture peaks at 160°F. Then proceed with the blending process.

Dairy-Free Strawberry Pudding
SERVES 6

12 ounces frozen unsweetened strawberries, thawed, with their juices
Juice of 1 lemon (about 3 tablespoons)
¼ to ½ cup sugar
2 large egg yolks
2 tablespoons cornstarch
½ teaspoon pure vanilla extract
¼ teaspoon salt

Blend the strawberries with the lemon juice and ¼ cup sugar in a blender or food processor until smooth and liquefied. Taste and increase the sweetness, if necessary. (The amount of sugar required will really depend on the sweetness of your berries.) Blend in the egg yolks and cornstarch.

Press the mixture through a fine-mesh strainer into a 3-quart saucepan. This will remove any remaining strawberry pulp and some of the seeds; expect to find a few tiny seeds in the final pudding. Bring the strawberry mixture to a full boil, stirring frequently. (When the fruit begins to boil, you may not notice it at first, since large bubbles will rise up very slowly, making a noise like "gloop" or "plop.") Lower the heat and let the pudding simmer for 2 minutes, whisking constantly, working the angles of the pot. Turn off the heat and whisk in the vanilla and salt.

Immediately pour the hot pudding into a container or into individual serving dishes. (If you notice lumps in the pudding, you can pour the pudding through a fine-mesh strainer to make it smoother.) To avoid the "skin" that develops on top of cooling puddings, cover the surface with plastic wrap or buttered wax paper. Put a lid on the container and refrigerate for 2 hours or until completely cold before eating.

Serve this custard in pretty bowls with whipped cream or Whipped Coconut Cream (see page 263).

The strawberry pudding can be stored in the refrigerator for up to 3 days.

MERINGUE *and* NECTARINE TRIFLES

SERVES 6

Crisp, airy meringues with whipped cream and bright, tangy nectarines offer a crispy, creamy, juicy dessert, layered in a glass. Every component can be made ahead of time (although the dessert is best assembled at the last moment). If you really need a quick dessert, use store-bought meringues instead of homemade. Try other fruit in this, too: Strawberries, fresh mango, or kiwi would all be delicious. This recipe presents another gift: It's naturally gluten-free. To make it a dairy-free version, see the Whipped Coconut Cream option at the end of the recipe.

FOR THE MERINGUES

- 4 large egg whites, at room temperature
- 1 teaspoon pure vanilla extract
- ½ teaspoon cream of tartar
  Pinch of salt
- 1 cup sugar

FOR THE WHIPPED CREAM AND FRUIT

- 1 cup heavy cream
- 1 tablespoon confectioners' sugar
- 1 tablespoon dark rum (optional)
- 1 teaspoon pure vanilla extract
- ¼ teaspoon freshly grated nutmeg, plus more for serving
- 4 to 6 small ripe nectarines, cut into 1-inch pieces (about 3 cups)

TO MAKE THE MERINGUES

Heat the oven to 250°F and line two baking sheets with parchment paper. Add the egg whites, vanilla, cream of tartar, and salt to the bowl of a stand mixer fitted with the whisk attachment (or in a wide metal bowl, using a hand mixer). Start the mixer on low speed. As the whites turn opaque and foamy, add the sugar in increments—1 table-spoon at a time.

Continue adding the sugar, and gradually increase the speed of the mixer to high. Keep beating the egg whites for 8 to 15 minutes until they hold sharp, stiff peaks and are smooth and silky.

Spoon twelve 2- to 3-inch ovals of meringue on the prepared baking sheets. (Bake any leftover meringue as well, but 12 total meringues are what you will need for this recipe.) Bake the meringues for 90 minutes. The meringues are done when they twist off the parchment paper easily without leaving anything behind. They should not have browned. When they're done, turn off the oven and prop the oven door open with a wooden spoon. Leave the meringues in the oven for 60 minutes to cool and exhaust any remaining moisture. Remove the meringues from the oven and let them cool completely. Store them in an airtight container for up to 2 weeks.

TO MAKE THE WHIPPED CREAM

Whip the cream with a hand mixer or in the bowl of a stand mixer for 5 minutes or until it holds soft peaks (page 125). Whip in the confectioners' sugar, rum (if you're using it), vanilla, and nutmeg. The whipped cream can be held in the refrigerator in an airtight container for up to 3 days.

TO ASSEMBLE THE DESSERT

Break a meringue cookie into several pieces and place in the bottom of each of 6 tall glasses or Mason jars. Top with a couple tablespoons of chopped nectarine, then a spoonful of whipped cream. Repeat, finishing with whipped cream and a little extra nutmeg. Eat immediately.

Whipped Coconut Cream
MAKES ABOUT 1 CUP

For a dairy-free version of this recipe, skip the whipped cream and make this coconut cream instead.

Place a can of full-fat coconut milk in the refrigerator overnight. When you open the can of coconut milk there will be a firm, waxy layer on top. Scoop out this firm layer, stopping as soon as you reach the water toward the bottom of the can. (You can use the water in smoothies, or just drink it straight.) Place this cream in the bowl of a stand mixer or in a large bowl. Turn your stand mixer or hand mixer to high speed and whip the coconut cream for 3 to 5 minutes until fluffy and light, with soft peaks. Mix in the sugar, rum (if you're using it), vanilla, and nutmeg and proceed as directed in the recipe.

MEYER LEMON BARS

MAKES 2 DOZEN

You can make a pan of lemon bars and they will be wonderful, but if you happen to come across some Meyer lemons, this is your opportunity to make them even better. Meyer lemons are a cross between a lemon and possibly an orange or a mandarin, so they are less acidic than lemons in most produce sections. You may not find a Meyer lemon at your corner deli, but these days a decent grocery store will probably have them in the winter months. For this recipe we've increased the lemon and decreased the sweetness, so the citrus flavor shines through.

FOR THE CRUST

- 2 cups unbleached all-purpose flour
- ¾ cup confectioners' sugar
- 1½ teaspoons salt
- 1 cup (2 sticks) unsalted butter, very cold and cut into small pieces
- 1 to 2 teaspoons ice water

FOR THE TOPPING

- 5 large eggs, at room temperature
- 1½ cups sugar
- 1 tablespoon Meyer lemon zest
- ⅔ cup fresh Meyer lemon juice (from 4 to 5 lemons)
- ¼ cup unbleached all-purpose flour
- Pinch of salt

- 3 tablespoons confectioners' sugar, for garnish

TO PREPARE THE CRUST

Position a rack in the center of the oven and preheat the oven to 350°F. Grease a 9 × 13-inch baking pan and line it with parchment paper, leaving about 1 inch of paper hanging over the two long sides of the pan.

In the bowl of a food processor, combine the flour, confectioners' sugar, and salt. Process briefly. Scatter the butter on top and pulse until the mixture resembles a coarse meal. Add a teaspoon of ice water, or up to 2 teaspoons, if the mixture is too dry.

Press the dough into the bottom of the prepared pan and snugly against the inside edges to keep the lemon topping from running beneath the crust.

Bake the crust for 20 to 25 minutes, or until golden. Remove the pan from the oven and set it on a wire rack to cool slightly. Reduce the oven temperature to 300°F.

TO MAKE THE TOPPING

In a medium mixing bowl, whisk together the eggs and granulated sugar until they are well combined and the eggs are pale in color. Stir in the lemon zest, lemon juice, flour, and salt. Pour the topping over the warm crust. Return the pan to the oven and bake the lemon bars for 15 to 20 minutes, or until set.

Remove the pan from the oven and set it on a wire rack to cool completely. Remove the squares by grasping and lifting the edges of the parchment. Cut into bars. Dust the bars with the confectioners' sugar before serving. The bars will keep, covered and chilled, for 3 days.

HONEYED PHYLLO STACKS *with* PISTACHIOS, SPICED FRUIT, *and* YOGURT

SERVES 4

One of the surprising things we learned from one of our readers is that phyllo dough is actually vegan—it's made with oil, not butter. This versatile freezer staple is also a helpful component for assembling fancied-up desserts that look beautiful but are actually a snap to make, like this one. You can create little pastries with the dough, as we do here, and even layer them with soft cheese, preserved fruit, and aromatic honey.

The key to success with phyllo dough is understanding how to work with the paper-thin layers of dough, keeping them moist until you're ready for them, and handling them gently. This recipe may look long, but all the components of this beautiful and unique dessert can be made ahead of time.

FOR THE PHYLLO DOUGH

- 6 sheets phyllo dough, thawed
- ¼ cup sugar
- ¼ teaspoon ground cinnamon
- ¼ cup extra-virgin olive oil

FOR THE PISTACHIO AND FRUIT MIX

- Zest and juice of 1 orange (about ¼ cup juice)
- 2 tablespoons sugar
- 2 tablespoons honey
- ½ cup golden raisins, roughly chopped
- 1 cup roasted unsalted pistachio nuts, roughly chopped
- ½ cup pitted dates, roughly chopped
- ½ teaspoon ground cardamom

FOR THE YOGURT

- 1 cup whole-milk Greek yogurt
- 1 tablespoon confectioners' sugar
- Zest of 1 lemon

FOR SERVING

- ½ cup pomegranate arils
- ¼ cup pistachios, chopped
- Honey, warmed

TO PREPARE THE PHYLLO SQUARES

Preheat the oven to 400°F and line a large baking sheet with parchment or Silpat.

Stack the phyllo sheets on the countertop and cover loosely with a barely damp towel. Combine the sugar and cinnamon in a small bowl. Put the oil in another small bowl. Remove a sheet of phyllo and place it on the prepared baking sheet. Using a pastry brush, lightly coat the phyllo dough with the olive oil and sprinkle lightly with the cinnamon sugar. Top with another sheet of phyllo, oil, and cinnamon sugar. Repeat with all of the sheets, but when you get to the top layer, brush it lightly with oil. Use kitchen shears to snip the layered dough into 12 squares or rectangles of equal size.

Bake the phyllo dough for 7 to 8 minutes or until it is golden brown and crispy. Let it cool completely. The prepared phyllo squares can be stored in an airtight container at room temperature for up to 3 days.

TO MAKE THE PISTACHIO AND FRUIT MIX

In a small saucepan over medium heat, heat the orange zest and orange juice, sugar, and honey until the juice boils and the honey dissolves. Stir in the golden raisins and set the pan aside.

In a medium bowl, mix the pistachios with the dates. Stir in the cardamom. Stir the spiced pistachios and dates into the pan with the syrup and raisins. Set aside the pistachio and fruit mix to marinate for at least 30 minutes. This mixture can be made up to 5 days ahead of time and stored in the refrigerator.

To make the yogurt: In a medium bowl, thoroughly mix the yogurt with the confectioners' sugar and lemon zest. The yogurt mixture can be refrigerated for up to 5 days, well covered.

TO ASSEMBLE THE DESSERT

Smear about 1 tablespoon of yogurt on a phyllo pastry square. Place on an individual dessert plate. Top with a generous spoonful of the fruit mixture, then another phyllo square. Repeat, and top with a final pastry square and a small dollop of yogurt. Sprinkle the stack and the dish around it with pomegranate arils and pistachios, then drizzle lightly with warmed honey. Repeat, creating 4 phyllo square stacks, and serve immediately.

BROWNIES THREE WAYS:
Fudgy, Cakey, or Chewy

How do you like your brownies? Fudgy, cakey, or chewy? Whatever your desire, we provide the right dose of brownie to meet your needs. Our fudgy brownie has a creamy texture thanks to a dollop of mascarpone cheese. Don't skip the ganache topping, because it makes the brownies taste even creamier. The cakey brownie is a lighter, more tender version of the classic brownie, and it features a shiny cocoa glaze and a pinch of salt to set off the sweetness. Lastly, a good chewy brownie is the quintessential favorite. These chewy brownies have a flaky, shiny top that crackles as the brownie is cut, and a chewy, dense chocolate treat underneath.

Fudgy Mascarpone Brownies with Creamy Ganache
MAKES ABOUT 20 BROWNIES

FOR THE BROWNIES
- 1 cup (2 sticks) unsalted butter, cut into small pieces, plus more for greasing the pan
- 3 ounces bittersweet chocolate (70% cacao), finely chopped
- 1 cup sugar
- ½ cup mascarpone cheese
- 3 large eggs
- 1 teaspoon pure vanilla extract
- ½ teaspoon salt
- ½ cup unsweetened cocoa powder
- ½ cup all-purpose flour

FOR THE GANACHE
- 2 tablespoons unsalted butter
- 2 tablespoons heavy cream
- 2 ounces bittersweet chocolate (70% cacao), finely chopped

TO MAKE THE BROWNIES
Heat the oven to 325°F and line a metal 8 × 8-inch baking pan with parchment paper so that it hangs over two sides of the pan. Lightly grease the pan and the parchment paper with butter.

Melt the 1 cup of butter in a 2-quart saucepan over medium heat. Stir in the chocolate and melt it until it is smooth. Remove the pot from the heat. Let the melted chocolate rest for 2 minutes, then add the sugar and whisk until fully combined. Whisk in the mascarpone until smooth, then add the eggs one by one, whisking until smooth. Whisk in the vanilla and salt. Stir in the cocoa powder and flour until the batter is smooth.

Pour the batter into the prepared pan and smooth the top to ensure even baking. Bake for 45 minutes, or until a toothpick or tester inserted in the middle comes out clean. Set the pan on a wire rack to cool.

TO MAKE THE GANACHE
After removing the brownies from the oven, heat the butter and cream in a small saucepan over medium heat until the butter is melted and the cream is bubbling around the edges. Stir in the chocolate and remove the pan from the heat. Let the ganache sit for 2 minutes, and then whisk it until it is smooth and glossy. Pour it over the still-warm brownies. Spread with a knife until smooth.

Immediately put the brownies in the refrigerator. Cool them in the refrigerator overnight or for at least 4 hours before cutting and serving. Remove the brownies from the pan by grasping the parchment and lifting up and out. Cut the brownies into small pieces using a sharp, hot knife, to get smooth edges. The brownies can be stored in an airtight container at room temperature for up to 1 week.

Soft Cakey Brownies with Salted Chocolate Glaze
MAKES ABOUT 20 BROWNIES

FOR THE BROWNIES

- 4 tablespoons (½ stick) unsalted butter, softened, plus more for greasing the pan
- ¼ cup heavy cream
- 4 ounces unsweetened chocolate, finely chopped
- ¾ cup sugar
- 2 large eggs
- ¼ cup milk
- 1 teaspoon pure vanilla extract
- ½ cup all-purpose flour
- 1 teaspoon espresso powder (optional)
- ½ teaspoon baking powder
- ½ teaspoon salt

FOR THE GLAZE

- ½ cup confectioners' sugar
- 2 tablespoons unsweetened cocoa powder
- 1 tablespoon corn syrup
- 1 to 2 tablespoons hot water
- ¼ teaspoon pure vanilla extract
- Generous pinch of flaked sea salt, plus more to finish if desired

TO MAKE THE BROWNIES

Move an oven rack to the center of the oven and heat the oven to 350°F. Line a ceramic, glass, or metal 8 × 8-inch pan with parchment paper so that it hangs over two sides of the pan. Lightly grease the pan and parchment with butter.

Heat the cream in a small saucepan over medium heat until the edges bubble. Remove the pan from the heat and stir in the chocolate. Let the chocolate cream sit for 2 minutes, then whisk until glossy and smooth. Set aside to cool.

In the bowl of a stand mixer, or using a hand mixer, cream the 4 tablespoons of butter with the sugar until light and soft. Add the eggs, one at a time, beating until smooth. Beat in the milk and vanilla, then scrape in the melted chocolate mixture. Beat for 1 minute or until the batter is smooth and has thickened slightly. Add the flour, espresso powder (if you're using it), baking powder, and salt, and beat just until the batter comes together.

Spread the batter into the prepared pan and bake until a toothpick inserted in the middle comes out clean with a few moist crumbs clinging to it, 30 to 35 minutes.

TO MAKE THE GLAZE

Whisk the confectioners' sugar and cocoa together in a small bowl. Whisk in the corn syrup, hot water, vanilla, and salt. Set the brownie pan on a cooling rack and spread the glaze over the brownies while they are still warm. If desired, sprinkle the top lightly with flaked sea salt. Let the brownies cool for at least 1 hour.

Classic Chewy Brownies
MAKES ABOUT 20 BROWNIES

- ½ cup (1 stick) plus 2 tablespoons unsalted butter, cubed, plus more for greasing the pan
- 2 ounces unsweetened chocolate, finely chopped
- 4 ounces bittersweet chocolate (70% cacao), finely chopped
- ⅔ cup granulated sugar
- ½ cup (packed) brown sugar
- 2 eggs
- 1 large egg yolk
- 1 teaspoon pure vanilla extract
- ½ cup all-purpose flour
- ½ teaspoon salt
- ¼ teaspoon baking powder
- ⅔ cup chopped walnuts (optional)

Move an oven rack to the center of the oven and heat the oven to 350°F. Line a metal 8 × 8-inch baking pan with parchment paper so that it hangs over two sides of the pan. Lightly grease the pan and parchment with butter.

Melt the butter and both chocolates in a 2-quart saucepan over low heat, stirring frequently. Remove the pan from the heat and whisk in the sugars. The mixture will be grainy. Whisk in the eggs and egg yolk, one at a time, and then the vanilla. Whisk vigorously for about 1 minute.

Stir in the flour, salt, and baking powder, then fold in the walnuts, if using. Spread the batter in the prepared baking pan.

Bake the brownies for 25 to 35 minutes or until a toothpick inserted in the middle comes out with just a few crumbs. The edges of the brownies should look firm and well baked, and the center should be slightly moist. Immediately put the brownies in the refrigerator for at least 1 hour before cutting them in order to maximize chewiness. The brownies will keep well covered for up to 5 days.

JAM HAND PIES

MAKES 18 TO 24 HAND PIES

Pie that you can eat without a fork is the best thing ever. These hand pies get bonus points for having an even better crust-to-fruit ratio than a normal slice of pie. The filling can be made with any favorite jam or a few spoonfuls of chopped ripe fruit. Get fancy and add some minced ginger, a sprinkle of cinnamon, or a few chocolate chips. They're great for kids' lunchboxes, or tucked into a lunch bag and for work.

Double the recipe for Galette crust (page 245)
2½ cups Quick Berry Jam (page 145) or store-bought jam
¼ cup whole milk or heavy cream
Sugar, for sprinkling

Divide the galette dough into two disks and refrigerate for at least 1 hour before making the hand pies.

Preheat the oven to 375°F. Line a baking sheet with parchment or nonstick liner.

Rest one disk of galette dough on a flour-dusted counter for a few minutes until it's no longer hard and solid. Roll out the dough with a rolling pin to between ¼ and ½ inch thick—thicker than a normal pie crust. Use a 3-inch round biscuit or cookie cutter to cut the dough into circles. Gather the scraps, roll out the dough again, and cut additional circles. (If your kitchen is very warm and the dough is beginning to soften, chill the circles for 10 minutes before proceeding.)

Roll each circle of dough a second time to ⅛ inch thick and about 5 inches wide. Dust it lightly with flour and transfer it to the prepared baking sheet. It's okay if the circles overlap. Chill the circles in the refrigerator for 15 minutes.

Remove the tray of dough circles from the refrigerator. Working with one circle at a time, place 2 tablespoons of jam on the front edge of the circle, leaving about a ½-inch border. Brush the lower edges with a little milk and fold the top half of the dough over the fruit or jam. Use the tines of a fork to gently seal the edges. Repeat with the remaining dough circles.

Arrange the pies at least 1 inch apart on the prepared baking sheet. Cut a few small slits in the top of each pie with a knife, brush the tops with milk, and sprinkle with sugar. Bake for 35 minutes or until the tops begin to turn golden brown. Don't worry if some of the filling leaks out.

While the first batch of pies are baking, roll, chill, and shape the second batch using the second disk of galette dough.

Allow the pies to cool for 10 to 15 minutes before eating. Hand pies are best the day they are made, but will keep in a sealed container at room temperature for up to a week. Baked pastries can be frozen for up to 3 months.

GATHERING

Once you've tackled the messy tasks of setting up (page 13) and caring for your kitchen (page 69), mastered the essential cooking techniques (page 107), and tried out a few dishes from the recipe section (page 129), it's time to celebrate by planning a meal and gathering around the table with a few friends.

We've always said that anytime you sit down for a meal, you are in a sense gathering, but now that you're feeling confident and honed about the state of your kitchen, and your cooking skills, why not have a whole group over?

Wait. When you hear the word *entertaining*, does the image of an intricately planned dinner party with place cards and a stressful day of cooking come to mind? Erase that! We are here to convince you otherwise with our low-pressure, no-nonsense, anti-perfect antidote to entertaining.

In many ways, every gathering is a feast; every meal is a cause for joy. Some, like weddings or funerals or our first dinner party, feel especially weighted, but, really, any occasion we sit down to a plate of food it is an opportunity for celebration and gratitude. When we do this in good company, be they family, friends, or strangers, we are participating in one of the oldest human activities: the shared meal.

Some believe that learning to cook is what civilized us. As we evolved from being singular gatherers of plants into a group huddled around the fire to roast a beast, we developed patience to wait for our food; we learned about trust and empathy when we shared in a meal. We became human.

If we ate together more often—dining not only with our families and close friends, but also with people who are not so familiar to us—the world would be a much better and more interesting place. At the dinner table, we share (and perhaps fumble with) our food and drink, manners and customs, expectations and pleasures. We debate our values and ideas, and we regale one another with our stories. We laugh, we cry, we get upset, we forgive. In short, we connect with each other, and, consequently, we begin to understand and, we hope, accept the deeper truths about who we are.

When times are tough, we gather together. When we want to mark an important day, a rite of passage, an arrival or a departure, we gather together. And as we feed each other, as we enter into the ancient dance of guest and host, giving and receiving, we discover that we are beholden to one another, in the most positive of ways: intertwined, sustained, grateful. We can't help ourselves. It's what we do.

GATHERINGS:
OUR PHILOSOPHY

We write stories at The Kitchn in the hope that you will see a workable approach to gathering in style, with grace and with ease. We try to counterbalance much of the advice about dinner parties that portrays an unattainable level of perfection and the myth that entertaining must be expensive and time-consuming.

Entertaining sounds like an intimidating household event requiring a lot of preparation and skill, so we prefer to remove that weight and call such events "gatherings" instead. Gathering to eat is not just something we do on weekends when guests come over and we bring out the candles and cloth napkins; it's what we do every single day when we cook for ourselves and our families. Cooking for the everyday people in your life is as deep an offering of joy and sustenance as an all-out dinner party. We wish

"One thing I often forget when I am having friends over is to enjoy myself. We entertain to share our time and create memories with friends, but sometimes the preparation of the dinner overshadows the greater purpose. If the difference between being able to mingle and catch up with friends and being stuck standing over the stove for half of the night means cutting a few corners, why not make things easy on yourself? After all, what good is throwing a party without having fun in the process?"

—*Stephanie Barlow, a writer for The Kitchn*

that sort of offering didn't share a word that also describes frivolous, stuffy affairs.

Gathering is the whole experience of a meal—from the shopping, to the playlist you create for chopping onions, to being able to tell your guests who grew that carrot or raised this piece of meat (or to wonder together where it all came from), to the tipsy game of charades to finally saying good-bye to the guests after dessert and cranking up the music to get through loading the dishwasher. That's what we see in our minds when we think of a gathering.

The social interaction that surrounds a meal feeds the soul; we tell tales and seek advice, we laugh and cry, we learn and teach, and sometimes we even fall in love around chopping blocks and dinner tables. The point is to have fun, make memories, learn new tricks, connect people, and eat really good food.

The tips in this chapter may sound like they are geared toward formal dinner parties, but remember that it's just as important to set the table nicely and put flowers out for yourself as it is for guests. Cooking and eating are moments to honor, so light a candle and use a cloth napkin, even if it's wrinkled. Turn off the television and put away your phone, and you'll find that the act of gathering around food is sacred every single time.

THE ELEMENTS OF A GOOD GATHERING

A successful gathering is simple, really. You just need great food, a beautiful table, and a happy mood. We helped you with the food part in the earlier chapters. Let's talk about the table and establishing an overall mood.

THE TABLE

The food bound for our bellies deserves its own place of honor. Both Sara Kate and Faith's dining tables are custom made, simple, and quite thought out in design. Much of their work on The Kitchn and certainly on this book was done across both of these tables.

If you have an opportunity to bring in a new table, take some time to think about how you will use it and what kind of space you have for it. As with most things, spending more time planning and getting it right always pays off, even if it means you spend a little extra money in the process.

SETTING THE TABLE

There are a million ways to set a table. More important than anything is that you include everything you need. A water glass and a wineglass are simple offerings. The same goes for flatware: set out a separate dessert fork or spoon with the dinner flatware; it is relaxing to clear the table and eat dessert with a clean set. We see the table as an opportunity to help people feel comfortable and enjoy their meal, and, of course, some things go together well as they serve that purpose (silverware to the side of the plate, for example), but which spoon goes on which side is a question we usually ignore.

We can think of very few occasions now when it would be necessary to set the table in the traditionally formal way. Don't ask us the last time we did this. Formal table settings are probably still done for state dinners in the White House, at buttoned-up weddings, and in homes that adhere strongly to the traditional, but for the most part, we believe that setting the table is an opportunity to be creative, not bound by strict rules.

That said, if you want to be really traditional, here's how you do it.

Arriving at a table with a bountiful setting feels luxurious. And for those nights when you just can't be bothered with any extra washing, skip separate salad plates and dessert spoons, but don't apologize. Remember, the best host is a relaxed host. Perhaps that's the real luxury.

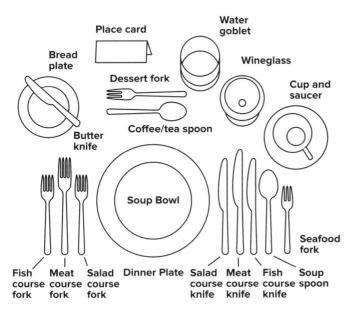

Place card · Water goblet · Bread plate · Dessert fork · Wineglass · Cup and saucer · Butter knife · Coffee/tea spoon · Soup Bowl · Fish course fork · Meat course fork · Salad course fork · Dinner Plate · Salad course knife · Meat course knife · Fish course knife · Soup spoon · Seafood fork

Sara Kate switched from a round table to a rectangular dining table as her daughter grew older; she craved some space for spreading out big projects and hosting larger dinner parties. There was one catch; she wanted a table that wasn't too wide, so she used German beer garden tables as her inspiration. Most dining tables are at least thirty-six inches and often up to forty-five inches wide, but she felt that such a wide table wouldn't allow for the intimacy she seeks for her dinner parties. With a cozy place to eat, even a simple meal laid across the table feels bountiful. When sitting at a slimmer table, people are physically closer to each other and feel connected. Sara Kate found Illinois-based woodworker Erin Norton True of Urban Wood Goods, who built a 30 × 60-inch table—a happy medium between the skinny German beer garden tables and the standard-issue dining tables found at most furniture stores. Her new table fits eight people comfortably; ten if she squishes two people on each end. Yet it fits perfectly into her very small New York City apartment. The benches at her table (one doubles as her coffee table) allow guests to squeeze in and children to fall asleep across grown-ups' laps.

FAITH'S TABLE

When Faith and her husband got married, they commissioned their first piece of "grown-up" furniture: an eight-foot-long table of reclaimed wood from Rhode Island craftsman David Ellison of The Lorimer Workshop. She and her husband regularly host large dinner parties, so they needed a table that could easily accommodate eight, ten, or more guests. She loves the reclaimed wood, which shows marks of saw blades and past use; it adds character and a sense of history to the centerpiece of the kitchen.

SETTING A BEAUTIFUL TABLE ON A BUDGET

Our writer Anjali Prasertong came up with a great idea for those who dislike spending money on things they rarely use, hate burning through the disposable instead of investing in the reusable, and can't find adequate space for party decorations and supplies in their small apartment closets. Enter the communal collection, or as she dubbed it, The Sisterhood of the Traveling Party Supplies.

The collection started when she and several of her friends began planning their weddings, spending inordinate amounts of time and money on party supplies. Already married friends began offering their leftover reception decor stash for the to-be-weds to borrow, saving them money and mental energy. The Sisterhood of the Traveling Party Supplies has evolved over time to include not only items needed for a wedding—twenty burlap table runners, anyone?—but also basic party equipment such as big metal tubs to hold ice and drinks at backyard shindigs and stacks of plain IKEA juice glasses to use instead of disposable wineglasses, as well as small decorative items such as vases.

Of course, she could have organized the Sisterhood with spreadsheets of who owns what, but for now she keeps things casual—just a group of apartment-dwelling, money-saving friends who love helping each other throw great parties.

To feed a family of between one and four people and to regularly have a few friends to dinner, you should have place settings for at least eight. That way, on a normal night after work, you should have enough clean dishes and forks to set down dinner. Anything beyond that can be kept in storage or borrowed from friends and neighbors. There's no rule requiring that your plates and bowls match and that your flatware be the same pattern. If you have more of a mix-and-match look going on your dining table, try to make it really original. Include some old things, go to garage sales and troll Etsy and eBay for great vintage finds. If you prefer a cleaner look, invest in a pattern you really love and plan to keep for a long time.

---

5 CHEAP WAYS TO SPRUCE UP YOUR GATHERING

▼

1. Two bouquets of flowers—one for the table and one to be split up around the house.

2. DIY cloth napkins. A yard of cotton fabric and a pair of pinking shears will get you about nine cloth napkins. No sewing required!

3. A few old jars to hold cutlery on the table and tea lights throughout your home.

4. Sparkling water in glass bottles and lemon or mint sprigs in water glasses.

5. A really good loaf of warmed bread, with butter and sea salt.

DECORATING THE TABLE

The table can be covered with a cloth, plates, glasses, and flatware, but there are occasions—holidays, celebrations, and hosting special dinner guests—when you will want your table to really come alive. When Sara Kate was growing up, her mother would send her to the park across the street to collect pine branches to decorate their holiday table. Even in the middle of the city you can find branches for your table (just wash them in the bathtub first!).

Over the years we've collected plenty of ideas for decorating a table. Here are a few of our favorites.

> **Turn bowls into woodland candleholders.** When tucked into regular white soup or noodle bowls, floral foam topped with dried moss creates the effect of little grassy meadows on your dining room table. The floral foam holds candlesticks while the moss dresses up the bowl.

tops, beaches, parks, etc.), the size of your table might frequently change. A roll of brown paper (look in the painting aisle at your local hardware store), applied as a runner to a tabletop creates a lovely neutral backdrop for your food and any style you'd like to add.

> **Invest a little in flowers.** Sara Kate spends $5 a week on flowers from her corner deli so there's always something pretty on the table. (Inexpensive bouquets may be one of the unsung benefits of living in a big city.) Flowers make a huge impact on a table. Pluck one from the bunch and put it in a bud vase in the bathroom for an extra-special touch.

> **For extra whimsy add small figurines, such as people, deer, or other woodland creatures.** (Check toy stores or model train stores for the best selection or find them online.) Don't forget about all the free accessories found in nature, such as pinecones, dried flowers, or small twigs.

> **Make vegetable centerpieces.** A blog we love called Brit + Co (www.brit.co) showed us how to make vases and candlestick holders out of vegetables such as turnips, radicchio, acorn squash, and pomegranate. Simply wash and dry the produce. If necessary, slice off a small piece on the bottom to create a flat surface so that the fruit or vegetable will stand upright. Slice off the top and cut out enough of the middle of the fruit or vegetable to accommodate a candle or a small shot glass for water and flowers.

> **Use simple brown paper.** Linens and tablecloths are fabulous things to own, but if you have a small space and do a great deal of entertaining elsewhere (alleys, roof-

---

10 EASY THINGS THAT WILL MAKE YOU AN ADMIRABLE HOST

▼

1. Cloth napkins and tablecloth or runner.

2. Well-thought-out music.

3. Flowers on the table and in the bathroom.

4. A house that has just been cleaned.

5. A preset table.

6. Candles.

7. A place for coats and bags (cleared hooks).

8. Being able to tell a story about the food you're serving.

9. Water on the table in a pretty pitcher

10. Being calm and happy.

SETTING THE MOOD

What goes into a party mood? Good music, nice lighting, drinks, a clean house, and a cheerful host. Theoretically, if you have the first four, you should have the fifth, right? Let us help you.

MUSIC

When we were growing up, our parents stacked four, five, sometimes six records on the record player, and hoped they wouldn't scratch. These days you can really go crazy with playlists and curated radio applications such as Spotify and Pandora. The sky's the limit, so there's really no excuse for dull dinner party music.

Think about separate kinds of music for cooking and cleanup (when we like to crank it up!) and dinnertime (when it's nice to be able to hear the conversation). Our staff has a lot of opinions about music, and the iPods to show for it. For more on music, visit the ever-expanding music category on our website.

LIGHTING

Bad lighting hinders relaxation and the party mood. It costs about $5 to get a sack of unscented tea lights at the hardware store and about two minutes to set them across your table. It takes another thirty seconds to turn off the overhead lighting. Well done.

DRINKS

Our resident wine expert, Mary Gorman-McAdams, has written dozens of posts over the years about specific bottles of wine, wine vocabulary, how to taste wine, and how wine is made. She still agrees that the best way to pick a bottle of wine for a meal is to talk to the folks in a good wine shop. Nothing beats that personal connection you get when you tell a wine person about your food. They love it. And if they don't, find a new wine store.

"I always like to start out with something bubbly—Champagne for special occasions. Bubbles always seem to put guests in an even better mood. I always try to have a selection of wines so that guests can mix and match and drink what they prefer."
—Mary Gorman-McAdams, wine writer for The Kitchn

In terms of quantity, our general rule of thumb is to plan on about a half a bottle of wine per guest for a sit-down dinner, and if you're only serving hors d'oeuvres, plan on one to two glasses per guest, per hour.

It's also important to offer an alternative to alcohol for those who don't drink, who are the designated drivers, or who are secretly pregnant. You never know if everyone will partake, so having something on hand besides tap water is a nice gesture. A glass filled with ice and a splash of just about any kind of juice or flavored simple syrup and topped with club soda is simple, inexpensive, and thoughtful.

A CLEAN HOUSE

There's really no point in cleaning your house top to bottom right before guests arrive. Assuming it isn't a complete pigsty, you should focus mostly on the food. (If it's a good party, there's going to be a mess later anyway.) But you want people to think your house is clean, even if you just kicked those yet-to-be-unpacked suitcases under the bed seconds before you opened the front door with a smile. Take care of the big messes if you can, and shove the rest into the closet. At the very least, clean the bathroom and light a candle so maybe, just maybe, people won't turn on the light.

THE POST-PARTY CRASH CLEANING PLAN

We can probably all agree that what feels best after the dinner is if the house is completely put back together, the dishes are clean, and all the leftovers are neatly packed away. However, when you've had a little wine and the party breaks up at a late hour, this ideal might not be realizable. The thought of washing pots and loading a dishwasher is making you cranky, yet the prospect of waking up to smelly, stuck-on food is no picnic, either. Here are the bare minimum tasks we do after guests leave to make cleanup the next morning much easier.

> Clear the table. Sounds like a no-brainer, but it's the one psychological move that will make you so happy the next morning. Even if the kitchen looks like a tornado hit, the dining area needs to be cleared, wiped down, and tidy (napkins refolded, chairs pushed in).

> Put leftover food in the refrigerator. Enough cocktails and you might forget there's soup in the covered pot on the stove. Make sure you wrap up leftovers and put them away or send them home with guests.

> Rinse off stuck-on food. Everyone leaves dirty dishes in the sink, but try to give them a rinse or light scrub so you don't have to use a jackhammer to pry off dried cheese or tomato sauce the next day. Fill a mixing bowl with warm soapy water and dump all of the silverware and serving utensils into it.

> Fill empty pots and pans with water. Don't leave a dirty pot to dry out overnight. Let the water do some of the work for you. If you have room to put your big meat-encrusted Dutch oven or casserole dish in the sink and let it soak overnight, do it! But even if you don't, pour some hot water into the pan and set it back on the stovetop or on the counter.

> Pour a little water into red-wine glasses. Wineglasses are the last thing to tackle. If you leave them out, even a tiny little bit of red wine will harden into a flaky residue that is hard to clean.

BEFORE THE PARTY 30-MINUTE CLEANING PLAN
▼

If you plan ahead, there's no reason why you can't devote thirty minutes on the day of your party to cleaning up your home. This isn't a deep cleaning, but a bare-bones approach to making the house look and feel fresh.

1. Fluff the couch cushions.

2. Vacuum the kitchen, dining area, living area, and bathroom (anywhere guests will be).

3. If you plan to use your bed for coats, make it nicely and pick up your bedroom.

4. Clean the toilet.

5. Set out an extra roll of toilet paper somewhere obvious.

6. Wipe down the bathroom sink.

7. Wash any dishes in the sink and/or load/run the dishwasher.

8. Put away the dishes.

9. Take out the trash and recycling.

10. Replace dishtowels in the kitchen and hand towels in the bathroom with clean ones.

WORKING WITH DIFFERENT DIETARY NEEDS

These days inviting a group of friends over for dinner usually means having to accommodate dietary restrictions such as vegan, gluten-free, egg-free, nut-free. Even within most families these days there is always at least one person—maybe it's you—who has to eat with a little bit of caution. It's easy to rise to the occasion and feed everyone.

For many engaged cooks these guests and challenges are not moments of exasperation, but opportunities for inspiration for creating something delicious and perhaps new. Anyone can make buttery foie gras on white toast taste good; it is the constraints that show what you're really made of as a cook.

We run the gamut of omnivores to sometime-vegans here at The Kitchn, with many food avoidances and allergies between us. Over the years we've come up with a few tips for accommodating every guest.

> **Keep it simple!** Three great veggie dishes will make a meal. Ask a guest to bring the dessert.

> **Let the season dominate.** Marinate, grill, and roast the bounty from the farmer's market. A plate of grilled asparagus and fennel, roasted carrots, marinated beets, and oranges will impress even the most devout meat eaters. Kale massaged with olive oil is also a crowd-pleaser.

> **Go meat-free.** Even if you are expecting omnivores, skip the meat completely, and use a little goat cheese to add richness to the dishes you prepare. Legumes and toasted and seasoned nuts can enhance a vegetable recipe, add texture, and also satiate hungry guests.

> **Be prepared for a vegan guest.** For an unexpected vegan guest, the quickest solution is to add a can of beans and a little diced onion into whatever vegetable dish is already available. Add toasted nuts to the salad or a side dish.

> Deliver flavor with dressings and sauces. Be generous, and have extra sauce and dressings available at the side in case guests want more.

"I know that planning a dinner party means much anticipation. You can't wait to see what your guests think of your food! But if you have to feed someone with a food restriction or different dietary needs than your own, well, it can be a panic. But in the event you have your dinner menu planned already, be sure to let your gluten-free guest know it's okay to bring some side dishes or bread that might make the meal more substantive. After all, the real point of having a dinner party is gathering friends around the table."

—Shauna Ahern, GlutenFreeGirl.com

GLUTEN-FREE TIPS

The most important thing when accommodating a gluten-free friend is to speak to them first about how they want to eat and how careful you need to be when preparing their food. They may have a slight intolerance, or they may have celiac disease. Don't be offended if they need to bring their own food to your party. While it's great to try to accommodate a guest, just because a food is gluten-free doesn't mean your guest will like it.

> Don't panic. Ask your gluten-free guest what he or she likes to eat. So many dishes are naturally gluten-free: roasted potatoes with salsa verde, carnitas with corn tortillas for taco night, quinoa salad with lemons and cherry tomatoes. If you really want to accommodate your guests, make the dinner gluten-free without announcing it!

> Plan a gluten-free dinner. This might seem extreme just to accommodate one person, but if you're expecting someone with a high sensitivity to gluten, even some residual flour on a plate can cause a reaction. Focus on serving vegetables, proteins, and grains (such as amaranth, buckwheat, millet, and quinoa) that are naturally gluten-free.

> Serve gluten-free dishes separate from other dishes. Gluten will mingle with anything it touches. Don't put rice crackers on the same tray as wheat crackers, for example, or expect guests to eat around wheat noodles in chicken noodle soup.

> Do a quick refresher on what eating gluten-free means. Gluten is hidden in some unexpected places such as soy sauce, beer, vinegar, and marshmallows. Read food labels and know what to avoid so that you won't realize when it's too late that your guest can't eat what you've prepared.

> Don't reinvent the gluten wheel. Substituting gluten-free flours for traditional flour is trickier than it sounds. Stick with simple dishes and well-tested recipes.

> Avoid wooden tools. If you're cooking for someone with celiac disease, don't use wooden spoons or cutting boards that have been used in your regular cooking.

WHAT'S THE DIFFERENCE BETWEEN A VEGAN AND A VEGETARIAN?

Here's a quick refresher course on what's vegetarian and what's vegan. In general, vegetarians don't eat any animal flesh, such as chicken, beef, pork, turkey, and so forth, but they do eat other animal products, such as milk, butter, yogurt, eggs, and honey. Vegans do not eat any animal products whatsoever.

OUR BEST ADVICE FOR HOSTING A BIG GATHERING

As laid back as we may be about entertaining, we recognize that there are important differences between cooking a normal, though special, meal for your family and having a bunch of people over for a meal. With a big gathering, you might set the table the night before, or plan to borrow extra platters or wineglasses from a neighbor. You might even make playlists for dinner music.

One of the most frequently asked questions we get is how to prepare a meal and get the dishes all ready at the right time and on time. This means that you've balanced your work precisely to be finished when your guests arrive, with the entrée hot and ready to serve, and each side dish at the appropriate temperature. First of all, that's a lot to expect of yourself. Leave a little to be done when guests arrive—preparing the garnishes and mixing drinks and making the salad dressing—so you can involve them in the preparation of the meal. To aim for everything to be done at the same time, here are a few tips:

> **Schedule.** Work backward. Make a schedule of your evening. If your guests are due to arrive at 7 p.m. and you are getting home from work at 4:30, then work your schedule backward from 6:45, so you have some breathing room. Then read your recipes closely to make sure that each fits into that time frame, planning well enough ahead that you have the option to prepare portions of the meal in advance. If this is your first dinner party, use recipes you already know.

> **Diversify cooking methods.** Broiler, stove, oven, microwave, raw. A classic mistake is to plan a roast chicken, baked bread, roasted vegetables, and a cake, all of which need to cook in the oven at the same time. Unless you plan to serve most things at room temperature and you make things ahead of time, or you have several ovens, it's unlikely that dinner will get on the table at a reasonable hour. A cook with even a tiny bit of confidence can probably multitask a cake in the oven and a stir-fry on the stove.

> **Look carefully through your recipes, and choose a variety of cooking methods.** Maybe this means blanching the asparagus instead of roasting it. Maybe you should bake a custard instead of making a stovetop pudding if the stove will be crowded with boiling pasta and simmering ragu.

> **Do ahead, do ahead, do ahead.** If we had to choose just one tip, it would be to work as far in advance as possible. So many dishes can be made early and stored, especially when you're planning spring and summer dishes that can be served cold. The salad and dessert can easily be made ahead (think pretty berries in individual cups with heaps of whipped cream and ginger biscuits waiting on the side, or plated ice cream bombes in the freezer). Set up your coffeepot early so all you need to do is boil water or push a button. So many shaved cabbage and green salads are easy to toss and store in the fridge until guests arrive. Cook the meat early, too, if you can—braised dishes can be cooked the night before and warmed up on the stove while you're tending to other tasks.

"Whether hosting two or twelve for dinner, I invariably serve soup as the first course. I make it a couple of days in advance (what soup isn't improved by a few days' mulling in the refrigerator?). Then, day-of, while I prepare the rest of the meal, I slowly reheat the soup in a pot on the back of the stove. It's a perfect first course requiring almost no prep time during those crucial few hours leading up to dinner. Plus, there are fun-to-serve seasonal soups for any time of year, and you can get as complex with the preparations as you like since you do it all ahead of time." —*Regina Yunghans, writer for The Kitchn*

> Don't forget appetizers (and cocktails). Buy yourself a little extra time (just in case) by setting out a dish of cheese, nuts, and crackers with the wine already open. When your guests arrive, you can ease into the evening and do any last-minute tasks while they are happily appetizing—less pressure for you and a nice start to the evening for them.

> Work in a cleaning break. Don't forget to clean as you go; it helps you feel less stressed and more ready to welcome guests. As you prepare the meal don't let your cooking tasks flow right into each other; take a few moments to tidy up as you go. This helps you stay on top of your cooking tasks, feel more prepared, and think clearly. Also, in small kitchens it's nice to clear as much clutter out of the way as possible!

BUDGET-MINDED? SHOP MINDFULLY FOR MEAT AND POULTRY

▼

Meat can be one of the biggest expenses when you're hosting a dinner party, but that doesn't mean you have to cut it out completely if you're trimming your budget this year. In fact, cheaper cuts of meat are often juicier, more flavorful, and easier to prepare ahead, and that makes them ideal for entertaining.

Meat tends to be less expensive when it includes bones, connective tissue, or other bits that take a little more time for the cook to deal with. The reward for this time is extra flavor, both in the meat itself and, in the case of braised meat, the sauce it simmers in. Another plus: Most dishes that use less expensive cuts actually taste even better when made a day ahead and reheated before serving, leaving you with some extra time to hang out with your guests.

With poultry, look for bone-in legs and thighs and ground meat. With pork, look for shoulder or butt and ground meat. With beef, look for chuck roast, short ribs, flank steak, shanks, and ground meat.

POTLUCKS AND BUFFETS

A great dinner party doesn't have to wear you down. Make it more of a casual affair by having other people bring a dish, or by setting up a buffet to remove some of the pressure of creating a completely set table.

POTLUCKS

Sometimes you can't do it all. The obvious way to ask for help is to turn your gathering into a potluck. If you decide to go that route, there are two very important things you need to do:

> "I've actually never been at a potluck in which the balance of food (veggies, chips, main dish, dessert) didn't work out. I know some people feel anxious about balance, but if it's a group of, say, eight people, it just works somehow. Potluck magic."
>
> —reader jmccourt

> **Ask guests to commit to a course.** The cardinal sin of potluck parties is a dinner table loaded with three kinds of hummus, four salsas, and chips. To make sure a number of different courses show up, include a line in the invitation asking friends to reply with what they'll bring. Or once the RSVPs have come in, ask several friends to bring a main course, salad, appetizer, or dessert. Someone will always change it up at the last minute, but at least having an idea of what to expect makes serving a well-rounded meal more likely.

> **Have backup dishes ready.** As the host, it's a good idea to pull together the main course, since you're the one in charge. Make sure it's something filling and universally appealing. Having something like a roast chicken or lasagna at the ready helps bridge any gap in courses or not having enough food. Since you know guests will at least eat what they brought, your main dish is a great opportunity to get them to try something a little different.

BUFFETS

When a ton of people are coming over and you just can't seat them all around your table, a buffet is the way to go. Here is our guide for setting up a successful buffet.

> **Think two-sided.** If at all possible, set up your buffet table so that people can approach it from all sides. This cuts down on traffic congestion and helps them get food faster.

> **Build upward.** Tiered cake plates and dessert servers create extra space. Put your highest serving dish in the center of the table and layer down from there. The more you can stack and layer, the more room you create. Also, layering the serving dishes makes it easier for guests to reach in for the food.

> **Plates first, the rest last.** Nothing is more annoying than a buffet where you have to pick up your cutlery, napkins, and cup at the beginning of the buffet line. Everything except plates should go at the end so you don't have to balance all that other stuff while scoping out the food.

> **Make it easy.** As much as possible, serve food already portioned-out and place anything in individual cups—like small shot glasses of soup, or individual servings of mousse—at the end of the tables, where grazing guests can reach in and snag one without going through the whole line.

> **Have backups.** If this is an especially large party (yes, we've catered weddings!), it's impossible to replenish the table while people are still clustered around it. Have backup platters full of food close by so that you can quickly replenish any food items that are getting low or any platters that are looking sparse.

> **Rent.** If this is a really big event, you may need to rent supplies. Every city has a party rental business. This is the place you can go for everything from even Porta-Potties, food warmers, and tables to serving platters, flatware, and wineglasses.

MANAGE YOUR TIME
LIKE A PRO FOR A BIG PARTY

Let's say you're hosting a really big party—dare we say Thanksgiving? Here's how we plan out and break down the work for a bigger gathering.

> A week before. Make the menu and then the shopping list. Identify anything on the list that should be purchased ahead of time; pears that might need to ripen, meat that needs to be special-ordered from the butcher, for example. If there's anything you plan to buy at a farmer's market, find out the market schedule and plan on when you can get there. Are there any platters or serving pieces you need to borrow from a friend? Get on that.

> A few days before. Tackle those make-ahead components of the meal (salad dressing and piecrusts). If you need to move anything from the freezer to the refrigerator, consider doing this now. If anything requires a long marinade or a long rest in the refrigerator (Perfected Chocolate Chip Cookies, page 246) make it now.

> The day before. Buy flowers and wine. If you're going to need ice, start making it now, or plan to buy a sack of it. We like to set out platters and serving trays the day before and imagine how it will all fit on the table or if we'll need a side table. This is also the day to gather the fresh ingredients, and the other ingredients if you haven't already purchased (or harvested!) them. You might even set the table.

> Party day. Get up early, have a strong cup of coffee, and start cooking. Put on some great music. Get as much done as possible, so you can spend the second part of the day making the table, and yourself, gorgeous. We like to have a drink before anyone arrives; there's nothing wrong with being ahead of the curve.

RESOURCES

Dana's Meditation:
SOURCING INGREDIENTS
▼

There's an old, and very accurate, statement that cooking is mostly shopping. If you want to cook well, first you must shop well. And by shopping we don't necessarily mean going to the market, although that certainly is how we get a great deal of our food these days. You can also explore the garden, find a wild fennel stalk in the fields, visit a farm stand, borrow a cup of sugar, or exchange pickles and jams with your neighbor. Keeping your cupboards full has never been more fun, or full of possibilities.

Foraging, rummaging, borrowing, exploring, digging, discovering, creating—even if your life is busy and it's all you can do to make it to the grocery store, be sure to allow for some moments of playfulness and imagination in the kitchen. Every now and then, pick up one ingredient that's utterly new and unfamiliar, or something you were convinced you could never pull off, and bring it home to your pantry. What will you do with this challenge? Where will this take you? Go find out!

Keep your larder, cupboards, refrigerator, and freezer as well stocked as possible, given the constraints of your space and pocketbook, so you can be spontaneous both in your daily routine and in entertaining guests. Knowing that you have something as simple as a packet of good pasta, some decent grating cheese, a few cloves of garlic, a few herbs, and your favorite olive oil on hand means that you can give in to that impulse to invite someone to dinner at the last minute. It also means that, no matter what happens in your day, you can arrive home and feed yourself and your loved ones with some ease. And that, while sounding deceptively mundane, is actually key to living a happy and satisfied life, and worth more than gold.

EQUIPPING A KITCHEN FROM SCRATCH:
A Checklist

We shared our essentials and philosophy of kitchen equipment in Chapter 2 (page 41). If you're starting from scratch after a move, graduation, or other big life change, here's a fast checklist of the things we consider to be most essential to a kitchen equipped for any meal. Of course, this is just one set of guidelines to consider; let your own cooking habits and preferences be the final arbiter of what you need. For information on stores, see our favorites later in Resources (page 291).

ESSENTIAL UTENSILS

☐ Wooden spoons, with long and short handles

☐ Basic metal tongs

☐ Flat metal spatula

☐ Fish spatula

☐ Ladle

☐ Large stainless-steel spoons, slotted and nonslotted

☐ Whisks, one large and one small

☐ Silicone or rubber spatulas in several sizes (GIR—Get It Right—makes an excellent spatula)

ESSENTIAL COOKWARE

☐ 10-inch skillet or sauté pan (we like All-Clad and Calphalon)

☐ Cast-iron skillet (such as American-made Lodge)

☐ 4- or 5-quart pot

☐ 2-quart (or 3-quart) saucepan

☐ 3- or 6-quart Dutch oven (we love Le Creuset, Staub, and Tramontina)

ESSENTIAL COOKING ACCESSORIES

☐ Wood cutting boards

☐ Big metal bowls

☐ Colander or strainer

☐ Scale (OXO makes great kitchen scales)

☐ Measuring spoons and cups—(Lee Valley, OXO, and Chef'n all have sturdy measuring spoons)

☐ Instant read thermometer (we love the Thermapen brand)

ESSENTIAL BAKING TOOLS AND PANS

- ☐ Silpat and parchment
- ☐ Pastry blender
- ☐ 9-inch round cake pan
- ☐ 9 × 13-inch metal baking dish/roasting pan (ideally with matching lids)
- ☐ 8 × 8-inch (or 9 × 9-inch) square metal or glass baking dish
- ☐ Pie dish
- ☐ 9 × 5-inch and 8 × 4-inch loaf pans
- ☐ Half (or ¾) commercial-quality sheet pans

ESSENTIAL KNIVES

- ☐ 10-inch (or so) chef's knife
- ☐ Paring knife
- ☐ Peeler
- ☐ Kitchen shears
- ☐ Serrated knife for bread, some vegetables
- ☐ Cleaver (best deals are at Chinese restaurant supply shops)

FAVORITE SMALL APPLIANCES

- ☐ Slow cooker
- ☐ Toaster/toaster oven (We like Breville's toasters)
- ☐ Blender (Vitamix is the Rolls-Royce)
- ☐ Food processor (Magimix and Cuisinart are both good brands)
- ☐ Mini chopper (Look for Chef'n and KitchenAid)
- ☐ Stand mixer or hand mixer (KitchenAid, Breville)
- ☐ Immersion blender
- ☐ Ice cream machine (Cuisinart machine or attachment for KitchenAid stand mixer)

ESSENTIAL STORAGE

- ☐ Mason jars (with lids) that can double as drinking glasses and flower vases
- ☐ Glass containers in various sizes with snap-on lids (Snapware Glasslock is our favorite)
- ☐ Glass, ceramic, or metal canisters for flour and sugar

COMMON UNIT CONVERSIONS

1 tablespoon = 3 teaspoons	
1 cup = 16 tablespoons	
1 pint = 2 cups	
1 quart = 2 pints	
1 gallon = 4 quarts	

LIQUID MEASUREMENT CONVERSIONS

1 tablespoon = ½ fluid ounce

¼ cup = 2 fluid ounces

⅓ cup = 2⅔ fluid ounces

½ cup = 4 fluid ounces

1 cup = 8 fluid ounces

1 pint = 16 fluid ounces

1 quart = 32 fluid ounces

(To convert fluid ounces to milliliters, multiply by 30. 1 fluid ounce = 30 milliliters)

WEIGHTS OF DRY INGREDIENTS

All-Purpose flour (unsifted)
1 cup = 4½ ounces

Bread flour (unsifted)
1 cup = 4½ ounces

Whole-wheat flour (unsifted)
1 cup = 4½ ounces

Cake flour (unsifted)
1 cup = 4 ounces

Pastry flour
1 cup (unsifted) = 4 ounces

White granulated sugar
1 cup = 6½ ounces

Brown sugar (packed)
1 cup = 7½ ounces

Confectioners' sugar
1 cup = 4 ounces

Chopped nuts
1 cup = 4 ounces

(To convert ounces to grams, multiply by 28. 1 ounce = 28 grams)

MEAT DONENESS (INTERNAL TEMPERATURE)

USDA RECOMMENDED:

Poultry: 165°F

Ground beef, pork, lamb: 160°F

Beefsteaks/roasts, and cuts of pork: 145°F

WHAT THE CHEFS SAY:

Whole chicken: 160°F

Beef: 125°F (rare); 130°F (medium-rare); 135°F (medium)

Pork: 140–145°F

COOKING SUPPLIES

▼

AMAZON.COM

Become a Prime member for $75/ year and get free two-day shipping on most items—convenient for party planning.

CRATE & BARREL
(crateandbarrel.com)

One-stop shop for cookware, appliances, cutlery, tabletop, and more with a extensive collection of house-brand items.

ETSY
(etsy.com)

Like an open craft fair, an e-commerce site with thousands of sellers of vintage and hand-made items. Check out vintage kitchenware and handmade wooden items, such as spoons and cutting boards.

FULL CIRCLE
(fullcirclehome.com)

Kitchen supplies made from sustainable and renewable resources.

SUR LA TABLE
(surlatable.com)

Everything for the kitchen from cooking supplies to the tabletop.

THE WEBSTAURANT STORE
(webstaurantstore.com)

A great resource for baking sheets, hotel pans, spatulas, metal tongs, or any other piece of restaurant-style kitchenware.

WILLIAMS-SONOMA
(williams-sonoma.com)

High-end cookware, appliances, cutlery, cookbooks, tabletop, and more. Their e-commerce site includes recipes and video tutorials on how to use their products.

INGREDIENTS

▼

ASTOR WINES & SPIRITS
(astorwines.com)

A great selection of wine and spirits shipped to all the states that allow liquor to be shipped.

BOB'S RED MILL NATURAL FOODS
(bobsredmill.com)

Natural, certified organic, and gluten-free grain products as well as beans, seeds, nuts, spices, and herbs.

JACOBSEN SALT CO.
(jacobsensalt.com)

Ben Jacobsen harvests fluffy sea salt from the North Oregon coast. The consistency is like Fleur de Sel or Maldon, but it's domestically sourced.

KALUSTYAN'S
(kalustyans.com)

Originally an Indian grocery in New York City, now carrying a large variety of international specialty foods, in their brick and mortar location and online.

MARKET HALL FOODS
(markethallfoods.com)

Specialty food store carrying a wide variety of baking ingredients, condiments, grains, oils, and vinegars.

MASSA ORGANICS
(massaorganics.com)

A small family farm in California that produces organic whole-grain brown rice. We're addicted and order in bulk.

NUTS ONLINE
(nuts.com)

Premium bulk nuts, dried fruit, coffee, tea, baking ingredients, beans, grains, herbs and spices, and dried mushrooms. We're always amazed at how quickly they ship.

RANCHO GORDO
NEW WORLD SPECIALTY FOOD
(ranchogordo.com)

Specialty producer of heirloom beans.

VITACOST
(vitacost.com)

Discount supplier of organic health and grocery products.

TABLETOP

ALDER & CO.
(alderandcoshop.com)

A Portland-based design shop selling a rotating collection of curated objects for the home, including everything to set your table.

ANTHROPOLOGIE
(anthropologie.com)

This store carries quirky, colorful, and internationally inspired linens, serving pieces, dinnerware, and other tabletop items.

CANVAS HOME
(canvashomestore.com)

Stylish tabletop items with a handmade edge.

CB2
(cb2.com)

The younger sibling of Crate & Barrel, CB2 has a good selection of modern tabletop items and at a lower price.

COST PLUS WORLD MARKET
(worldmarket.com)

Known for its inexpensive tabletop items with some cookware and kitchen supplies.

FISHS EDDY
(fishseddy.com)

Restaurant and vintage-inspired serving pieces, glasses, dinnerware, and flatware.

GRETEL
(gretelhome.com)

Design shop with a clean, feminine aesthetic. Trays, vases, flatware, dinnerware, glassware, textiles, and candleholders.

HEATH CERAMICS
(heathceramics.com)

Some of our favorite dinnerware, serving pieces, and vases, made in California.

SCHOOLHOUSE ELECTRIC & SUPPLY CO.
(schoolhouseelectric.com)

A mix of vintage-inspired and modern kitchen and tableware.

WEST ELM
(westelm.com)

A Williams-Sonoma company, carrying a range of modern and functional dinnerware, servingware, cookware, and kitchen tools.

FAVORITE WEBSITES ABOUT FOOD

101 COOKBOOKS
(101cookbooks.com)

What started in 2003 as a written and visual chronicle of her wanderings through Heidi Swanson's personal cookbook collection is now a site with recipes from books, friends, and Heidi's own kitchen, focused mostly on natural, whole foods and ingredients.

A WAY TO GARDEN
(awaytogarden.com)

A gardening site from Margaret Roach that naturally includes food—from growing it to canning it to cooking it.

BAKING 911
(baking911.com)

This is the site to visit for every bit of information you could possibly want to know about baking, from pan conversions and ingredient substitutions to tried-and-true recipes.

CANNELLE ET VANILLE
(cannellevanille.com)

Aran Goyaga publishes thoughtful, well-tested, and beautiful food on her site that will appeal to just about anyone, but it also happens to be child-friendly and gluten-free.

DAVID LEBOVITZ
(davidlebovitz.com)

For inspiration from Paris, professional guidance on pastry, and all-around wit, David is one of our favorite reads.

ESQUIRE
(esquire.com)

Esquire's writing on food is smart and often very entertaining.

EVERYDAY FOOD
WITH SARAH CAREY
(marthastewart.com/946620/ everyday-food-sarah-carey)

Sarah's videos are practical, down-to-earth, and always inspiring.

FOOD52
(food52.com)

The photos and recipes our friends at Food52 create are always wonderful.

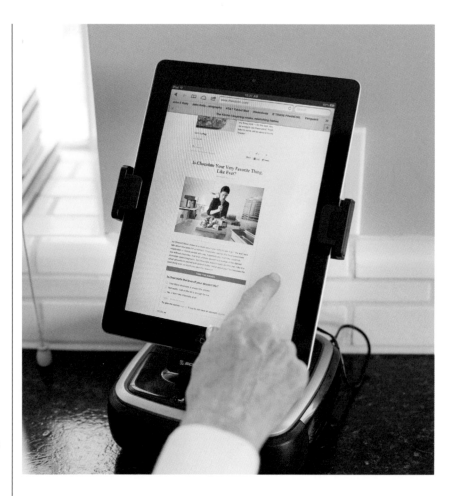

GLUTEN-FREE GIRL
(glutenfreegirl.com)

We love Shauna Ahern's blog for reliable and tasty gluten-free resources and recipes.

IMBIBE
(imbibemagazine.com)

Imbibe turns out some of our favorite writing on cocktails, beer, wine, tea, coffee, and other libations.

LEITE'S CULINARIA
(leitesculinaria.com)

We appreciate David Leite's commitment to making available online not just good recipes, but longform food writing and essays as well.

OH HAPPY DAY
(ohhappyday.com)

Cheery, inspiring party resources and ideas that are still practical and within reach.

SERIOUS EATS
(seriouseats.com)

Our go-to for practical recipes, American casual dining, and the science of cooking.

SIMPLY RECIPES
(simplyrecipes.com)

Google a common recipe title and one of Elise Bauer's will come up. Her recipes are detailed and tested. Since her site has been going for so long, she has a giant archive of reliable recipes and helpful comments.

FROM THE TOURS

MARIANNE LANNEN AND JOHN KELLY

Leather finish ("Ubatuba") granite: Walker Zanger

Cabinets: made and designed by Lannen Construction

Appliances: Viking

Outdoor table: Target

Espresso machine: Breville

Custom window treatments: 3-Day Blinds

Silver throughout: handed down through the Kelly family

iPod stand: Scosche

Plates: R. Wood Studio Ceramics

BRIDGET POTTER

Architect: Leo J. Blackman Architects

Countertop: Pietro Cardoso

Cookware: Le Creuset (*lecreuset. com*)

Tomato knife: Messermeister

Stand mixer: KitchenAid (*kitchenaid.com*)

Food processor: Cuisinart

Teapot collection: various gifts and family heirlooms

Antiques: inherited

English specialty ingredients: Myers of Keswick

ROZANNE GOLD AND MICHAEL WHITEMAN

Ranges: LG

Platters: personal collection from travels

Desk/chair in dining area: Desk made by Michael Whiteman, desk chair from a dining set belonging to Michael's mother

Goldtone flatware: Pieces inherited from Rozanne and Michael's mothers

KIM AND JOHN KUSHNER

Stainless-steel coiled kettle: Simplex Heritage

Stand mixer: KitchenAid

Dishwashers: Miele

Microwave and wall oven: Thermador

Coffeemaker: DeLonghi Nespresso

Glass light fixtures: Juliska Lighting

Tiered glass cookie jars: Barreveld (purchased on Gilt Group)

KRISTEN OSSMANN AND JACKIE WERNER

Flowers and plants: Pretty Streets Botanicals

Porcelain fork, knife, spoon: Creatures of Comfort

Speckled enamel milk pot: Brooklyn Kitchen

French press coffeepot: Bodum

Hanging fruit/vegetable basket: Thrift store

Plates: Brook Farm General Store

Blue bookshelf and wire rack above: found on street

Dining table and chairs: flea market finds

NANCY NEIL AND ETHAN BROSTEDT

Table linens: Heather Taylor (*heathertaylorhome.com*)

Napkins: Botanik (*botanikinc.com*)

Organic Local Coffee Concentrate: We Have Many Surfboards (*wehavemanysurfboards.com*)

Handmade ceramics: Rebekah Miles (*rebekahamelia.blogspot.com*)

Juicer: Local Latino market

LAUREN CHANDLER

Cookware: Vintage Dansk Kobenstyle (*dansk.com*)

Olive oil: Corto Olive Co. (*corto-olive.com*)

Grasshopper print: Neko Case concert poster by Gary Houston of Voodoo Catbox (*www.voodoocatbox.com/*)

White plates with cutouts: Handed down from Lauren's grandmother

Speckled bowls: Anthropologie

Salt and pepper bowls: A gift from Lauren's friend Cassie, made by her aunt, artist Bobbie Specker (*bobbiespeckerceramics.com/*)

Kitchen towel: Heather Moore (*www.etsy.com/people/skinnylaminx*)

Towels hung as curtains in dining room: New Seasons (*www.newseasonsmarket.com/*)

GRETCHEN AND CHRIS HOTZ

Lighting: Nelson Bubble Lamp (*modernica.net*)

Wallpaper: Cole & Son (*cole-and-son.com*)

Faucet: Hansgrohe (*hansgrohe.com*)

Stove: KitchenAid

Stools: Lem Piston, designed by Shin and Tomoko Azumi.

VICKI SIMON AND TIM COHRS

Design: Vicki Simon Interior Design (*vickisimoninteriordesign.com*)

Paint: Pratt & Lambert in Chalk Gray (*prattandlambert.com*)

Paint (Accent): Eddie Bauer in Linen (*lowes.com*)

Paint (blue accents): Yolo Colorhouse in Water .02 (*yolocolorhouse.com*)

Lampshades: Schoolhouse Electric (*schoolhouseelectric.com*)

Artwork: Creative Growth Art Center (*creativegrowth.org*)

Brass Ager (to refinish new lamp hardware): Hippo Hardware (*hippohardware.com*)

Dutch ovens: Le Creuset in Flame

Butcher-block island: Custom-designed by Vicki Simon Design, using maple on the base and end-cut cherry on the top

Canisters: Vintage

Sink: Reproduction by Sign of the Crab. Distributed by Strom Plumbing.

Cooktop: Wolf

Vase on windowsill: Handmade by friend Victoria McOmie

Plates: Biordi

Faucet: Belle Forêt

BEATRICE VALENZUELA AND RAMSEY CONDER

Brown clay mugs: Imported from Mexico by Beatrice (*beatricevalenzuela.com*)

Chai tea: Kneeland Mercado (*kneelandmercado.com*)

Radio: Tivoli (*tivoliaudio.com*)

Kitchen tools: Tortoise (*tortoisegeneralstore.com*)

Brushes and dish soap: Caldrea (*caldrea.com*)

Dried chiles: The Farmer and the Cook (*farmerandcook.com*)

Dishtowels: Feal Mor (*fealmor.com*)

Knives: Global (*global-knife.com*)

Moroccan tile: Casbah Cafe (*casbahcafe.com*)

Ingredients and cookbooks: Cookbook bookstore (*cookbookla.com*)

ACKNOWLEDGMENTS

FAITH & SARA KATE

▼

To Leela Cyd, who gave our message light and color. To Chelsea Fuss and Adrian Hale, who breathed life and form into our food.

To Angelin Borsics, the editor who makes house calls, whose persistent yet flexible touch helped make this book come alive in a seemingly impossible amount of time. And to Aliza Fogelson, who took the reins with grace.

To Emma Christensen, for pitching in with the recipes and keeping the site alive simultaneously.

To Nealey Dozier, who diligently tested our recipes and brought us monkey bread.

To Dana, for being our Zen master of food writing. If reincarnated, we'd like to come back as your pen and notebook, for you give them so much care.

To all the writers of The Kitchn. Eight years ago Sara Kate sat alone in a tiny apartment thinking about how she could help the world cook more. You all make that dream come true on the site every day with your wit, humor, textbook knowledge, and humility.

To the subjects of our tours in this book and on the website—it is such an intimate act to open up your homes to our cameras and diligent note-taking; know that you inspire millions of readers to cook more and flourish in every kind of kitchen.

And of course, to our readers. You made The Kitchn. Without you, we'd just be a bunch of home-bodies Instagram-ing our dinners.

SARA KATE

▼

To Julia, who chopped, organized, measured, tested, washed, and brainstormed her way into my heart.

To Janis Donnaud, my agent, who always has my back.

To Faith Durand, my collaborator for close to a decade. Thank you for everything you've done for The Kitchn, and for our friendship.

FAITH

▼

To Sara Kate, for giving me my first break in food writing and teaching me just about everything I know about writing a good recipe. Thanks for your friendship and all that you've taught me.

To Maxwell, who also gave me a chance and who has nurtured and encouraged The Kitchn into what it is today.

To Jenni Ferrari-Adler, my small yet mighty red-headed agent.

To everyone who did dishes in my kitchen and ate the results of recipe testing throughout this madcap process. You know who you are.

INDEX